Crossroads of Modern Warfare

Crossroads of Modern Warfare

DREW MIDDLETON

DOUBLEDAY & COMPANY, INC.
Garden City, New York
1983

Library of Congress Cataloging in Publication Data

Middleton, Drew, 1913–
Crossroads of modern warfare.

Includes index.
1. Battles—History—20th century.
2. Military history, Modern—20th century.
I. Title.
D431.M5   1983   904′.7
AACR2
ISBN: 0-385-14937-9
Library of Congress Catalog Card Number 79–7873

PREFACE

War, unfortunately, is part of the human condition. This strident century has seen two global wars, at least a dozen minor ones, and scores of politico-military situations such as that in Northern Ireland that involve the military to some degree in the support of the civil power.

The selection of decisive battles in this century has been difficult. In general I have followed two criteria in my selection. First, battles which clearly were turning points and which thus altered the course of history. Second, battles which introduced or exploited a new technology in warfare and, consequently, changed the nature of war.

The Battle of Saratoga in 1777 is an example of the former. It broke the back of the most ambitious, and logical, war plan evolved by the British for the conquest of the United States. The war dragged on. The British won other battles, but "never again bright morning." The course of the war was fixed unalterably in the fighting on the plains above the Hudson.

The encounter between the U.S.S. *Monitor* and the C.S.S. *Virginia* in the American Civil War was an example of the second type of battle. It was inconclusive as a battle but decisive in its effect on naval war. Those cannon firing off Hampton Roads in March 1862 sounded the knell of all the wooden ships of all the world's navies, and ushered in the age of the battleship and the dreadnought.

Each conflict, no matter how limited in scope or time, introduces some new weapon or tactic which alters the established modes of war. For example, the brief war between Britain and Argentina over the Falkland Islands in the spring of 1982 marked the debut of three new weapons that are likely to increase the hazards of the projection of naval power.

Exocet, a French-made missile, was the most spectacular. Loosed from an aircraft—the Exocet also can be fired from ships and land bases—the missile drops to about six to ten feet above the sea and homes in on its target guided by a radar in the nose cone. The Exocet was the instrument for two of the few Argentine successes: the destruction of the destroyer *Coventry* and the merchantman *Atlantic Conveyor.*

The South Atlantic war also saw the operational debut of long-range, wire-guided torpedoes. One of these, fired at extreme range from the British submarine *Conqueror,* sank the Argentine cruiser *General Belgrano* as she led a division of ships toward the British task force. With the loss of the *Belgrano,* the massive Argentine naval attack collapsed.

The Harrier fighter was another new weapon that proved its worth in the Falkland Islands fighting. The Harrier is a jump jet capable of taking off vertically or after a very short run. Designed and intended as a ground-attack aircraft, the Harrier demonstrated an unanticipated effectiveness as a fighter against the Argentines' faster and better-armed Mirage.

There is a natural tendency among historians to consider a battle decisive because of the number of men involved. Gettysburg belongs in this category. It was a huge battle. But was it decisive? Would victory at Gettysburg have turned the tide of the war in favor of the South? I doubt it. The Gettysburg campaign was a raid, one of the greatest raids in history and, until the encounter battle that was its climax, a successful one. But its impact on the course of the war seems to me to have been less than the Federal victory at Vicksburg, which split the Confederacy in two.

There is another category of battles for which, unfortunately, there is no room in this book. These are the minor, often isolated actions that lay the groundwork for later, greater successes. The British repulse of the Afrika Korps at Alam-el-Halfa, Egypt, on Aug. 31, 1942, is an example.

My selections, I expect and hope, will provoke argument. I have watched minor actions which, to those involved, appeared to be of critical importance. I apologize in advance to all those who feel that an operation in which they were concerned has been omitted through ignorance. Perhaps the truth is that the end result of all battles, large and small, decisive or otherwise, is the same: The soldier killed in a Vietnam ambush is as dead as the one who died on the Normandy beachhead.

Drew Middleton

New York City
Westport, N.Y.
Weston, Conn.

CONTENTS

LIST OF MAPS

Crossroads of Modern Warfare

I

The Guns of the Rising Sun

TSUSHIMA

The Battle of Tsushima virtually ended the Russo-Japanese War of 1904–5. It was a Japanese naval victory as complete as that won by the British over the French at Trafalgar. But whereas the outcome of the Napoleonic wars had to wait until Waterloo, Tsushima had enormous and immediate political consequences for the Pacific world. Japan emerged from the battle as the first military power of the Far East, a position it held for another forty years. The Japanese navy, indeed all its fighting services, drew from Tsushima and other battles of that war a tradition of victory and supreme confidence. Neither was shattered until the Battle of Midway in World War II.

Tsushima had another important political consequence. It was the last and most conclusive of a series of military defeats that exposed in that war the fundamental weaknesses of imperial Russia. The vast, brittle Russian edifice tottered, but did not fall, in the subsequent 1905 Revolution. But the seeds were sown. The harvest was reaped by Lenin twelve years later, after (it should be remembered) another series of crushing defeats for the imperial forces inflicted, in that instance, by Wilhelmine Germany.

There is a striking similarity between the operations of the Japanese navy at the start of the war with Russia and operations at the start of the war with the United States thirty-seven years later. On Feb. 8, 1904, two days before the declaration of war, Japanese torpedo boats, under the command of Admiral Heihachiro Togo, entered the Russian naval base at Port Arthur, now part of Liaoning Province of the People's Republic of China, and damaged two battleships and a cruiser. The stricken ships were beached at the mouth of the harbor. The heavier Japanese ships then opened fire and damaged another battleship and four cruisers, with negligible losses to themselves.

The Japanese then blockaded Port Arthur. The new Russian commander, Admiral Stepan Makarov, sallied out to engage the blockaders. His flagship, *Petropavlosk,* hit a mine and sank with the loss of 700 lives including Makarov's. The battleship *Pobieda* and a destroyer were torpedoed but made it back to the base. Thereafter the Russians stayed in harbor.

The Russians, sailors and soldiers both, tended to discount the fighting quality of the Japanese and the efficiency of their ships. Again there is a similarity to 1941, when the officers and men of the United States Navy held their potential enemies, commonly referred to as "those little yellow monkeys," in contempt.

The defeat at Port Arthur left the Russian Imperial Navy without a significant naval force in the theater of war. The relief of Port Arthur, now besieged by land as well as sea, and significant reinforcement of the Pacific Fleet were urgently necessary if the war was to be won. But it was not until June 20, almost five months later, that Czar Nicholas II convened a meeting of the Higher Naval Board to appoint a commander for the fleet that was to steam to the Far East. The board's choice, or really the Czar's choice, was Vice Admiral Zinovy Petrovich Rozhdestvenski, whom the Czar found efficient and confident. The new commander was accounted one of the ablest Russian naval officers. Able leaders in the higher ranks of the navy were rare. As in the army, the choice commands and staff jobs went to well-born young dilettantes or to bumbling survivors of the Russian Empire's earlier, and largely unsuccessful, wars. The navy in which they served was in little better condition than the army.

The significant advances that had occurred in warship design, building, and equipment worldwide in the preceding decade had had little effect on the Russian navy. For example, ten years earlier the

British Royal Navy, then the undisputed mistress of the seas, had introduced a new electric firing mechanism. But at the start of the Russo-Japanese War, the Russian navy's most modern and powerful ships still employed the noninstantaneous lanyard procedure for firing guns. The British, American, Japanese, and French navies all used telescopic sights. These were introduced into the Russian fleet midway through the war.

Russian naval construction, to put it mildly, smacked more of the eighteenth than the twentieth century. Five or six years were required to fit out a ship after it had been launched. Often the guns and armor with which she was equipped were obsolete by the time they were installed.

Aristocratic tastes and needs affected ship construction. Admiral Rozhdestvenski's flagship was the battleship *Suvorov,* sister ship to the *Orel, Borodino,* and *Alexander III.* Russian officers expected to be comfortable at sea. Their quarters and wardrooms were both elaborate and well protected by armor. The result was that these ships, the backbone of the fleet, were top-heavy. The secondary armament could not be used in a heavy sea, and all but two feet of the main belt of armor was submerged when the ships were loaded. This not only cut the vessels' speed but made them unstable in any sort of weather. Rozhdestvenski ordered the crews to strip the superstructures of his ships of unnecessary weight. They did so, to the discomfort of his officers, but still the battleships remained unwieldy.

The Russian sailors were not, as is commonly supposed, ripe for mutiny. They were, however, ripe for defeat because of insufficient training. Drawn largely from the peasants, the largest class in imperial Russia, their seagoing training was limited to the six yearly ice-free months in the Baltic. These peasant-sailors, largely illiterate, were assigned to weapons that, for their time, were highly sophisticated (technology *was* creeping into the Imperial Navy, albeit at a slower pace than elsewhere). The intricacies of engines and gun turrets had to be forcefully fed to the sons of peasants for whom a sewing machine was a mechanical wonder.

Rozhdestvenski's fleet was manned by these peasant conscripts, plus a smattering of reservists and some merchant seamen. Aside from the reservists, none had battle experience—and that of the reservists often went back to the days of sail! Richard Hough quotes a gunnery lieutenant on the *Suvorov* as saying, "One half will have to be taught everything because they know nothing, the other half because they have forgotten everything; but if they do remember anything, then it is obsolete."

Four new battleships, considered modern by the Russian Admiralty, were to form the backbone of the Russian Second Pacific Squadron ordered to raise the siege of Port Arthur and destroy Togo's fleet. For their day they were huge, scheduled for 13,500 tons. But the "improvements" in the course of construction, cited above, had raised the displacement to 15,000 tons. The main armament was two turrets, one fore and the other aft, of twelve-inch guns theoretically able to throw a 700-pound shell more than ten miles. Twelve six-inch guns provided the secondary armament. The battleships also were armed with lighter guns to be used against torpedo boats, which were then considered to be the capital ships' most deadly enemy. The ships were protected by strips of steel ten inches thick at the waterline, and there was four-inch armor on the decks and fourteen-inch armor protecting their vitals. The battleships' engines gave them a speed of over eighteen knots.

The four new battleships were supported by three older battleships. These were less heavily armed and armored. The *Oslyabya,* the most modern of the trio, bristled with guns, including ten-inch guns as the main armament and a medley of guns of other calibers firing from ports along her sides. The second division of the squadron was completed by two ancient armored ships, the *Sisoy Veliky* and the *Navarin*. The latter had been built for coastal defense and, in fact, was more a monitor than a battleship. Optimists put the speed of these two vessels at twelve knots.

The remainder of the squadron was the result of the Admiralty's scouring of shipyards and anchorages. The cruiser *Dmitri Donskoy* had been designed in the seventies and had been first used as an armored frigate with sailing rig. Her speed was estimated at ten knots. The *Svetlana,* a naval designer's nightmare, was a cross between a cruiser and a yacht. The only effective secondary element in the squadron was a force of four cruisers—*Oleg, Aurora, Zhemchug,* and *Izumrud*. These were modern, relatively fast ships. They were backed by nine destroyers, or as they were called at that time, torpedo-boat destroyers. Each had a displacement of 350 tons, hardly enough for a journey halfway around the world from the Baltic to Tsushima.

The fighting ships were supported by a heterogeneous collection of support craft: transports, merchantmen, tugboats, a hospital ship, and the *Kamchatka,* a maintenance vessel.

The squadron, forty-two ships in all, faced a mission that would have daunted any navy in the world except one served by courageous, fatalistic Russians. To be sure there was a revolutionary element among the crews. After the battle, it was charged that many of the sailors were more interested in the expedition's failure than in its success. There was evidence of sabotage on the *Orel* and some odd construction faults; her rivets opened in dock. Revolutionary fervor in the Russia of that day was strongest in the semieducated class from which a portion of the crews for the new ships were drawn. But the influence of the revolutionaries among the crew was probably no more detrimental to the ships' efficiency than the ineffectiveness of peasants faced with the problems of modern machinery. Russia did not then, nor did she for another forty years, possess a technologically educated work force.

The mission was to steam from St. Petersburg to the Far East and defeat the Japanese fleet! In retrospect the first part of this challenge was as daunting as the second.

A supply of coal was essential. At cruising speed the squadron would consume 3,000 tons of coal a day; at full speed, about 10,000 tons. Unlike the British, the Russians had no coaling stations scattered around the globe. A modest estimate was that they needed half a million tons of coal to reach the Far East. Neutral ports would be closed to a combatant fleet. The British, who inclined toward Japan's favor, were unlikely to be co-operative. The only solution was to buy or rent colliers (coal ships) that would supply the fleet on its voyage. The German Hamburg–Amerika Line agreed to provide sixty colliers to supply the fleet with coal from the Baltic to the Yellow Sea. To the Admiralty in St. Petersburg, this probably sounded feasible; to Rozhdestvenski it meant another nightmare. He would have to halt his fleet at sea or in a strange harbor while coal was transferred by hand from colliers to warships, sack by sack. It was an enormous problem. But in retrospect it was less important than others that arose.

In all wars misinformation about the enemy plays a part. Nine months of war against the ingenious and enterprising Japanese had formed in Russian minds a ludicrously exaggerated idea of their enemy. Even before the fleet left Kronštadt for Reval and an inspection by the Czar, St. Petersburg was rife with rumors that the Japanese had collected a torpedo-boat squadron (how this was done was never explained) and intended to ambush the Second Pacific Squadron on its voyage. It was a self-perpetuating rumor. Russian consuls in Baltic and Scandinavian ports asked merchant captains to be on the lookout. The captains returned to consuls in other ports with stories of shadowy warships on the horizon. But after Togo's successes with torpedo boats at Port Arthur, the Russians had real reason to fear an attack by these vessels.

Rozhdestvenski, therefore, took the maximum precautions. An attempt to sweep the Great Belt (the Kattegat) between Denmark and Sweden of nonexistent mines was unsuccessful although, perhaps, heartening to the crews. Nine days out of Reval, on Oct. 21, a more serious incident occurred.

The night before, the *Navarin* had reported sighting two balloons. No one else ever heard or saw the balloons, but in their jittery state the Russians were willing to believe anything. The sighting of these early UFOs forced the admiral to discontinue coaling and to order an immediate departure into the North Sea.

There the squadron encountered heavy fog. This was trial enough for inexperienced sailors, but worse was still to come. In the early afternoon the *Kamchatka*, ahead of the flagship, reported that it was being chased by eight torpedo boats. Officers on the bridge of the elderly supply ship said that they could not see any torpedoes and later reported that they had lost sight of the boats. But the first message was enough to make the Russians, officers and enlisted men alike, even more nervous. Here was proof that those stories which had circulated around dinner tables in St. Petersburg and in the wardrooms were true. There might be more than torpedo boats out there in the mists—there might be destroyers or even cruisers. Well, the fleet was prepared. No Japanese force could turn them from their holy mission of relieving Port Arthur and destroying Admiral Togo!

A fleet of 100-ton, single-screw British trawlers had left Hull on the English coast on Oct. 19 and had reached the familiar fishing grounds of the Dogger Bank in the North Sea between England and Denmark, on the evening of the twenty-first. The trawlers had been seen by several merchantmen who skirted the grounds to avoid collision. Just after midnight, however, the fishermen sighted a line of battleships. The captains reckoned that this was the Royal Navy's

Channel Fleet, which invariably respected the trawlers. The fishing vessels, known collectively as the Gamecock Fleet, continued their fishing. To warn the approaching battleships of their presence, one trawler fired two flares. There was no answer from the warships, so the trawlers steamed to the windward, out of the course of the on-coming battleships.

Suddenly the little ships were engulfed in the harsh glare of searchlights. Three trawlers were singled out. The *Suvorov* began firing at a range of one hundred yards. One trawler, the *Crane,* had two men killed and many wounded. Three other trawlers took off the dead and wounded. The *Crane* sank. Slowly the firing died and the searchlights went out.

The Russians' bearing in this, the squadron's only successful operation, sheds no great luster on the Imperial Navy. Officers and sailors alike believed they were in the midst of a full-scale Japanese attack and that the torpedo boats were supported by cruisers. The two flares sent up to signal the presence of the trawlers were interpreted as a Japanese battle signal. The flagship ordered, "Engage enemy," and the tragicomedy aboard the squadron began. Even in those circumstances, it took the Russians some time to sight their supposed "enemy."

The firing was heavy. Some of the lighter Russian guns soon ran out of ammunition. The sailors' discipline, never especially rigid, all but disappeared. The boom of the flagship's heavy guns sounded to some like torpedoes hitting. Although, of course, the trawlers could not return fire, many of the sailors and some of the officers fell flat on the decks. However, three of the "enemy" had been hit and one sunk, and the officers, repairing to their elaborate wardrooms, toasted their victory with champagne and vodka.

It is almost incomprehensible that neither Rozhdestvenski nor his senior officers realized what they had done. Their attitude was one of self-congratulation. What they had done, of course, was not simply to shell an inoffensive fishing fleet, but to ignite a diplomatic incident that brought the British and Russian Empires perilously close to war. The British of that day considered the Russians as their principal enemies, although some far-sighted admirals and generals discerned a greater threat in Germany's naval-building program. But there had been a long duel with Russia in Central Asia beginning with Afghanistan, where Russian ambitions were clear. So the news that a Russian squadron had fired on inoffensive British trawlers and had killed two British subjects touched off waves of indignation.

Crowds protested in Trafalgar Square. Earnest deputations waited on the Prime Minister, the First Lord of the Admiralty, and members of Parliament. Condolences poured into Hull. The British ambassador in St. Petersburg delivered a strong note of protest demanding an explanation, an apology, and assurances that the guilty officers would be disciplined. The London *Times* commented magisterially that "the mind of the Government, like the mind of the nation, is made up." The British of that day did not take such incidents lightly.

The Royal Navy's Mediterranean, Channel, and Home Fleets were readied for war. By the evening of Oct. 26, the Royal Navy had twenty-eight battleships at sea or with steam up, prepared to intercept and destroy the Russian Second Pacific Squadron.

That squadron steamed on through the Channel and southward toward Spain without knowledge of the to-do it had occasioned. It was not until Rozhdestvenski reached Vigo near the northwestern tip of the Iberian Peninsula that the admiral realized the effect of the Dogger Bank incident on European opinion. The Spanish were cold. The squadron was entitled to stay twenty-four hours and no longer as warships of a belligerent power. Spanish policemen boarded the ships to prevent coaling or any other replenishment. When the newspapers—continental as well as British—arrived, the Russian officers found that Berlin, Paris, and other capitals were almost as aroused as London.

The admiral's version of the incident, telegraphed to St. Petersburg, hardly satisfied the British. He insisted that the Russian attack was "provoked by two torpedo boats which, without showing any lights, under cover of darkness advanced to attack the vessel steaming at the head of the detachment. When the detachment began to sweep the sea with its searchlights and opened fire, the presence was also discovered of small fishing vessels. The detachment endeavored to spare these vessels."

He also expressed sympathy "in the name of the fleet" for "the unfortunate victims." However, he claimed that neither his fleet nor any other could have acted differently under the circumstances.

An international commission, always an attractive refuge for insoluble arguments of this kind, was established to investigate the incident. Units of the squadron involved were to be detained at Vigo and the responsible officers questioned. Rozhdestvenski paid little attention. He left in Vigo some junior officers from the three other battleships, and from the flagship he sent Captain Nicholas Klado whom the admiral considered an intriguer. Having thus, in his own mind, cleared his and the squadron's name, he steamed out of Vigo on the morning of Nov. 1, escorted, once the squadron cleared Spanish territorial waters, by a squadron of British warships. The first great trial was over.

The tragicomedy of the Dogger Bank incident has entered history. For nearly three quarters of a century since, the Russian officers and men involved have been ridiculed. And, indeed, it was in retrospect a ludicrous event. Yet in war, when few combatants are quite sane, such things do happen. A decade later the British, those supposedly hard-headed, no-nonsense people, were swept by a frenzy of enthusiasm as a result of a rumor that Russian troops were passing through England on their way to the relief of the hard-pressed Allies in France. Incredibly, the Russians were identified because "they had snow on their boots."

From that point the squadron, continuing its 18,000-mile voyage, encountered the difficulties that might be expected from crews hurriedly assembled and ships badly found. The steering gear of the *Orel* broke not once but twice. Exercises at sea revealed startling inexperience on the part of officers and crew. The fleet reached Tangier, coaled in fierce heat, and then divided. Rozhdestvenski took four battleships on the long voyage around the Cape of Good Hope. The *Sisoy Veliky, Navarin,* three light cruisers, and the destroyers were sent eastward to take the Suez Canal and the short route to the Indian Ocean.

The battleships steamed down the coast of Africa, pausing to coal at Dakar, in French West Africa (now Senegal). The French had forbidden the squadron to coal at Libreville, the next stop, so the Russians loaded as much fuel in Dakar as they could. Coal was dumped into every available space, including the cabins of officers up to the rank of commander. The ships left Dakar in clouds of coal dust that had sifted into every part of the vessels. The battleships, never particularly handy at sea, moved sluggishly under this new burden. They were no longer warships but glorified colliers. They plodded on into the sodden heat of the West African summer, coal dust in the water, the food, the bearings, the guns—everywhere!

This woeful armada turned past the Cape of Good Hope and

started up Africa's east coast and the harbor of Nossi-Bé, in Madagascar. There it was to await orders and the arrival of the Third Pacific Squadron, a reinforcement hastily scraped up from the Czar's few remaining naval forces.

Almost everything that could happen to a fleet far from enemy shells happened to the Russians at Nossi-Bé. The climate was brutal —the few Frenchmen in the area told them they would be lucky to last three months. Their food was totally unsuited to the climatic conditions. Officers and men went drinking and whoring ashore. Demoralization among officers was almost as great as among the sailors. Rozhdestvenski became ill and threatened to resign. There was mutiny on the Third Pacific Squadron's *Nakhimov* with 400 angry sailors in arms. The mutiny was quelled, and ten of the ringleaders were shot. Other offenders were transferred to a cruiser whose crew joined them in another mutiny.

The admiral, recovering his health but not his confidence, set the fleet to firing practice. This was marked by bad navigation and worse marksmanship. The fleet was short of ammunition, and realistic maneuvers were out of the question because of the coal situation. Once they assayed a torpedo attack with live weapons. A fiasco.

Rozhdestvenski, never a particularly sanguine man, daily grew more pessimistic. St. Petersburg sought his appreciation of the situation. It was stark:

"I have not the slightest prospect of recovering the command of the sea with the forces under my orders," he replied. "The dispatch of reinforcements composed of untested or badly built vessels would only render the fleet more vulnerable. In my view the only possible course is to use all force to break through to Vladivostok and from this base to threaten the enemy's communications."

This is not the attitude of a victor. But it is the attitude of a realist. The admiral knew that the Third Pacific Squadron, under the command of Rear Admiral Nebogatov, was something less than terrifying to its putative enemies. It consisted of one ancient battleship, *Czar Nicholas I,* a relatively efficient cruiser, and three armored coast-defense vessels of dubious value in a fleet action.

Rozhdestvenski waited. But the reinforcements did not come. So he sailed east again, passing Singapore on April 5 and reaching Cam Ranh Bay on the coast of Vietnam, then French Cochin China, on April 14. Cam Ranh Bay was, and is, a magnificent anchorage. Almost three quarters of a century ago, it was that and no more.

Today, by grace of the millions of dollars spent by the United States to construct shore facilities, Cam Ranh Bay is the most modern naval base on the Asian mainland between Singapore and Shanghai. Admiral Nebogatov's Third Squadron caught up with Rozhdestvenski at Cam Ranh Bay. The new Far East Fleet was assembled.

No one can exaggerate the Russians' difficulties on their way to Tsushima Island. Indeed, a day-to-day account of the voyage would disclose mental and physical agonies, ghastly mistakes of seamanship, and mutinous attitudes far exceeding the rough outline provided above. In all their aspects, from the vainglory of the stupid old men in the Admiralty in St. Petersburg to the drunken, mutinous crews, from the amateurish firing practices to the continual breakdowns of ill-tended machines, they illustrate the basic weakness of the Russian Empire. In retrospect the entire command reflects the doddering inefficiency of the empire it served. So the fleet steamed north to Tsushima and disaster.

The fleet left Cam Ranh Bay on May 14. In all there were forty-two ships—some, as we know now (and Rozhdestvenski knew then), totally unsuited to meet a Japanese fleet. But whatever their problems with engineering, whatever their revolutionary instincts, however bad their health, these were Russians. If there was one bond that united them, it was that of high personal courage. They entered the battle in a fatalistic mood.

Rozhdestvenski was headed for Vladivostok. Admiral Togo's task was to intercept and destroy him. The Japanese leader held almost all the cards.

The Japanese battle fleet was deployed at Masampo near the southern tip of Korea. Across the Tsushima Strait, Togo arrayed his cruisers. Tsushima, from which the great battle took its name, is about fifty miles from Korea and about one hundred miles from the then-Japanese naval base at Shimonoseki. Tsushima means "the island of the donkey's ears." Southeast of Tsushima is the smaller island of Ikishima. The true width of the strait is only forty miles. Rozhdestvenski had to pass through this to reach Vladivostok.

The Russian position was in some ways comparable to that of Spain's Invincible Armada when it sailed against the English. On the Russian side were ill-found ships, faulty machinery, discontented crews, and badly trained officers. They faced a fleet already wearing the laurels of Port Arthur. Japan's ships had been repaired. There was no shortage of ammunition. The fleet was commanded by the first sailor of his day, an admiral whose genius it was to employ tactical orthodoxy at the highest peak of efficiency. But this cold, calculating mind was moved by a highly developed combative instinct. Togo was quite ready to risk himself, and his fleet, if the risk ensured the destruction of the enemy. There were no self-doubts among the Japanese.

"We all ought to rejoice" that we are under the command of Admiral Togo, a Japanese destroyer commander wrote shortly before the battle. But, he added, he was happy that he would be a "certain distance" from his formidable commander. For Togo was more respected than loved by his officers and men. If, as the admiring British thought, he had "the Nelson touch," the touch was confined only to his brilliant handling of his fleet. He was brave, thought with clarity even at the height of action, and was a rigid disciplinarian. These qualities sufficed for a people naturally inclined to authoritarianism.

Russian security under the czars was lamentable. The Japanese Emperor had held a secret conference on Nov. 14, 1904, to plan the destruction of the Second Pacific Squadron, which had sailed a month earlier. As a result the guns and machinery of the Japanese fleet were refitted and the crews, already veterans of the Port Arthur fighting, went through a training program to ensure that there would be no slackness when next they met the Russians. The refitting and retraining were completed by late February 1905.

Togo based his fleet at Chinhae Bay on the southeastern coast of Korea. From there he directed patrol activities in the Sea of Japan by a Special Service Squadron of armed merchantmen and his light cruisers. His battleships and armored cruisers waited in the bay for the arrival of the Russians.

There is something pathetic about the Czar's last fleet as it steamed north from Cam Ranh Bay. Those clumsy floating castles, those ill-found cruisers carried with them the military traditions of the vast empire for which they fought. Russian naval tradition was composed largely of lost battles, often fought at great odds.

Rozhdestvenski set course straight for Vladivostok through the strait between Tsushima and the Japanese mainland. There was an alternative. The Russian admiral could have sailed around Japan's eastern coast and through the Strait of La Pérouse. The Russian admiral's decision to "put it to the touch, to win or lose it all," was dictated by the fear of torpedo-boat attacks, the Russian naval nightmare, the difficulties of coaling in the long Pacific swell, and the prospect that in any case they would be observed and intercepted by Togo before they neared Vladivostok.

For a few hours the Russians enjoyed a momentary elation. Had they outwitted Togo? When the morning of May 26 came, there were no Japanese ships in sight. But the reckoning had only been postponed. The morning was bright, the sea calm. The fleet steamed on in two columns; the seven battleships and the *Nakhimov* of the original, and now-destroyed, Second Pacific Squadron to starboard and to port Admiral Nebogatov on the *Czar Nicholas I* ahead of the coast-defense ships and four cruisers. Between the two lines of warships straggled the transports—the *Kamchatka,* the *Rousse,* and the *Svir*—along with two hospital ships and seven destroyers. Five other cruisers acted as scouts.

The next morning the mist had returned. Russian hopes rose still further. They might yet elude Togo. The end of their 18,000-mile journey was near. As the morning advanced, the mist thinned and they could see to port the cleft mountain that gave Tsushima its name. As Richard Hough comments, "They had come 18,000 miles to be greeted by an ass."

They were alone but not unobserved. The Japanese auxiliary cruiser *Shinano Maru* had sighted them in the early morning. The Russians, their speed dictated by that of the slowest ships, were moving at nine knots and continued to do so for most of that fateful day. Togo, on the other hand, maneuvered at slightly less than twice that speed.

Later in the morning the cruiser *Idzumo* appeared out of the mist from the northeast. She did not open fire, and the fleet steamed slowly along. Togo, meanwhile, had started for his chosen battle area east of Tsushima Island, where the straits were narrowest. Three battleships—the *Mikasa,* the *Fuji,* and the *Asahi*—led the Japanese fleet. The battleships were accompanied by two heavily armored cruisers. Admiral Hikonojo Kamimura commanded six other armored cruisers attached to the battleships.

Togo's plan was simple. The battleships and larger cruisers would attack the largest Russian ships. Another cruiser squadron under Admiral Dewa would fall on the slower Russian ships. The large torpedo-boat fleet would be held in reserve for action at night.

A naval action, we have it on the authority of Winston Churchill, is the most hazardous of all battles. But Admiral Togo that day

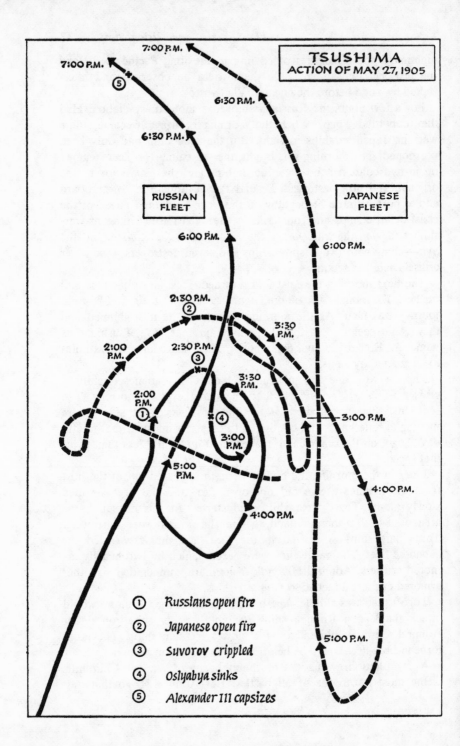

TSUSHIMA
ACTION OF MAY 27, 1905

7:00 P.M.

7:00 P.M.
⑤

6:30 P.M.

6:30 P.M.

RUSSIAN
FLEET

JAPANESE
FLEET

6:00 P.M.

6:00 P.M.

2:30 P.M.
②

3:30
P.M.

2:00
P.M.

2:30 P.M.
③

3:30
P.M.

3:00 P.M.

2:00
P.M.
①

3:30
P.M.

④

5:00
P.M.

3:00
P.M.

4:00 P.M.

4:00 P.M.

5:00 P.M.

① Russians open fire

② Japanese open fire

③ Suvorov crippled

④ Oslyabya sinks

⑤ Alexander III capsizes

commanded with calm deliberation. The *Idzumo* was replaced by the elderly battleship *Chin-Yen* accompanied by four cruisers. The Japanese ships remained just out of range, about five miles, surveying the Russian fleet which was now steaming in line and reporting its strength, speed, and composition to the flagship. Tsushima was the first naval battle in which radio was used in action. The Japanese employed it freely, but the Russians feared that its use would disclose their location and so used it sparingly, relying during most of the action on signal flags and semaphores.

The moment of battle was approaching rapidly. In the fleeting minutes of calm remaining, Rozhdestvenski made his greatest mistake of the battle. The first and second divisions of heavy ships were ordered to turn ninety degrees to starboard to interpose a shield between themselves and the weaker ships. They were also ordered to raise their speed to eleven knots. Then, unexpectedly, the admiral countermanded the order and told the fleet to return to the in-line-ahead formation it had previously kept.

Nebogatov reported later that the movements led to "absolute confusion."

The Russian fleet went into action, buoyed at the last moment by one of those obeisances to tradition that form so large and unexpected a part of the Russian character, be it Czarist or Communist. They remembered aboard the flagship that it was the anniversary of the coronation of the Czar and Czarina. There was a thanksgiving service, a swig of vodka for every crewman, and (of course) champagne in the wardroom. Glasses were raised to the toast: "On this, the great anniversary of the sacred coronation of their Majesties, may God help us to serve with him our beloved country. The health of the Emperor! The Empress! To Russia!"

As they downed their champagne, the alarm rang for action stations. Togo, having hoisted his own Nelsonian order—"The rise and fall of the Empire depends upon today's battle; let every man do his utmost"—turned westward to cross the line of advance about 8,500 yards ahead of the Russians with his flagship, *Mikasa,* in the vanguard. The Russians opened fire at shortly after two in the afternoon, and the Japanese responded as they began to cross the "T."

Togo was accomplishing what every admiral sought. He was bringing his ships' broadsides upon the head of the Russian column. Crossing the "T" was a naval maneuver comparable in land warfare to the double envelopment of Cannae, the *ne plus ultra* of command expertise.

As they came on, the Russians opened a heavy and accurate fire. But the return fire of the Japanese was more lethal. Their twelve-inch shells exploded on contact, and it was not long before the upper works of the *Suvorov* were badly battered. The Russian flagship had scored some hits with its six-inch guns on the *Mikasa* and on the cruiser *Shikishima,* but the damage was negligible compared to that on the *Suvorov,* the *Alexander III,* and the *Borodino.*

Now the fleets were steaming in parallel lines. The Russians concentrated on the *Mikasa,* the Japanese on the *Suvorov* and the *Oslyabya,* fifth in the Czarist line.

At this point the Russians were giving as good as they got. The *Mikasa* had been hit ten times (some authorities say twelve) by twelve-inch and six-inch shells. The obsolescent vessels of Nebogatov's third division, firing at extreme range, had put one turret on the cruiser *Yakumo* out of action; the *Asana,* hit by a twelve-inch shell from the *Nicholas I,* was forced out of line, and the *Nishin* was badly mauled by a ten-inch projectile.

The accuracy and volume of Japanese fire slowly began to tell. The instantaneous-fuse shells ripped apart the upper works of the Russian ships, tore holes in the armor, started fires, and smashed lifeboats. They also killed or hideously wounded Russian sailors. The *Suvorov*'s dressing station was hit; two gun turrets were put out of action; the conning tower, from which the ship and the fleet were commanded, was hit twice, wounding Rozhdestvenski and killing his gunnery officer. The flagship was unable to control its own actions from the conning tower, and the fleet proceeded unlead into disaster.

Togo—he had been slightly wounded but paid no attention to the gash in his leg—now decided to switch to armor-piercing shells. Through his glasses, he could see clouds of smoke pouring from the superstructures of the enemy battleships and fingers of flame leaping from below decks.

A shell hit the *Suvorov* astern, jamming her steering gear. At approximately 2:30 P.M. the flagship lurched out of line. Twenty minutes later the *Oslyabya,* her guns out of action, her decks a shambles, sank. She was the first armored warship ever to be sunk by gunfire.

The Russians are, and were, a very brave race, but neither they nor any other previous seamen had had to face the incessant hurricane of fire that now enveloped their battleships. Many, still miraculously unwounded in that hail of steel and explosives, stood or lay, mute and uncomprehending. They neither heard nor obeyed orders. They were shell-shocked, a condition which ten years hence could be readily found on the western or eastern fronts of World War I.

Togo's audacious maneuvering and accurate gunnery had forced the Russian fleet to starboard. There was an interval during which the Czarist battleships circled the helpless *Suvorov*. Then they reformed line and resumed their course to the north at about 3 P.M. Togo, having already crossed the head of their line, now recrossed it, and the second phase of the battle began with the *Mikasa* at the head of the Japanese line.

In retrospect the expert maneuvering of the Japanese leaders commands as much respect as the gunnery of their crews. The turning of great ships at high speeds in battle is a maneuver that demands the highest levels of seamanship from captains, navigators, and crews. The Japanese navy, a relative newcomer on the world's stage, performed such intricate maneuvers at Tsushima as though it had been doing them in battle for centuries.

The Russians came on, led now by the *Alexander III* and harried from the south by the Japanese cruiser squadrons. Their fire drove the Russian transports to the rear of the fleet where the *Ural*, a big, ex-German liner, was sunk.

Rozhdestvenski, now wounded in the head, the back, and the right leg, was transferred to the destroyer *Buiny*.

The *Borodino* took over leadership of the Russian line as the *Alexander III* fell back. At about 7 P.M. the *Alexander III* capsized, and a few minutes later the *Borodino* exploded. Darkness was falling. Togo withdrew his big ships, leaving the battle to the torpedo boats and destroyers—eighty of the former, twenty-one of the latter. One important casualty was the *Suvorov*. The flagship, hit by four torpedoes, went down about sundown. She was a wreck when she sank; nothing about her bore the slightest resemblance to the ship that had left St. Petersburg the preceding year. A few minutes later the ill-fated *Kamchatka* was hit by another salvo of torpedoes and sank.

All night the Japanese torpedo boats darted through the battered Russian fleet like wolves through a herd of sheep. But although the odds were in favor of the Japanese, the Russian losses were not as high as might have been expected.

Togo resumed the battle at dawn on May 28. "Battle" is a misnomer. It was a mopping-up operation. Nebogatov on the *Czar Nicholas I* was caught eighteen miles south of the island of Takeshima with two other battered ships. The Japanese gunners resumed their drumfire upon the Russian ships. Russian ammunition was running out. At noon the admiral ran up the white flag, a tablecloth, and surrendered "as the only means of saving our crews from destruction."

The cruiser squadron, commanded by Admiral Enkvist, ran for it. After a nightmare night of dodging Japanese torpedoes in which the *Ural* rammed the stern of the *Zhemchug* and the *Andadyr* rammed and sank the *Rousse,* Enkvist set course for Manila and internment. He left behind the ancient *Dmitri Donskoy,* which in her death agonies performed far more efficiently than other, newer warships. She sank two torpedo boats, damaged a third, and hit four Japanese cruisers. Afire, badly holed, the *Dmitri Donskoy,* with not an unwounded man aboard, managed to grope into the shelter of an island where she sank. She had been laid down in 1885, and she fought on alone for two hours.

The *Monomalk* and *Sisoy Veliky,* two other ironclads, had been hit by torpedoes and surrendered to the Japanese at dawn without firing a shot. The *Oushakov,* on the other hand, fought to the water's edge before going down.

Rozhdestvenski had been transferred a second time, this time to the destroyer *Biedovy.* The ship was captured in the late afternoon along with her commander in chief. Another destroyer, the *Groznyi,* by burning most of her wooden fittings for fuel, avoided surrender. She was one of the ships, together with another destroyer and the light cruiser *Almax,* to reach Vladivostok with the tidings of a defeat unparalleled in Russian naval annals.

Eight Russian capital ships had been sunk and four captured. Five cruisers and seven destroyers had been destroyed. The Japanese, on the other hand, had lost three torpedo boats, and the *Mikasa* and other battleships had sustained some damage. The Russian casualties in manpower were staggering: 4,830 dead and 5,917 wounded or captured. The total Japanese losses, including 117 killed, were 700.

Togo lived on as the author of the Japanese navy's greatest victory and the founder of a tradition of triumph on the seas. He was not, as he is so often pictured, the "father" of the Japanese Imperial Navy. The tools already had been made when he showed the world how to use them. But he was more important; his naval genius catapulted Japan into the first rank of naval powers.

Rozhdestvenski was taken to a Japanese naval hospital at Sasebo. There he was visited by Togo, who paid him his "highest respects" for his bravery. By late September, the admiral was recovered to the point where he could start the long journey by land from Vladivostok to St. Petersburg. Revolution was abroad in the land, and the convalescent admiral was heckled by drunken sailors and workmen. The towns through which the Trans-Siberian Railway train passed were tumultuous with revolt. Only at Tulun, a tiny hamlet, did the defeated admiral receive any reception. There he was first cheered and then questioned by a group of soldiers and workmen. Had Nebogatov failed him? Had there been treason?

"No, there was no treason," Rozhdestvenski said. "We just weren't strong enough—and God gave us no luck."

A court martial in St. Petersburg acquitted Rozhdestvenski. He retired on an adequate pension. When Nebogatov was court-martialed, Rozhdestvenski generously supported his subordinate. It was not enough. Nebogatov was sentenced to be shot, but the sentence was commuted to a long prison term. Rozhdestvenski died in 1909.

To the world of 1905 Tsushima was a wonder. As it was seen in Washington, London, Berlin, and Paris, a weak Asian power had defeated one of the great powers of Europe. The comparison between David and Goliath was done to death.

Of course, the battle was nothing of the kind. It was a one-sided contest between an efficient, highly motivated fleet commanded by an admiral of genius and an ill-matched collection of vessels, the most modern of which were poorly served by officers and men alike. The commander, Rozhdestvenski, was a man of great physical courage but little suited to high command. Even had he been a captain of great ability, the sloth, incompetence, and jealousy of his subordinates might have wrecked him as effectively as Togo's twelve-inch shells. Russia in 1905 was not the great military power it professed to be. It was an empire tottering to its fall. Tsushima hastened the process.

Few of the great figures at Tsushima played any important roles in World War I. One, however, was reserved for a larger fate in the second. Midshipman Isoroku Yamamoto was present. Twenty-four years later he commanded the Japanese Combined Fleet for the attack on Pearl Harbor.

II

Germany Loses, No One Wins

THE MARNE

The Battle of the Marne was the strangest decisive battle in history. It was fought in September 1914 at the very outset of a war that was to continue for four and a quarter years. It covered, at the most conservative estimates, 150 miles of forest, meadow, valley, and upland. Decisive though it was, nowhere were great masses of men locked in desperate conflict. It was instead a battle of maneuver and movement. The casualties were small in comparison with the butcher's bill for Verdun or the Somme.

The Marne epitomizes Liddell Hart's theory that the true history of battles can be found only in the minds of opposing commanders. On each side the generals' appreciation of the other side's plans, their reaction to changes in plan, and their energy or lack of that vital force were the decisive factors. One more element must be mentioned; the intrusion onto the battlefield of a figure alien to the combatants, a staff officer exercising powers that today would be reserved to a commander in chief.

The Marne was a decisive battle. But at the time few realized it. There is an analogy here to the Battle of Britain a quarter of a century later, which we shall discuss in Chapter 6.

Why was the Marne decisive? Because it frustrated the basic German plan to first defeat the French and British in the west and then to turn upon the fumbling, ill-led legions of imperial Russia. After the Marne, the German Empire resorted to other plans, some of them brilliant, but never again was it to have complete victory so nearly within its grasp.

A man long dead when it began conceived the Battle of the Marne. This man was Graf Alfred von Schlieffen, Chief of the German General Staff from 1891 to 1906. Like many of his colleagues, he had been surprised and alarmed by the rapid recovery of the French from the stunning defeat of 1870–71 in the Franco-Prussian War. Unlike Kaiser Wilhelm II and the sycophants of the court circle, Schlieffen expected the renewal of war between the two ancient enemies. And as France allied herself first with imperial Russia and second with her old foe, Britain, the new war appeared to him inevitable.

Schlieffen and his staff planners were not, as they have sometimes been portrayed, highly confident soldiers unaware of difficulties. They knew that Germany and her main ally, Austria, would be inferior in manpower at least to France, Russia, and Britain. But Germany held the center of Europe. From that position, using interior lines of communication, it might be possible with meticulous planning to defeat the French before the slow-moving Russians could complete their mobilization and advance into East Prussia. Once the French and their British allies, of whom the Germans thought little, were defeated, then the forces of the German Empire could turn on the Russians and destroy them.

The implementation of this strategic conception presented a series of problems. A smashing invasion of France across the frontiers would face formidable geographical difficulties. The frontier was only about 150 miles long. For seventy miles it followed the Vosges Mountains. It was studded with the fortresses of Verdun, Toul, and Épinal, each mothering minor strongholds. The French had left open the area between Épinal and Toul in the hope that the Germans would advance through the gap, the Trouée de Charmes, and be destroyed. North of Verdun lay the frontiers of Luxembourg and Belgium, neutral states, each covered by the hills and forests of the Ardennes.

Faced with this situation, Schlieffen conceived a plan that would concentrate thirty-five of the forty German army corps against France. The bulk of these were to be placed on the right wing for a wheeling movement through France that would pivot on the fortified area of Metz-Thionville. A total of fifty-three divisions supported by *Landwehr* divisions, comparable to National Guard divisions, was to lend power to the right wing. This enormous mass of infantry, cavalry, and artillery was to sweep through Belgium and northern France, wheeling gradually to the east, passing west of Paris, crossing the Seine River near Rouen, and driving the French back toward the Moselle River where they would be smashed.

Everything depended on speed. Schlieffen died in bed murmuring, "Keep the right wing strong." In his original plan he allotted only ten divisions for the defense of East Prussia against the Russians.

The Schlieffen Plan surprised the French, although had they been willing to listen to others, they might have been better prepared. As early as 1911 Henry Wilson, a brilliant but eccentric British general, outlined the Germans' plan to the British cabinet. But the French were busy with their own plan which they kept secret. It was a harebrained enterprise, especially when one realizes that the lessons of the Boer War were available to the French general staff.

The French general staff was presided over by General Joseph Joffre, an engineer who had served faithfully but without great distinction in the colonial wars France had waged since 1870. In physique plump to the point of obesity, by nature indolent, Joffre relished his meals and insisted on an undisturbed night's sleep—not inspiring characteristics for the commander of over a million men in the Battle of the Marne. Yet this unemotional ex-colonial soldier possessed a signal qualification for high command: he was never rattled. Neither casualties—and the French casualties in the opening days of the war were very high—continued retreat, nor the loss to the enemy of old and famous cities ever disturbed his outward calm. Joseph S. Galliéni, Ferdinand Foch, Louis Franchet d'Esperey, and other French generals made significant contributions to the winning of the Marne. Yet without the phlegmatic Joffre, seeing the battle as a whole, all might have come to naught. In his approach to war, he resembles Ulysses S. Grant more than he does Napoleon or other French leaders.

The French forces commanded by Joffre were the victim of a national delusion. Field and staff officers alike believed that the *élan* of the French forces would make up for the Germans' numerical superiority, that the bayonet supported by the seventy-five-millimeter gun would provide them with superiority on the battlefield. All that was needed was *cran,* or guts. Disregarding the power of the German machine gun and heavy artillery, the French wallowed in the glories of the offensive. Consequently the general staff evolved what was called Plan 17. This called for a general offensive to the east and northeast by four French armies, with one army in reserve. The spirit of the offensive, they were sure, would carry these armies deep into the lost provinces of Alsace and Lorraine. No account was taken of the possibility that while the French were engaged in the congenial occupation of recovering these provinces, the Germans might come sweeping down on their left. Nor did the planners speculate on the possibility that unbroken infantry armed with machine guns and heavy artillery would smash attacks by soldiers in red pants and blue coats led by brave and ardent young men wearing the white gloves of St. Cyr. General Charles de Gaulle, musing on that offensive in his old age, concluded that "at least it taught one what not to do."

Thus there were two battle plans at the start of the war. Joffre had under his command 1,082,000 men, including the British Expeditionary Force. The part that the BEF played in the Marne was minor, but the part it played in the retreat to the Marne was important. Of all the Allied armies at this stage of the war, this was the most nearly professional, as was its successor in 1940. Blooded in obscure frontier battles around the world, trained to a high rate of fire and outstanding accuracy in riflery, stubborn in defense but somewhat unenterprising in pursuit, the BEF possessed the characteristics of the class from which a professional, long-service force was drawn. However, it was ill-led. General Sir John French, its commander, was a cavalryman who had made a great reputation in the Boer War. With some reason, he distrusted his French allies at the outset and alternated between unrealistic optimism and profound depression. Unlike Joffre or Galliéni, General French never perceived the whole battle.

The German commander was General Helmuth von Moltke, nephew of the great Prussian Helmuth C. B. von Moltke of 1870 renown. The younger Moltke was of a different stamp. He never exercised the control of his army commanders that was essential to success as his uncle had done in 1870–71. He was irritated and perplexed by the Kaiser. Montrose could have had men like Von Moltke in mind when he wrote, "He either fears his fate too much, or his deserts are small, who dares not put it to the touch, to win or lose it all."

Behind the plans and the commanders were the men. The Germans, who had shouted *"Nach Paris!"* as they boarded the trains that bore them westward to battle, constituted the best-trained and -armed army on the continent. Its strategy, tactics, and logistics had been worked out with infinite care and skill by the Great General Staff whose members formed a privileged elite within the officer corps. Their staff officers frequently assumed powers on the battlefield that ran well beyond their statutory rank and responsibilities.

Perhaps the staff's greatest feat was the transportation by railroad of over 3,000,000 soldiers to the western front. From Aug. 6 onward, 550 trains a day crossed Rhine bridges in 11,000 cars. The soldiers represented forty years of steadily growing military strength illuminated, as letters of the time show, by a boundless confidence in Germany's mission. The declaration of war had swept away political differences; Socialists, high and low, were as enthusiastic as Junkers (Prussian landed aristocrats) about the war. *Deutschland* was *über alles* and (they felt) God was with them.

And in the first weeks this seemed so. By Aug. 20 the German armies, well ahead of schedule, had reached Namur, the last fortress barring the Meuse River path in Belgium, and had entered Brussels. The Belgian field army, outnumbered, fell back to the fortified camp at Antwerp. The main French thrust in Lorraine to the south meanwhile made little progress at the cost of terrible casualties.

The German eruption into Belgium, particularly the taking of Liège, alerted the French high command to the gravity of the movement on their left flank. But Joffre and his intelligence officers misjudged the extent of the enemy's envelopment. They estimated that the Germans would move south between the Meuse and Ardennes. No one knew that the Germans had deployed twice as many troops as the French had estimated for an enveloping movement whose scope was far greater than the defenders had foreseen. Attempting to turn what was perceived as a German weakness to France's advantage, Joffre launched an unsuccessful offensive with twenty divisions against the center of the German line in the forest of the Ardennes. It was repulsed with heavy losses. As happened in the Battle of the Frontiers, French infantry charging with bayonets were mowed down by the German machine gunners.

To the northwest of the Ardennes, the situation was even more ominous. There the French Fifth Army of thirteen divisions and the BEF of four were menaced by the German First and Second Armies

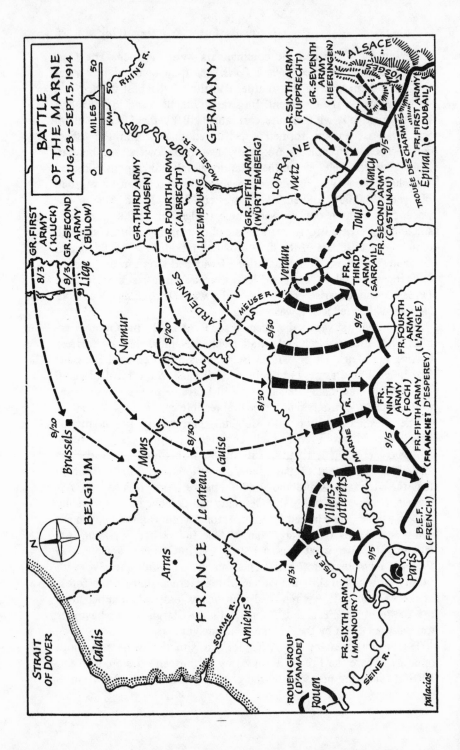

driving fast from the north and by the Third Army attacking from the east. The Allies escaped the German trap largely because General Charles Lanrezac, the French commander, showed commendable caution in advancing over the Sambre River and because the British, who somehow had eluded German intelligence, arrived on the French left. The German Second Army helped by attacking prematurely.

The Allied retreat in the northwest began on Aug. 23. The BEF, which had withstood the attacks of six German divisions that day, was doubtless glad to get away. The British returned the next day in conformity with the French movement, and the withdrawal south to the Marne had begun.

The Germans harried the Allies as they retreated. The First Army, commanded by General Alexander von Kluck, fell on the British. The British halted and gave battle, checking the enemy's onslaught. The Second Army engaged Lanrezac. Elsewhere the news was not as good as the Germans pursued the Allies. The French attacks had failed. The four British divisions were a negligible quantity in so vast a battle. The pursuing Germans were convinced, despite the absence of hordes of prisoners, that they had won a decisive victory.

This led to one of the greatest blunders of the war. The Germans had been defeated by the invading Russians at Gumbinnen in East Prussia, and the German commander, General Max von Prittwitz, had telephoned imperial headquarters begging for help. The Kaiser was upset by the news. The German people, until then fed on a diet of exaggerated good news, were appalled. Von Moltke, although personally dubious about the extent of his victory in France and Belgium, agreed to send help.

He sent four divisions. Two of these were plucked from the extreme right wing of the German movement into France, the position where they would be most needed in the coming days. Ironically, the division played little part in the great German counteroffensive in the east that ended in the Battle of Tannenberg.

At the moment the transfer passed almost unnoticed on the western front. The news continued to be good. The Kaiser was in what staff officers described as a "shout-hurrah mood" as the French and British continued their retreat. But, as a few astute German staff officers noted, the two Allied armies were still there; they were retreating, but they had not been destroyed. The French at Guise and

Nancy and the British at Mons, Le Cateau, and Villers-Cotterêts had turned and inflicted heavy casualties on their pursuers.

The operations of Von Kluck's army now became all-important. This aggressive and ambitious general, who impressed French civilians as the epitome of Prussianism, had swung to the southwest as part of the Schlieffen Plan's objective of enveloping Paris. In doing so, Kluck had battered the newly formed French Sixth Army, which Joffre intended to use in an offensive. At this point there is the first sign of a turn in the tide.

Lanrezac had attacked General Karl von Bülow's Second Army. Bülow asked for help. Kluck was ordered to provide it and, at Moltke's order, changed direction so that the axis of his advance would take him inside—that is, east of Paris. It was the end of the Schlieffen Plan, as originally conceived, for Von Moltke now envisaged a much more modest envelopment of the French center and right. The Fourth and Fifth Armies in the center were to drive to the southeast. The left wing of the Sixth and Seventh Armies was ordered to smash through the French in their fortifications between Toul and Épinal. Meanwhile the First and Second Armies on the right wing were to face west and deal with any French attack from Paris. The destruction of the Allied armies remained the objective. But the means were more limited, the planning more pedestrian.

The French had been doing some planning on their own. Joffre, whose calm never deserted him throughout the retreat, had decided to reinforce the Paris garrison with General Michel J. Maunoury's Sixth Army, which had already been mauled by Von Kluck. But judging by the orders he issued on Sept. 1, a general offensive was far from Joffre's mind. On that day he directed the Allied forces to retire to a line behind the Seine, Aube, and Ornain Rivers.

Joffre already had received a warning from above that France expected more than continued retreats. On Aug. 25, Messimy, an ex-soldier turned politician and Minister of Defense, sent a directive to Joffre that a force of "at least three active corps should be directed upon the entrenched camp of Paris to secure its protection." This directive prepared the way for the emergence of General Galliéni. History shows no scarcity of claimants for the title of Victor of the Marne, but Galliéni's claim is better than most, certainly than those of Joffre or Foch.

The new Military Governor of Paris, for such was Galliéni's title, was a rather professorial soldier under whom Joffre had served in

Madagascar. Galliéni held the title of *successeur éventuel* or, as Churchill translates the phrase, "contingent successor to Joffre."

The latter was still convinced that the retreat should continue. Joffre told Sir John French, "I do not consider it is possible to envisage a general action on the Marne with the whole of our forces. But I consider the co-operation of the English army in the defense of Paris is the only course that can give an advantageous result." But if Joffre was not thinking of an offensive role, others were. The change in Von Kluck's direction to the southeast had been noted and reported by British pilots flying over the battlefield. Galliéni, studying this report and those of cavalry patrols from Maunoury's force was convinced that the Germans, Von Kluck's First Army, were moving past the French forces concentrating in Paris and were offering their flank to a French attack. Maunoury was ordered to prepare for an attack. Speed was essential.

The hierarchial system of the French command structure was so inflexible, however, that before Galliéni could launch his attack on Sept. 3, it was necessary to convince Joffre that a glittering opportunity was beckoning French arms. Galliéni telephoned the commander in chief and urged him to approve an offensive. Joffre promised at least to consider the move. Meanwhile Galliéni was driven to Melun to describe the new situation to Sir John French. Neither Sir John nor his chief of staff, Archibald Murray, was present, and Galliéni made little impression on the dispirited, and snobbish, staff officers. There he was, after weeks of retreat, in spectacles, an untrimmed moustache, black boots, and yellow leggings calling on the British to end their retreat and return to the offensive in co-operation with the French. When General Murray finally arrived, he showed no interest in Galliéni's plans. The information on the German turn to the southeast was meager and had been reported by pilots. Who could trust these harebrained young men? Murray's refusal to do so reflects the oddities of the military mind at the time. In 1914 it was the conventional wisdom of all European general staffs that the airplane's principal value in war was in reconnaissance. But here, when pilots brought in news of the greatest moment, neither the British nor the French were disposed to believe it.

Joffre, like Murray, was unimpressed. The British were told that the French commander's intention was to retire behind the Seine, that he would not attack until all forces were united, and that the

BEF's role should be confined to a defensive position between the Marne and the Seine.

Every historian of the battle—German, French, and British—has emphasized the difference between Galliéni's instant perception of the opportunity and Joffre's sluggish reaction. The former, seeing Von Kluck's right flank presented to the Allies, exclaimed, "I dare not believe it, it is too good to be true." Joffre was still ruminating, doubtless on a full stomach and eight hours of sound sleep.

Nevertheless the Allied commander in chief was moved to telegraph Franchet d'Esperey, who had succeeded Lanrezac as commander of the French Fifth Army. The telegram was hardly an incitement to vigorous action. It merely asked the new commander if he thought his force was ready for offensive operations. Franchet d'Esperey was a tough, realistic soldier. Considering the weariness of his men and the weaknesses of the reserve divisions, he informed Joffre that he could attack on Sept. 6, but that "the situation is not brilliant."

Galliéni had been told by Joffre that he could use Maunoury's army, the Sixth, but only in an attack south of the Marne. Galliéni, conscious that the opportunity was fleeting and might not recur, telephoned the commander in chief, now comfortably ensconced in a new headquarters at Bar-sur-Aube.

In Joffre's behalf it must be acknowledged that he and his staff did intend to take the offensive. But the plans were vague. Then over the telephone line came the squeaking of Galliéni's voice. It is probable that in the conversation Galliéni's vibrant personality and vigorous language gained an ascendancy over Joffre. After all, Galliéni had been the commander in Madagascar and Joffre the subordinate.

For whatever reason, Galliéni succeeded. Permission was given for an attack by the Army of Paris north of the Marne as part of a general offensive by the armies on the left wing, Joffre having promised to win the co-operation of Sir John French. The British commander at the time was lost in gloom, contemplating, among other courses, a retreat to the Channel ports.

The final orders issued by French General Headquarters set Sept. 6 for the offensive.

The "friction of war" intervened. Nothing went completely according to plan, nor does it ever so go. Delays in enciphering and sending orders occurred. The next morning the BEF and the French Fifth Army continued their retreat. Not until midafternoon was the order for the offensive received by Franchet d'Esperey and General French. Ironically, this continued Anglo-French retirement in the end helped the Allies. Von Kluck, having "lost" the British army, pulled back two corps from that sector to bolster the flank that was now being attacked by Maunoury's forces thrusting out of Paris.

At this point came one of the most famous incidents of the Battle of the Marne, an incident so elaborated in fiction that its true dimensions have been almost forgotten.

A French division had reached Paris by train. It was at least forty miles from the battle. How could it be gotten there in time to fight? Railroad transport was meager. Someone—there is no statue to him in Paris, and his name is unknown to military historians—had a novel idea. Why not send the troops in taxis?

The Paris police rounded up approximately 600 taxis and sent them to Gagny, a suburb. There they were loaded with soldiers and set off for the front. Two journeys brought about 6,000 soldiers to the battle area. The difficulty, of course, was that no "march discipline" was imposed on the drivers so that it took many hours to sort out the troops and re-form the units when the journey was over. The 6,000 men conveyed to the front by this novel means were not sufficient, of course, to turn the tide at the Marne. But the operation, the first motorized reinforcement in history, was magnified in time by imaginative novelists and scenario writers so that it seemed the decisive stroke in a vast battle.

No single action by troops contributed to the victory. The historian cannot put his finger on this decision or that advance, as is possible at Waterloo or Gettysburg, and say with confidence that here the battle was won—or lost.

The Germans' situation was worsening. Von Kluck, having pulled back two corps, was left with a gap of thirty miles between his army and Von Bülow's Second Army. He tried to fill it with two cavalry divisions and some light infantry, but the gap uncovered Bülow's flank. Bülow responded by withdrawing his right. The BEF marched into the gap. Franchet d'Espery's Fifth Army advanced slowly. The critical point in the great battle had arrived, although no one can say at precisely what point the fortunes of war deserted the Germans.

The operations on the Allied left wing commonly are considered the most important. But this is a parochial view. In the center, the armies of Foch and General Fernand de L'Angle de Cary also attacked. But it was on the French right, or German left, that the invaders encountered the most serious trouble.

The initial German offensive had driven the French armies, General Marquis Jacques de Castelnau's Second and General Auguste Dubail's First, back to the protection of the French fortress line, stretching from Verdun to Belfort, with the exception of the Charmes Gap. At least one piece of prewar planning worked to France's advantage. As envisioned, a German offensive withered under French artillery fire. The Germans were halted with heavy casualties, and Joffre transferred two divisions to the still-precarious Allied left wing.

The German Fifth and Fourth Armies in the center, commanded respectively by the Duke of Württemberg and the Imperial Crown Prince, fared little better. General Maurice Sarrail's Third Army, pivoting on Verdun, checked the Crown Prince's advance as a result of accurate artillery fire and steady resistance by the infantry. The Fourth Army continued to attack until Sept. 9, when it was obvious that no further gains against the French were possible.

Another critical but not decisive point was on the front of General Max von Hausen's Third Army. This German army's role was divided. The formations on the left were used to help the Duke of Württemberg in a costly and unsuccessful attack on the French Fourth Army. The divisions on the right crossed the Marne and attacked Foch's Ninth Army, a new, hastily assembled force, in company with some of Von Bülow's divisions.

Like many other generals, Ferdinand Foch believed that he had won the Battle of the Marne. He claimed that his counterattack against the attacking Germans had driven them into the marshes of Saint-Gond. Sober historical research shows, however, that the Germans retired not because of Foch's attack but because the battle was being decided elsewhere. Nor did Foch, as he claimed, prevent a German breakthrough in the center of the Allied line. By that stage of the battle, Von Bülow was not seeking a breakthrough but a new position, facing west, from which he could deal with Franchet d'Esperey and the BEF.

Foch's true role, which he played with distinction, was to guard Franchet d'Esperey's flank. There was hard fighting, some of the most costly of the entire battle; and Foch, at one point, had to ask Franchet d'Esperey, known to the British rank and file as "Desperate Frankie," for help. The Germans made some progress, but on

Sept. 9 their attack was halted—not by Foch and his battered divisions, but by an order from Von Bülow for a general retirement.

At this point in the battle, both sides had been fighting and marching for nearly a month. The Germans, emboldened in the first days of their advance by visions of the delights of Paris, had plodded on, coated in the white dust of the French roads. But this miraculous advance brought them nothing. There was no entry into Paris or, for that matter, into Nancy or Verdun or Belfort. Each morning there were only more and more miles of road stretching before them.

The Allies were in slightly better condition. They had not marched as far, although they had suffered heavier casualties. But now, suddenly, the long retreat was over. They turned and struck their pursuers. The momentum of battle, so long on the German side, was transferred to the Allies. But there was not a grand, cohesive offensive. Only weary formations pushing the retreating Germans and, here and there, fighting isolated, bloody actions.

The sides even then were well matched. Why did the Germans retreat? Here again, there is no single answer. Part of the answer lies, however, in the singular command system of the German army.

Von Moltke by this time had transferred his headquarters from Coblenz to Luxembourg. But the all-powerful is the all-unknowing. The German army commanders kept the commander in chief in the dark about their operations. When they won a victory, Von Moltke was told of it, often in exaggerated terms. Otherwise, General Headquarters lived on a sparse diet of rumors, bits of information from neutral countries, and the usually untrustworthy reports of wounded.

It seems incredible, but most historians agree that during the crisis of the battle, Von Moltke had no real information about Von Kluck's whereabouts or the change in fortune and direction on the German right flank. Already concerned about the absence of large batches of prisoners, the commander in chief on Sept. 8 sent an emissary to the five German armies operating to the west of Verdun. Such a mission could be performed only by a member of the Great General Staff, that military priesthood which dominated the German command. The man selected was Lieutenant Colonel Richard Hentsch. His instructions included power to co-ordinate a retreat should one have been started.

Hentsch, traveling by car, found the Third, Fourth, and Fifth Armies still in good shape but lacking that supreme confidence that marks victorious armies. But it was the elderly Von Bülow at the Second Army's Headquarters who made the greatest impression on the emissary. There was unrelieved gloom, and although Hentsch himself could not give the order for a retreat, he left Bülow sure that it would soon be issued. As it was.

Aerial reconnaissance reported to Bülow on the morning of Sept. 9 that six Allied columns, one of French cavalry and five of the BEF, were approaching the Marne and entering the mouth of the gap between his army and the First under Von Kluck. That was at 9 A.M. Two hours later, he ordered his army to begin its retreat at 1 P.M. Von Kluck was informed of this action.

Meanwhile, Hentsch, his car threading cautiously through supply columns and marching infantry, did not reach Von Kluck's head-quarters until early afternoon. He reported to General Headquarters that the orders for retreat already had been issued and that his sole function was to order the retreat to follow a northeasterly direction. After the war, Von Kluck's chief of staff said that Hentsch had is-sued the orders for retreat. Such was the power of a member of the Great General Staff!

The stark reality, which outweighs these German claims and counterclaims, most of which were made after Hentsch was dead, is that the two westernmost of the German armies, the forces on which implementation of the Schlieffen Plan rested, had begun their re-treat. With the BEF and Franchet d'Esperey's army on their heels, the Germans withdrew. Behind them they left imperial Germany's last chance of absolute triumph.

Spare a thought for that shadowy figure, Lieutenant Colonel Hentsch. He does not appear in the company of World War I's deci-sion makers. But, in his way, he had a more decisive influence on the Marne, and thus the war and history, than many greater men. As he went from army headquarters to army headquarters bundled in his greatcoat against the cool September nights, he carried with him the accumulated wisdom of the Great General Staff.

Von Moltke was half-convinced of the necessity for retreat. Why else would he have told Hentsch to be prepared to co-ordinate one? Was Von Moltke too pessimistic? The German hosts were tired but undefeated. Possibly commanders of the caliber of Von Kluck and Von Bülow should have been able to wring one more spasm of suc-cessful offensive action from their forces. This would not have filled the gap between the two armies, but granted Joffre's ambivalent attitude toward an offensive, it might well have induced him to restrain the advancing Allies. Had that been done, the Germans could have resumed the offensive.

"Sufficient unto the day." The German invasion of France had been reversed. The Battle of the Marne had entered history.

Although the battle had covered a front of roughly 150 miles from west to east, it had not been significantly costly to either the Allies or the Germans in comparison with the earlier fighting along the frontiers, in which the French suffered terribly, or with the greater losses incurred by the French and Germans at Verdun and the British on the Somme. The tragedy of the Marne is that Joffre failed to exploit the victory. The Germans retreated in a fashion almost as orderly as that in which they had advanced. As they went, they continually extended their right wing toward the sea—that is, toward the English Channel. The French followed, but they were always "too little and too late." The Germans established their line on the Aisne River, and both sides were condemned to four years of bloody trench warfare.

Churchill aptly wrote: "It was less like a battle than any other ever fought. Comparatively few were killed or wounded, no great recognizable feat of arms, no shock proportionate to the event can be discerned."

Exactly. The results of the Marne were strategic, not tactical. Had Joffre been quicker to pursue, had Sir John French goaded the BEF to greater efforts, the battle might have resulted in a complete tactical as well as strategic victory.

The battle also had a psychological impact upon the German high command that is immeasurable. Von Moltke broke under the strain. Von Stein, his chief of staff, failed to assume the responsibility. As we now know, there were young, innovative officers at German headquarters, men fertile with plans for retrieving the situation. But they were not heard. The war of maneuver, of instant generalship as expressed by Galliéni, was over.

Galliéni emerges as the single most important tactical commander of the battle. If any general has a claim to enthronement as the Victor of the Marne, it is he—not Joffre, not Foch. But if the Marne was on one level a generals' battle of insight, resolution, and energy, all displayed to the fullest extent by Galliéni, it was also a soldiers' battle. The true victors then were the *poilus* and the Tommies of the two Allied armies. Mauled and hounded through a long retreat, weary in body, confused in mind, they marched mile upon dusty mile away from the enemy. Then, with little warning, they were told to attack, to retrace their steps. That they were able to do so, that their morale was largely unimpaired by their experience, testifies to their courage and their flexibility under stress. And, it should be emphasized, it was not the German soldier who cracked, not old *Landser* Fritz, but the great ones who lived in *châteaux* far from shells and bullets. In the Battle of the Marne, as in every engagement until the end, the German soldier exhibited those qualities of valor, discipline, and enterprise that for four long years were the greatest threat to the Allied cause.

III

The Bloody Twilight of the Dreadnoughts

JUTLAND

Jutland was the last great battle-line encounter in naval history. The British and German fleets met at the height of their powers; battle cruisers against battle cruisers, battleships against battleships. The resources of two empires had gone into the making of those fleets which embodied the highest technological advances of the day. Yet the battle was far from being the conclusive conflict expected by both sides. Instead Jutland is a story of lost opportunities, misunderstood signals, and questionable leadership. Instead of the majestic and terrible spectacle of two fleets pounding each other into ruin, there is a hazy picture of two giants groping for each other through the North Sea mists, making occasional and bloody contact and then failing to follow fortune.

In one sense Jutland resembles the Marne. The strategic victory went to the side that suffered the heavier losses, the British. Jutland also, it may be argued, was the last gamble of the German High Seas Fleet. Had that fleet won, the whole course of the war might have been changed. The gamble failed. The High Seas Fleet returned to port, never again to sortie with battle flags flying.

The Allies' situation at sea in May 1916 was far more favorable than their position in the land war. For nearly three years, Britain's Royal Navy had enforced a blockade upon Germany. The blockade's impact upon the German and Austro-Hungarian economies at that time was serious but far from critical. There were those in the German naval war ministry, however, who foresaw that if the blockage were to continue, the consequences for the two powers could be grave.

On the high seas, the British had methodically run down the surface raiders loosed by Germany at the start of the war, while the submarine menace had not yet developed fully. When Admiral Alfred von Tirpitz on Feb. 4, 1915, proclaimed that "every Allied merchant vessel found within the waters surrounding the British Isles would be destroyed," he was indulging in wishful thinking. At that time the Germans had between twenty and twenty-five submarines, of which only seven or eight could be at sea at any given time. Later this situation was to change—partly as a result of the events recounted in this chapter—and the U-boat campaign came close to bringing Britain to her knees.

Through 1916 the High Seas Fleet, Germany's maritime pride, had been bottled up in its ports, aside from one or two daring but ultimately unprofitable adventures. To the patriotic German, this fleet represented his nation's challenge to Britain's position as Mistress of the Seas. The High Seas Fleet had been a quarter of a century building. At the time of Jutland, its crews were imbued with a high sense of purpose. In the wardrooms, officers drank to *der Tag* when their ships would humble the British.

The developing German sea power challenged the Royal Navy as it had not been challenged since the Napoleonic Wars. Once the challenge was understood—and it took a long time to bring understanding to some admirals and most politicians—the British service, goaded and guided by two human dynamos, Admiral Sir John Fisher, the First Sea Lord, and Winston Churchill, First Lord of the Admiralty, made enormous efforts to maintain British naval superiority. This had to cover not only the North Sea and the North Atlantic but every quarter of the globe in which British merchantmen operated.

Admiral Sir John R. Jellicoe commanded the British Grand Fleet. He had every professional qualification for the post. He had been given command of the largest battle fleet of modern times, served by officers and seamen who, emerging from the doldrums of the last century, had raised their effectiveness to a very high mark.

The command responsibility was awesome. Winston Churchill

after the war stated Jellicoe's position in stark terms: "Jellicoe was the only man on either side who could lose the war in an afternoon." It might fall upon the admiral "as on no other man—Sovereign, Statesman, Admiral, or General—to issue orders which in the space of two or three hours might nakedly decide who won the war." For it was taken by Churchill and by the conventional military wisdom of the day that the "destruction of the British battle fleet would be final."

It is not necessary to accept this view. Sixty years later it appears extreme. But Jellicoe accepted it. His acceptance of it explains much that happened in those confused hours of conflict in the North Sea.

The two most important weapons of contemporary naval war, the airplane and the submarine, played no important roles at Jutland. There were no aircraft present, and submarine activity was minimal. But the torpedo, a weapon that could be launched by either submarine or destroyer, affected British tactics throughout the battle. Although torpedoes played a minor role in the Jutland fight, in the minds of the British commanders, particularly Jellicoe's, they were a significant, perhaps dominant, factor. And it is in the minds of commanders that battles are won or lost.

Conscious of his overwhelming responsibility to preserve British naval superiority, Jellicoe not unnaturally was wedded to tactics that enjoined caution upon the fleet. Very nearly the opposite was true of the German commanders, Admiral Reinhard Scheer, commander of the High Seas Fleet, and Admiral Franz von Hipper, who led the battle cruisers. The Germans from the outset of the war had avoided a major naval action with a British fleet which they knew to be superior in numbers, speed, and weight of metal. They hoped that in any engagement mines and torpedoes would sink enough British ships to redress the balance. In this they had been unsuccessful in terms of ships sunk but eminently successful in convincing Jellicoe that caution was to be his watchword. This was a dreary slogan to offer a fleet, and a nation, imbued with memories of Nelson's "England expects every man will do his duty."

No account of Jutland is understandable without recognition of a salient factor on the intelligence side. The German light cruiser *Magdeburg* had been sunk in the Baltic in August 1914 by the Russians. After the encounter, the Russians recovered the body of a German noncommissioned officer whose dead arms clasped the cipher and signal books of the Imperial German Navy. For good measure the books also contained the Germans' squared maps of the North Sea.

British naval intelligence, after receiving this vital information from St. Petersburg, was able to intercept and decipher much of the Germans' most important operational orders. This should have been a vital element at Jutland. It was not. Intelligence is useful only when commanders are prepared to accept it and act upon it.

The plan evolved by Admiral Scheer was simple. He would sally from the North Sea ports with the High Seas Fleet, tempt the Grand Fleet into action, and inflict enough damage on some squadrons to redress the balance of naval power in the North Sea. He did not place great reliance on torpedoes; his vision was of isolated gunnery actions that would further whittle the strength of the British already depleted by mines and submarine attacks.

The world is unlikely to see again a parade of naval power comparable to that exhibited by the two fleets as they moved toward battle. The British deployed twenty-eight "dreadnought" battleships, the all–big-gun battleship championed by Churchill during his tour at the Admiralty. In addition there were nine battle cruisers, thirty-four light cruisers, and eighty destroyers. The Germans, despite their excellent gunnery and, in some cases, more modern ships, were at a numerical disadvantage. Admiral Scheer had sixteen dreadnoughts, which from this point will be described as battleships, which is what they were, and five battle cruisers. These were supported by eight old battleships, eleven light cruisers, and sixty-three destroyers.

The British also had the advantage in speed and weight of metal. Their slowest battleship could steam at twenty knots, and the four new ships of the Queen Elizabeth class were capable of twenty-four to twenty-five knots. The fastest German ship had a top speed of twenty-one knots. The British superiority was even greater in gun power: 48 15-inch, 10 14-inch, 132 13.5-inch, and 144 12-inch guns against the Germans' 144 12-inch and 100 11-inch. The British also held a 382–362 lead in torpedoes, those hobgoblins that haunted Jellicoe.

Of the commanders at Jutland, the most interesting, if not on that famous day the most successful, was Vice Admiral Sir David Beatty, who commanded the battle cruisers. To a British public less than enthusiastic over Jellicoe, a small taciturn figure or over the more imposing but equally taciturn Field Marshal Sir Douglas Haig, commander in chief of the British armies in France, Beatty with his cap

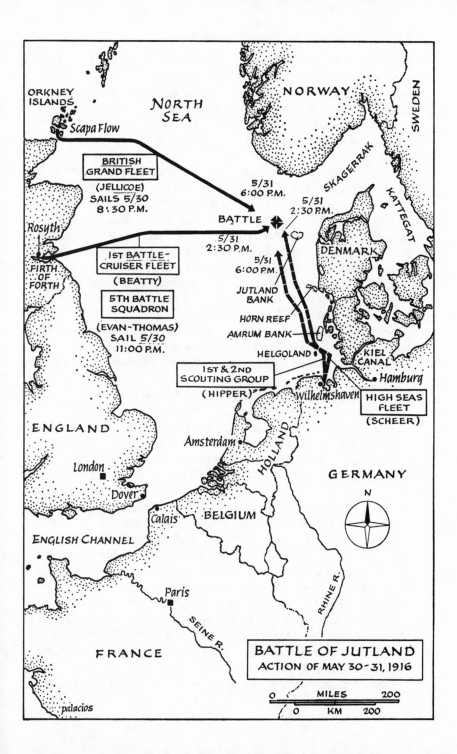

ORKNEY ISLANDS

Scapa Flow

NORTH SEA

NORWAY

SWEDEN

BRITISH GRAND FLEET
(JELLICOE)
SAILS 5/30
8:30 P.M.

5/31
6:00 P.M.

5/31
2:30 P.M.

SKAGERRAK

KATTEGAT

BATTLE

Rosyth

5/31
2:30 P.M.

DENMARK

FIRTH OF FORTH

1ST BATTLE-CRUISER FLEET
(BEATTY)

5TH BATTLE SQUADRON
(EVAN-THOMAS)
SAIL 5/30
11:00 P.M.

5/31
6:00 P.M.

JUTLAND BANK

HORN REEF

AMRUM BANK

HELGOLAND

KIEL CANAL

1ST & 2ND SCOUTING GROUP
(HIPPER)

Wilhelmshaven

Hamburg

HIGH SEAS FLEET
(SCHEER)

ENGLAND

Amsterdam

HOLLAND

GERMANY

N

London

Dover

Calais

BELGIUM

ENGLISH CHANNEL

Paris

RHINE R.

SEINE R.

BATTLE OF JUTLAND
ACTION OF MAY 30-31, 1916

FRANCE

palacios

0   MILES   200
0   KM   200

aslant, his vigorous language, and his "hell-for-leather" tactics was the closest approximation to "the Nelson touch," that combination of tactical genius and charisma which led to victory at Trafalgar and made Nelson the greatest admiral of his time.

It fell to Beatty and his battle cruisers to make the first contact and fight the first of the two actions that made up the Battle of Jutland.

By late May, Admiralty intelligence in London was reporting unusual activity in the High Seas Fleet, and at 5 P.M. on May 30 Jellicoe was informed that the Germans were at sea. Although the British did not know it, the German plan was to send Admiral Von Hipper with a force of battle cruisers and light cruisers up the Norwegian coast. The assumption was that this would lure the Grand Fleet into battle. Scheer hoped to destroy part of it.

The British fleet put to sea in two divisions, Beatty and his battle cruisers in the south, Jellicoe and the Grand Fleet in the north. By the evening of May 30, both were at sea.

Seldom in war do operations go according to plan. Jutland was no exception. Beatty was turning north to unite with Jellicoe when one of his light cruisers sighted an unknown steamer. The *Galatea* steamed to investigate. Simultaneously, one of Hipper's cruisers sped on the same errand. The cruisers signaled "enemy in sight" to their flagships, and the first action of Jutland began.

Beatty on the *Lion,* his flagship, increased the speed of his squadron and turned about to meet the Germans. But the battleship squadron, the four ships of the new Queen Elizabeth class commanded by Rear Admiral Hugh Evan-Thomas, continued to steer in the opposite direction. He continued on this course for eight minutes, losing touch with the battle cruisers. When, finally, the battleships turned, they were ten miles behind Beatty's ships.

Here is the first of the errors that mark Jutland. Why did Evan-Thomas fail to turn? Beatty could have sent the order to turn by searchlight, a more reliable means than signal flags. But he did not. When Evan-Thomas finally did turn, Beatty gave him no time to catch up with the main body but steamed full-tilt toward Hipper. Evan-Thomas claimed that he did not see Beatty's signal flags until 2:40 P.M. But ten minutes earlier his flagship, the *Barham,* had received by wireless a message from the *Lion* about Beatty's new course.

The controversy raged for twenty years in the Royal Navy and rages still in the writings of historians. It is difficult to assign the blame. But the fact is that in the first half-hour of Beatty's fight with Hipper, the heavy guns of the battleship squadron played no part.

By 3:45 P.M. the two battle cruiser squadrons were in action at a range of about nine miles. They fought for two hours. Beatty had the numerical advantage, six ships to four, but this advantage was soon eliminated.

The *Indefatigable,* hit by a salvo of shells from the *Von der Tann,* was driven out of the British line and soon sank with a thousand men. The *Lutzow,* Hipper's flagship, hit the *Lion* twice. One of the shells penetrated the midship turret. Major F. J. W. Harvey of the Royal Marines, the turret commander, managed before he died (both his legs had been blown off) to call the order down the voice tube to flood the magazines. Thus the *Lion* probably was saved from the fate of the *Indefatigable.*

No naval officer on either side had lived through so fierce an encounter. The battle cruisers were firing four rounds at a time, each shell weighing about half a ton.

The *Queen Mary* was the next British ship to go. Plunging fire from the *Derfflinger* hit the *Queen Mary,* which burst into flame and exploded. About this time the *Princess Royal* vanished into a cloud of smoke and a signalman on the bridge of the *Lion* reported to Beatty, *"Princess Royal* blown up, sir."

The Vice Admiral's reaction was characteristic. Turning to his flag captain, Chatfield, he said, "There seems to be something wrong with our damned ships today. Turn two points to port"—that is, two points nearer the enemy battle line.

This was the crisis of the first battle. The remaining British battle cruisers were firing more effectively, and the German ships began to take heavy punishment. The German fire became less accurate. Then, shortly after 4 P.M., the ships of Evan-Thomas's Fourth Battle Squadron, out of the fight until then, began to hurl their 15-inch shells at the last ships of Hipper's formation. The situation from the German standpoint had worsened. The trap had not sprung. Admiral Scheer now had to come to Hipper's aid.

Just before 5 P.M. ships of Beatty's light-cruiser screen sighted the German High Seas Fleet. The admiral then turned his battle cruisers north to entice Scheer's ships toward the Grand Fleet to the north. Again Evan-Thomas's squadron missed the signal and was engaged by the van of Scheer's battleships before he too turned north.

Scheer's conduct reflects, as general orders say, "the highest credit on his service." Despite the threat posed by the Fourth Battle Squadron, he hastened to Hipper's rescue. By doing so, he moved toward the Grand Fleet under Jellicoe now advancing south in six parallel columns. As Churchill points out, the situation had been reversed. Beatty now was attempting to lead Scheer into range of Jellicoe's guns. Hipper and Scheer, without knowing it, were advancing toward the superior Grand Fleet.

The question of Jellicoe's tactical use of his fleet becomes all-important. As he advanced, he was not in a combat formation. To deliver his maximum "payload," as it would be called today, he had to turn each column to the left or right so that the broadsides of the entire fleet could be directed at the enemy. In exercises the Grand Fleet had taken only four minutes to carry out this maneuver.

Now the fog of war intervened. At 6 P.M. Jellicoe wanted to know the location of the enemy battle fleet. At first Beatty, still intent on Hipper's battle cruisers, failed to answer. Then both Beatty and Evan-Thomas signaled the location and course of Scheer's ships.

Jellicoe now ordered the deployment that has been the subject of continued and violent controversy. He deployed on his left wing. Critics contend that he should have deployed on his right wing, although that might have meant that Scheer would have crossed the head of the British line, "crossing the T" before the British could fire. In any event, it was twenty-two minutes before the British line was straightened out, and the time lost was priceless.

Churchill argued that Jellicoe might have given a third possible order. Jellicoe, he claims, could have run up the old and famous signal, "Follow me," and taken his own division out of the formation, to be followed by the other divisions. The argument is buttressed by Churchill's estimate that Jellicoe would have saved three miles and ten minutes by this maneuver.

Scheer was now rushing toward the British battle line. But he was reluctant to risk the High Seas Fleet, inferior in numbers, speed, and weight of metal, against the Grand Fleet. On the German side, too, there were tactical misconceptions. Scheer sighted the battle cruisers, decided it was the main battle fleet, and turned about. The time was 6:30 P.M. Mist obscured the North Sea. Darkness was gathering. Scheer turned west toward England.

While the two vast fleets had been jockeying for position, single units delivered heavy fire. The German cruiser *Wiesbaden* was sunk.

But Hipper succeeded in sending the *Invincible,* another battle cruiser, to the bottom.

The tactical situation was odd, to say the least. Scheer was steaming away from his bases and a superior fleet. The British, having come into action, had now lost their quarry. Now Scheer made one of the battle's many controversial decisions. After nearly half an hour steaming toward the west, he suddenly reversed his course and headed east.

The German official history endorses Scheer's explanation that he turned back in order to "seek contact with the enemy again." Contact is a word of wide application. It seems probable, sixty years later, that Scheer hoped to head for harbor and, if lucky, to attack ships at the end of the British line of battle.

Whatever his thoughts, he gambled, for the German fleet now encountered the heaviest cannonage ever recorded at sea. Those British battleships within range opened fire, and the crew of the leading German ship saw a horizon alight with gun flashes. The lighter German ships suffered most. The *Lutzow* and the *Seydlitz* were badly damaged. Shells rained on the leading battleships of the Koenig class.

Scheer embraced discretion. Just after 7 P.M. he again turned his fleet westward, screening the withdrawal with torpedo attacks from his destroyers and ordering the already badly battered battle cruisers to make another attack on the British.

The torpedo attack, in Jellicoe's mind at least, justified all his forebodings about the ability of this relatively new weapon to damage his fleet. The British admiral swung his fleet away by two quick turns of two points each or 22.5 degrees in all. The Grand Fleet left the battleground and never again sighted Scheer and his battleships.

Caution reigned on both sides. Only Beatty appears to have grasped the significance of the situation. He saw the opportunity of cutting off the enemy fleet before it could run for home. At 7:47 P.M. he sent a message to Jellicoe: "Submit that the van of the battleships follow me [in the *Lion*]; we can then cut off the enemy's fleet." It was fifteen minutes before Jellicoe replied in the form of a message to the Second Battle Squadron ordering them to follow Beatty. Beatty had continued on his course and at the end, as at the beginning, fought the enemy. The German battle cruisers were sadly battered. British gunnery on the *Tiger* knocked out the two remaining turrets of the *Derfflinger,* and the *Seydlitz* and *Lutzow* were hammered hard. Night fell and the Germans escaped to the west.

The German position was dangerous. Jellicoe still commanded a much superior fleet. Scheer knew this and had to go home. The British commander avoided a night battle which, in retrospect, seems wise. Why hazard his superiority in a nighttime encounter which of all naval operations is the most risky? Scheer, on the other hand, had to return home. He wisely was reluctant to risk a daylight battle with a relatively undamaged Grand Fleet. Three courses were open. Each led to a channel swept throughout with German minefields which covered the approaches to the home bases. One led past the Horn Reef on the east. A second led past the island of Helgoland. The third on the southwest would take the High Seas Fleet to the German coast and the mouth of the Ems River.

Scheer, we may assume, was in his cabin studying his charts, pondering his choices. Jellicoe had sent his battleships into night-cruising formation—three parallel columns, with his destroyers five miles astern. Beatty was at the head of the western flank with his battle cruisers. The two great fleets were no more than six miles apart in the night, a fact that is almost inconceivable to a generation reared on radar and its magic.

Jellicoe was also weighing his choices. Which route would Scheer take—the Ems, Helgoland, or the Horn Reef? Meanwhile the Grand Fleet was steaming southward at seventeen knots. And Scheer? He took the short route home via the Horn Reef while Jellicoe's attention increasingly was fixed upon the Helgoland and Ems routes.

The quiet progress of the two fleets did not last long. From about 10:30 P.M. onward, the scouting forces of both fleets were in contact as Scheer moved across the tail of the British fleet toward safety. The night actions were inconclusive, following the pattern of the operations of the preceding day. The German cruiser *Frauenlob* was sunk. Two British cruisers were heavily damaged. The light cruiser *Elbing* was rammed by the destroyer *Posen,* and the British destroyer *Spitfire* rammed the German battleship *Nassau.* It was a hit-or-miss action, blows struck in the dark. But the German fleet, with some variations, continued its course.

It cannot be repeated too often that on the British side, Jutland was a melancholy series of missed opportunities. Another was now to arise.

Admiralty intelligence in London had been monitoring German

signals traffic. At 9:14 P.M., the Admiralty intercepted and decoded the signal from Scheer to his fleet. At about 11:30, Jellicoe received the message: "German battle fleet ordered home at 9:14 P.M. Battle cruisers in rear. Course S.S.E. 1/4 east. Speed 16 knots."

The message could only mean that the High Seas Fleet was retiring by the Horn Reef. By turning his fleet onto a parallel course, Jellicoe would have the opportunity of engaging the Germans with a superior force at first light.

Jellicoe's course, however, was to reject the Admiralty's report and continue to head south at seventeen knots. It is a reasonable assumption that Jellicoe thus threw away his last opportunity to engage the High Seas Fleet.

For over half a century, controversy has raged around this and other decisions in the battle. Churchill, no admirer of Jellicoe's leadership, concedes that the admiral had received one clearly erroneous report from the Admiralty earlier in the day and that at 10:15 P.M. he had a signal from the cruiser *Southhampton* that Scheer's fleet was still to the west. Another report from the cruiser *Birmingham* reported German battle cruisers still to the westward. There was another fatal error, however. The Admiralty had also omitted from its message the fact that Scheer was asking for airships—that is, Zeppelins—for reconnaissance over the Horn Reef, a reliable indication of the route he had chosen.

So the great floating fortresses steamed southward in the night. Scheer was making for the Horn Reef passage and home at sixteen knots. As he turned to the southeast, his squadrons encountered the British destroyer flotillas covering the rear of the Grand Fleet. The British took their toll but also lost the destroyers *Fortune* and *Ardent,* sunk in an action that began with the loss of the *Frauenlob.*

The Germans drove on. The British cruiser *Black Prince* was immolated by the fire of German battleships, and 750 men died. The destroyer *Turbulent* was sunk. By 2:10 A.M. the Battle of Jutland reached its last desperate spasm. The British twelfth destroyer flotilla dashed to the attack and sank the German cruiser *Pommern* and the destroyer *V-4.* The firing stopped. The Grand Fleet continued in stately procession toward the south until 2:30 P.M., when it turned northward away from the German coast. Scheer and his ships by now were beyond the range of pursuit. The battle was over.

The Germans saw Jutland, which they called the Battle of the Skagerrak, as a great victory. So it was, in a tactical sense. The German battle cruisers had taken a heavy toll of Beatty's squadron. Scheer had escaped from a greatly superior enemy, partly through his own seamanship, which was flawed, and partly through British errors. The British Grand Fleet, the most massive assemblage of naval power in history, had hardly been engaged. Only one battleship, the *Colossus,* had been hit, and of 20,000 men on all the battleships, the casualties were two killed and five wounded. But the blunt appraisal so many years later must be that the Grand Fleet did not fulfill the hopes of the Admiralty, its commanders and seamen, and above all the people of Britain.

If losses are true indicators of victory and defeat, which they are not, then the Germans won. The British lost one battleship, one battle cruiser, four light cruisers, and five destroyers. The butcher's bill was 6,097 British killed to 2,545 Germans.

Why, then, should Jutland be included in a list of decisive battles? It was not, as some historians argue, the last sortie by the High Seas Fleet. The Germans went to sea again on Aug. 19. This time both Scheer and Jellicoe took counsel from their fears—Jellicoe on the assumption that the Grand Fleet was heading into a newly laid German minefield, Scheer on the supposition that he was about to be caught in a trap with a strong British force; actually there were only light British forces from Harwich, advancing upon Jellicoe from the south. Again there was the majestic but in the end futile picture of great fleets evading battle.

The significant fact is that after Aug. 19 and Jutland, the German High Seas Fleet never again emerged in strength from port. The Grand Fleet remained in being, its officers reappraising their tactics and noting the effect of plunging fire on ill-armored decks and turrets. But the fleet was there. Despite the submarine warfare around Britain's coasts and in the North Atlantic, the British were able to maintain their blockade of Germany. As the months wore on, with their frightful casualties on the western front, Germany's economic position steadily worsened. *Ersatz* became part of everyday language —ersatz coffee, ersatz soap, ersatz sheets, ersatz medical dressings for the wounded. The people of Germany's great cities became gaunt and hollow-eyed. Children suffered from malnutrition.

While the Grand Fleet maintained what Liddell Hart called "its passive superiority of strength," what of its great rival? The High Seas Fleet was condemned to spend the rest of the war in harbor. Seamen were transferred to submarines and other duties. Those who remained spent their time repeating meaningless duties. They soon became the target of left-wing agitators, and when the German revolution burst at the end of the war, sailors from the High Seas Fleet were in the vanguard. The High Seas Fleet never fought again. *Der Tag* had come and gone. So from the strategic standpoint, the Royal Navy won Jutland and the naval war.

IV

A Tractor, Machine Guns, and the Rebirth of Mobility in Battle

CAMBRAI

Something was stirring out there beyond the mist. The German infantry in their comfortable, even capacious dugouts, their well-lined trenches in the north of France, could hear at intervals the coughing of motors, the clank of tracks. Whatever it was, there was no need to worry. This was November 1917, the fourth autumn of the war; and every German, soldier and officer alike, knew that any attack would be preceded by a prolonged artillery bombardment. This would do a certain amount of damage to barbed wire, communications, and front-line formations, but when it ended and the British or French infantry began the deadly journey across no-man's-land, the Germans would drag their machine guns out of the dugouts, the infantry would tumble out to the firing steps, and the attack, no matter how gallantly pressed, would shrivel into a few score desperate men content to have pierced for a few hundred yards one section of the trench system.

This was war as both sides knew it in 1917. Sunk in the mud and caught on the barbed wire was the theory and practice of war as it had hitherto been fought. There were no maneuvers, no break-throughs, simply the headlong rush of men under artillery barrages against other men who were sheltered, supported by their own guns. The combatants died in great numbers. At Verdun, the French admitted to losing 377,231 men, of whom 162,308 were listed as dead or missing. The German losses amounted to 337,000, and the total butcher's bill probably was around 800,000. All of this in an area no larger than Burlington, Vermont.

This was the negation of warfare. The generals on both sides were helpless. In C. S. Forrester's image, they were like savages trying to extract a screw from a block of wood. Try as they might, they could not pull the screw from the block by main force. But they continued to try. They used poison gas and even heavier bombardments. Nothing worked. The British lost 60,000 men in a day on the Somme. A communiqué reporting "all quiet on the Western Front" signaled the death of three or four thousand Germans.

Then, on the morning of Nov. 20, 1917, 381 tanks followed by a small infantry force rumbled out of the British positions against the German defenses of Cambrai. By the next night the church bells of London were ringing a peal acclaiming victory. By the last day of the month, the Germans had mounted a fierce counterattack that wiped out most of the gains won by the British in the interval. But the tank attack at Cambrai cannot be measured by the raw statistics of yards gained or lost. It marked the start of a revolution in warfare, one that has flourished until the present. The tank defied the power of the machine gun and restored decisive power to the offensive.

Through most of the Middle Ages the offensive—heavily armored knights and men at arms using shock tactics—dominated battlefields. Cavalry, whether it was the pony hordes of the Mongols or the mailed warriors of Charlemagne, was the decisive arm. Then in the fourteenth century, in the Hundred Years War between Britain and France, a new "leveling" weapon appeared, the long bow.

The bow, of course, was not new. It had been used as a battlefield weapon for centuries. But until that war, it had never been considered the decisive weapon it was to become. Now in battle after battle, the English archers, using bows of yew and "cloth-yard" arrows, knocked the French out of their saddles. They were more successful than previous archers because the bow was better, their discipline stricter, and, it must be admitted, their thirst for booty unslakeable. The Mongols, Normans, and other warlike races had used the bow but never with this degree of success.

Then came gunpowder. For a couple of centuries the long bow (because of its high rate of fire) and the cross bow held their own. But the evolution of the musket and subsequently the rifle did not change the fundamentals of tactics; the musketeer or the rifleman dominated the battlefield as had the archer. The greatest cavalry action of the Napoleonic Wars, at the Battle of Waterloo, proved only that the horsemen of Napoleon, the finest heavy cavalry in the world, could not break formations, in this case squares, of disciplined infantry.

Then, the breechloader and the machine gun were developed, improvements in the artillery's rate of fire and range. The infantry, with its own arms and supported by the guns, became decisive. And the long, futile bloodletting of the western front began.

It was commonplace among historians of half a century ago to assume that the general staffs on both sides made no attempt to discover a means of ending the trench warfare stalemate. Any intelligent man, though, faced with the enormous casualties of that stalemate, would have sought for a means of breaking it. The British, perhaps because they had been the least successful in such attacks, sought hardest to overcome it. Their goal was a machine impervious to machine gun bullets that could both move and fire. The tank was, in Basil Liddell Hart's words, "a specific antidote for a specific disease," the disease being the paralysis of the offensive.

Because the tank was successful, scores of officers, politicians, and engineers claimed credit for its development. Of these, two have valid claims. One was Colonel Ernest Swinton, a regular officer with an inquiring and reflective mind, who had studied the effect of machine gun fire on infantry as it had been demonstrated in the Russo-Japanese War and who, after his first visit to the western front, had put together some ideas for an antidote to the disease. The second was Winston Churchill.

Swinton proposed to Colonel Maurice Hankey, the Secretary of the Committee of Imperial Defense, the development of a bullet-proof, track-propelled vehicle capable of crossing trenches and armed with small, quick-firing guns. Hankey was impressed, others less so.

General Headquarters in France turned Swinton's proposal down. Field Marshal Lord Kitchener, the all-powerful Secretary of State for War, was not impressed. But Hankey, skilled in the wiles of the British bureaucracy, kept trying. He submitted a memorandum to Prime Minister Herbert H. Asquith on various methods of breaking the trench deadlock, including among them Swinton's suggestion. This was late in 1914, and the memorandum passed, among others, to the attention of Winston Churchill, then First Lord of the Admiralty. That fertile brain already had been grappling with the problem of breaking the trench line. Early in 1915, Churchill wrote Asquith supporting the Swinton idea in Hankey's memorandum. But as history shows, more than memoranda are necessary to move an entrenched military bureaucracy.

In their defense, it should be said that senior military officers, be they British, American, Israeli, or Russian, are not constitutionally adverse to new ideas. Their problem is that they have been given certain powers and sworn certain oaths and that, in addition, they feel a moral obligation to shy away from innovations that, no matter how attractive they may appear on the drawing board, may divert resources and manpower from the missions with which they are dealing. This was more true in World War I than in World War II—largely, I believe, because the great chiefs, General Erich F. W. Ludendorff, Haig, and Foch, were mostly unacquainted with the new age ushered in by such plebeian and highly unromantic developments as the internal-combustion engine. By 1939 the Second Industrial Revolution had impressed all commanders, and technological innovation was much more popular among generals.

Despite War Office coldness to the tank, Churchill was able to keep Swinton's idea alive. He formed what he called the Landships Committee. (The name "tank" came later and was used as a cover term to confuse German intelligence. But to this day, tank language owes something to its Admiralty support. You enter a tank through a "hatch," and to tankers their vehicles remain "she" or "her" as ships do for sailors.) Churchill kept the tank program breathing, but only just. After the Allied failure in the Dardanelles, he was booted out of the Admiralty, but his influence remained, exerted largely through Lord Eustace Tennyson-D'Eyncourt, the Director of Naval Construction. Churchill was sacked paradoxically because he had sought in Gallipoli and the Dardanelles another means of getting around the trench stalemate. The attempt failed. The concept, sixty years later, appears correct.

Meanwhile Swinton was active. He had appealed again to Haig at General Headquarters (GHQ) and by the summer of 1915, with Haig's approval, an interdepartmental committee was working on the new machines. The first experimental tank, called "Little Willie" by the incurably frivolous British, failed to meet requirements. A second, larger model met the army's specifications—it could climb a vertical wall of five feet and could cross an eight-foot ditch. This second tank became "Mother" or "Big Willie."

The tank was tested at Hatfield Park in England in the presence of King George V, Kitchener, and members of the cabinet. The reaction was positive, and an order for 40 tanks, later increased to 150, was placed. This was in February 1916.

The French, of course, faced the same tactical problem as the British and had been working along the same lines. They developed a smaller tank and placed an order for 400 of the vehicles. The British had the first operational tank, however. The French were to have one somewhat later.

Swinton's tactical concept was that the tanks should not be employed in small numbers but *en masse,* supported by strong infantry forces. However, when the tanks arrived in France in the late summer of 1916, this reasonable concept was discarded because of the impression the new weapons made on Haig and his staff. Tried behind the British lines, the tanks flattened barbed-wire entanglements and crossed trenches. GHQ wanted to employ them immediately on the Somme, where the fighting had gone steadily against the British.

Churchill records that he was "shocked" at a proposal to expose "this tremendous secret" to the Germans on a petty scale in what he was sure would be an indecisive operation. He protested to Prime Minister David Lloyd George, but GHQ in France had its way.

On Sept. 15, 1916, the tanks, their crews insufficiently trained, their mechanical performance uncertain, were thrown into the battlefield. Haig deployed sixty tanks into the Somme over country that under no stretch of the imagination could be called, in today's phrase, "good tank country."

The ground had been churned by thousands of shells. The German defense system was far more elaborate and much stronger than the one that had existed when the tank was first planned. Nevertheless the tanks, followed by the infantry, gained a minor success— enough to enable GHQ to salvage some acclaim from the Somme bloodbath, though not enough to win acceptance of the tank by the military incompetents who surrounded Haig.

The British Ministry of Munitions ordered 1,000 new tanks. The General Staff in France said the vehicles were not needed and the order was canceled. Fortunately, Major Albert Stern, who in civilian life was a prosperous broker, was not overawed by either the General Staff or the War Office. He went to Lloyd George and the order was restored. Stern, naturally, paid for it. He was removed from his post at the Ministry of Munitions. Swinton was ousted from his command of the tank unit in England.

But there were young, regular officers who had not lost faith in the tank's ability to accomplish its mission, just as in 1939 there were young regular officers in the USAAF who believed in the B-17, and in the RAF who believed in the Spitfire. The tank, despite all that the cavalry generals could do, was about to make its lasting impact on ground warfare.

It is a mistake in writing history to assume that what "they" expected to do at a certain time and place and what "we" half a century and more later expect are comparable. After years of tank warfare, most modern military writers see the first great tank battle in modern terms. But the tanks of those days were neither as mechanically reliable nor as heavily armed as those of World War II or later. It is quite apparent that if we put ourselves in those tanks, we will see that their primary impact was on the morale of the Germans, that their achievement was demoralization rather than destruction.

Clement Attlee, Prime Minister of the Labor government after World War II, was a young officer in the Tank Corps in, as he called it, "the German war." Sitting one night in my flat in London, he ruminated on that first great tank battle.

"We didn't have any wireless or radio, y'know. Mostly we signaled with flags like ships at sea. It was—what's the Chinese phrase? —'hot and noisy' inside. Machine guns popping off and those two-pounders in the side casements. Oh, we made a good deal of progress. Fairly rolled up their line. Couldn't see much of it. But I do remember looking out of one of the slits and seeing a Jerry [German soldier]. Standing there with his rifle across his knees. Frozen. Frozen with fear, I suppose."

Colonel Swinton, Churchill, and the other godparents of the tank were convinced that tanks would not be successful unless they were deployed in large numbers rather than in "penny packets." The tactics that were evolved called for a raid rather than a major offensive, the idea being that the tanks' aim, in the words of the British planners, would be "to destroy the enemy's personnel and guns, to *demoralize* [author's italics] and disorganize him and not to capture ground." This was a sound enough concept in view of the reliability and armament of the tanks, but it stresses the difference between Cambrai and the great armored battles of World War II and the 1973 Arab-Israeli War. What the Tank Corps, in the person of the then-Colonel J. F. C. Fuller, Chief Staff Officer, had in mind was a "hit-and-run" operation.

In early August the Tank Corps had worked out a plan for a raid south of Cambrai, an operation that would last no more than eight to twelve hours. This project might have been adopted had it not been for the deadly attraction of the Ypres battle to the north, to which Haig was committed. But as Ypres or Passchendaele became bloodier and less rewarding, Haig, looking for a success—somewhere, anywhere—agreed to the tank attack at Cambrai.

The job was given to Sir Julian H. G. Byng and the Third Army. That army, like others in the British Expeditionary Force, had lost tens of thousands of men at Ypres. Byng, an imaginative and thorough commander, realized that if the tanks did succeed in making the long-desired breakthrough, the reserves on hand would not be sufficient to exploit it.

But the objectives in Byng's plan were outrageous for a tank force as yet untried and, indeed, for infantry and artillery with no doctrine of all-arms co-operation. For his army and the Tank Corps, Byng prescribed four missions: to break the Hindenburg Line, which was the heart of the defense, between the Canal de L'Escaut and the Canal du Nord; to seize Cambrai, Bourlon Wood, and the passage over the Sensée River; to cut off the Germans in the area south of the Sensée and west of the Canal du Nord; and to exploit success toward Valenciennes.

This overly ambitious plan was to be carried out by two corps, each of three divisions, a cavalry corps of two divisions, a total of 381 tanks and approximately 1,000 guns.

Field Marshal Sir Harold Alexander in discussing Cambrai once explained, "They did it with so little because none of them"—he meant the generals at GHQ—"doubted that the British infantryman could, what's your phrase, 'lick his weight in wildcats.'"

Whatever the rationale, the character of the operation had changed. This was not a raid; this was a full-blooded offensive of the type that had been tried time and time again on the western front and had failed time and time again. But it was to be an offensive with insufficient reserves. No soldier, not even the cavalry generals who exercised such influence at Haig's headquarters (Haig himself, of course, was a cavalryman), could have believed after three years of war that cavalry could live with machine guns on a battlefield. Yet the reserve was two cavalry divisions.

The pioneers of the first armored staff did their work well. The preparations were thorough and, in most cases, proved adequate.

The Hindenburg Line, at that time, was the most elaborate system of fortifications ever devised by man. To cross its wide trenches, the British placed great bundles of brushwood on the nose of each tank. These were released when the tank reached the edge of a trench, providing a crossing for the vehicle. The tanks, working in sections of three, thus had the capability of crossing three successive trenches.

The young officers of the Tank Corps, remember, were experimenting with an entirely new weapon. Tactics had to be worked out by rule of thumb. There were no books to consult, no retired officers available for consultation.

The tactical approach was for one tank to move about one hundred yards ahead of the two others in its section, dominating hostile machine gun fire as it went. The other two tanks would lead the infantry advancing just behind them. The two forces, tanks and infantry, were to co-operate; the tanks would knock out enemy strongpoints, and the infantry would mop up the remaining enemy infantry. As Attlee later pointed out, these infantrymen were unlikely to present fierce resistance.

The tactics should have been adequately suited for the operation. The error, for which the Tank Corps and GHQ share the blame, was in loosing the tanks along the whole front rather than against the strongpoints of the Hindenburg Line. Yet this attack pattern persisted in the British and French armies until the Germans Guderian and Rommel introduced a new doctrine in 1940.

The tank was asked to do too much. The first operational tank, the Mark I, which Haig used on the Somme, was an unreliable weapon. It was 7 feet 4½ inches high, 32 feet 6 inches long, and carried a crew of eight. The engine was a 105-horsepower British-manufactured Daimler, which gave the tank a maximum speed when the going was good of about 3.7 miles per hour. When the going was rough, the tank made about half a mile an hour. These Mark I's were armed with either two six-pounder guns or two machine guns. Those armed with six-pounders were called "male," those with machine guns "female" (unfortunately Dr. Sigmund Freud was not available to trace the origins of this sexual differentiation). When the Cambrai fight started, the British were deploying the Mark IV, an improvement on the Mark I. Its dimensions were roughly similar, but it too was a weapon that was far from perfect.

These were the tanks that on Nov. 20, followed by the infantry, rolled forward on a six-mile front. In every area but one, the combination scored a striking success. The exception was in front of Flesquières where the German local divisional commander allowed the tanks to go forward unaccompanied by infantry, which had not been instructed in tactical co-operation with the tanks. The result was that the tanks passed through the gaps in the barbed wire but the infantry was too far behind to exploit the breakthrough. The Germans, with that striking ability to recover from a reverse which marked them in two world wars, pulled out their machine guns and butchered the infantry.

Elsewhere the tanks drove to success. On the right flank the Twelfth, Twentieth, and Sixth Infantry Divisions secured their objectives. The Twentieth Division swept on, capturing Masnières and Marcoing, seizing the passages over the canal and a bridge. The Sixty-second Division on the left drove as far as Anneux, two miles behind Flesquières.

Nothing like this had happened on the western front since the short-lived war of maneuver in 1914! Tanks and infantry actually had penetrated five miles behind the German lines. The three main lines of German defense had been overrun. The British faced only a half-completed final defense line and open country. No wonder the church bells pealed!

Although the element of surprise now was lacking, the offensive continued to prosper on Nov. 21. Many of the tanks used in the offensive were unserviceable because of mechanical breakdowns, not enemy fire. Enough remained, however, to lead the Fifty-first and Sixty-second Divisions to Fontaine–Notre-Dame.

This was the flood tide of the attack. Now the tide ebbed. The Tank Corps, both machines and men, was spent. The Germans recaptured Fontaine–Notre-Dame, although on Nov. 23, tanks and the Fortieth Division took the whole of Bourlon Wood. Without sufficient tanks, the pace of the battle slackened. Meanwhile the Germans were preparing their counterstroke.

The counteroffensive launched on Nov. 30 was preceded by a

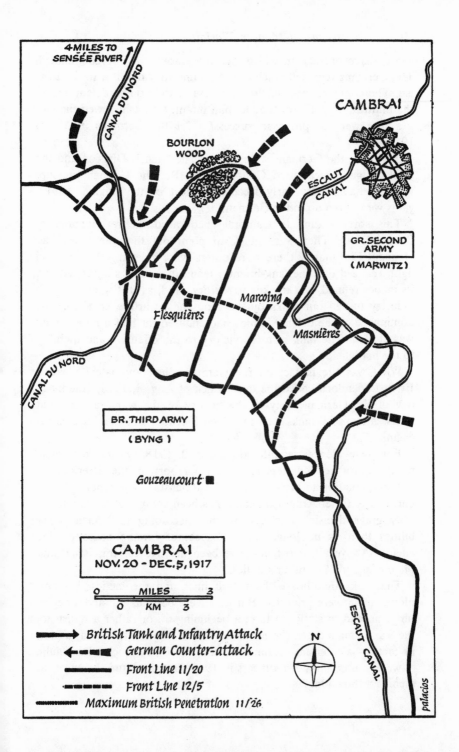

4 MILES TO
SENSÉE RIVER

CANAL DU NORD

BOURLON
WOOD

CAMBRAI

ESCAUT CANAL

GR. SECOND
ARMY
(MARWITZ)

CANAL DU NORD

Marcoing

Flesquières

Masnières

BR. THIRD ARMY
(BYNG)

Gouzeaucourt

CAMBRAI
NOV. 20 – DEC. 5, 1917

0   MILES   3
0   KM   3

N

ESCAUT CANAL

palacios

→ British Tank and Infantry Attack
← --■ German Counter-attack
—— Front Line 11/20
- - - - Front Line 12/5
····· Maximum British Penetration 11/26

short, fierce barrage in which gas and smoke shells predominated. The Germans regained much of the ground they had lost to the British. The counterstroke, in the shortness of the bombardment and in the infiltration tactics of the German infantry, foreshadowed the tactics that were to prove so successful for the Germans in March 1918.

This time the Germans were halted. The Guards Division and the Tank Brigade recaptured Gouzeaucourt. But the German pressure was maintained. By early December most of the original British gains were given up to the Germans.

This sorry ending to Cambrai encouraged the reactionaries at British GHQ. They were quick to point out that the tanks had "failed." Fortunately there were others who, assessing the Cambrai fight, realized that the tank-infantry team, its weapons improved and its tactics refined, was the key to victory. And, as British and French industry turned out tanks by the thousands, warfare changed. The dominance of the defense, which had endured for half a millennium, was eroded. The tank restored victory to the offensive and mobility to the battlefield.

What was the impact on the Germans then and later? General Erich Ludendorff called the tank attack of Aug. 8, 1918, "the black day of the German army in the history of the war," adding that "mass attacks by tanks . . . remained hereafter our most dangerous enemies."

Further evidence was offered on Oct. 2, 1918. On that day, German military headquarters submitted a report on the deteriorating military situation to the leaders of the Reichstag. The report said, in part: "The Chief Army Command has been compelled to take a terribly grave decision and declare that according to human possibilities there is no longer any prospect of forcing peace on the enemy. Above all, two facts have been decisive for this issue, *first the tanks. . . .*" (Author's italics.)

The tanks that broke the trench lines and the tactics that employed them were primitive. But they were both an end and a beginning: an end to static warfare; a beginning of, or rather a return to, the war of maneuver. The men who would take the tank and fashion its tactics—Guderian, Rommel, Patton, Fuller, Horrocks, De Gaulle —were young, unknown officers in 1917. But the future belonged to them. For how long?

It may be, as we shall see in a later chapter, that a new revolution in weaponry has sounded the death knell of the tanks, that the bell tolls for them as it did for horsed cavalry when the first archer loosed his cloth-yard shaft and brought down a knight at fifty paces.

V

The Storm that Swept Europe into Oblivion

THE BATTLE OF FRANCE

The storm that rolled over France, Belgium, the Netherlands (Holland), and Luxembourg in May and June of 1940 has been called the Battle of France. This is an omnibus term for a series of battles, on the ground and in the air, that in six weeks eliminated France as a military power. The French Third Republic was accompanied into limbo by the three minor states: Belgium, the Netherlands, and Luxembourg.

The campaign must be accounted the most decisive in the nearly six years of the war that followed in northwest Europe. New armor-infantry tactics, implemented with bewildering speed and enterprise, defeated the only important land power then on the Allied side. And the Germans had not only beaten the French, they had established themselves in positions from Norway's North Cape to the coast of Spain that provided unparalleled opportunities for waging sea and air warfare against Germany's sole surviving enemy, Britain.

It is understandable that, after the "Fall of France," as it was widely described, many Germans, Italians, Spaniards, Portuguese, and French believed that the war was over. In Moscow, too, there were those who considered the war in the west ended. But the Russians were not cheered by the prospect. They had expected a long, bloody struggle between the Axis and the Allies, one that would leave all Europe exhausted and an easy prey for Moscow's missionaries.

These then were some of the immediate consequences of the Battle of France.

One of the ironies of this tremendous victory is that the Germans did not expect it. They expected to win, of course, but not so swiftly and completely. They were as bewildered by the rapid collapse of the French as they were surprised by the stubborn bellicosity of the British. The German tendency to misjudge other nations influenced their operations. They thought the French to be stronger than they actually were; they discounted the British. Field Marshal Gerd von Rundstedt said to me after the war, "We should have known better after the first war. The French came close to collapse in 1917; *der Englander,* even after our 1918 offensive, never."

The first element in the German victory was the plan worked out by the German general staff. It was name *Sichelschnitt* (sickle stroke). In the long history of World War II, it is one of the few plans that worked. It is also a plan whose execution dealt a perhaps irreparable blow to the psychological state of the German planners' main opponent, the French high command.

Contemporary accounts to the contrary, neither the French nor the British, once war had been declared, expected the Germans to knock their brains out on the Maginot Line. Both the Allies and the Germans knew that the line itself ended at Montmédy, just southeast of Sedan. The Belgians had proclaimed their neutrality in 1936 and, three years later, there was little the French and British could do but prepare defenses along the Belgian-French frontier and pray that the government in Brussels would awaken to its peril.

General Maurice G. Gamelin, the Allied commander in chief, adopted an essentially defensive strategy. France, the dominant land power, was committed to a holding operation along the eastern frontiers. This strategy would provide France, and Britain, time to mobilize their military resources for a counteroffensive. The French planners anticipated a German drive through Holland and Belgium, and the British agreed.

The difference between the Allies lay in their appreciation of the strength of the German attack. General Noël Mason-MacFarland, the British Expeditionary Force's Chief of Intelligence, thought that the Germans would register decisive gains in the first five days. He was right. The French envisioned a German attack that would be repulsed in four days.

Belgium was a problem. The consensus among the Allied staff planners was that the Netherlands could not be defended against German forces advancing from the east. But it was believed that if the Belgian government co-operated, France's First Army Group under General Gaston Billotte and the British Expeditionary Force could move into Belgium. The force was to advance to the line of Meuse–Louvain–Antwerp. It was assumed, Churchill says, that the main Belgian forces would be east of this line and that they would be supported by the Allies or, should the Belgians retire, as they did, the main weight of defense would fall on the Allied forces.

Assessments of blame for this cataclysmic defeat have been directed largely at the French. And, indeed, they earned much of the criticism that was subsequently heaped upon them. But King Leopold of Belgium's stubborn refusal to join the western alliance once the fighting had begun and his niggling refusal of any realistic military co-operation also contributed to the defeat. I remember that when on May 10 the British Expeditionary Force advanced into Belgium, the leading units had to wait until the steel and wire antitank defenses, placed across the main roads to impede British and French troops, were removed by Belgian police.

In these circumstances, there is much in Churchill's suggestion that the whole of the French plan, Plan D, might better have been scrapped and that the French and British should have stood and fought on the French frontier.

The major weakness of Plan D was that it assumed that the principal German drive would follow the traditional route of invasion across the plains of Belgium. This, in fact, was central to the original German plan which sought no more than the defeat of Belgium and Holland and a lodgement on the English Channel coast facing Britain. Under this plan the major role was given to Army Group B, commanded by General Fedor von Bock, a subsidiary role given to Army Group A, commanded by Von Rundstedt. But the Germans altered their plan.

The architect of this victorious and decisive campaign was General Erich von Manstein, Field Marshal Rundstedt's Chief of Staff. It was the first and most strikingly successful of a long series of operations he was to plan during the war.

Like most inspired planners, Von Manstein took a chance. He

knew that the Ardennes sector was the weakest part of the French defense. It was held lightly because Marshal Henri Philippe Pétain, whose military education had stopped at Verdun, had concluded that the Ardennes were "impassable" to armor. The sector was "not dangerous," he told the French Senate's Army Committees. Pétain was oblivious to the advances that had been made in the range and durability of tanks since 1918. "A Rip van Winkle" was General Bedell Smith's description of the Marshal.

So the Germans shifted the weight of their attack from their frontiers south to Army Group A, which received seven of the ten available armored divisions and two masters of mobile, armored warfare, Generals Heinz Guderian and Erwin Rommel. Army Group B retained an important task, that of advancing into Belgium and engaging the Allied armies there, but the principal role of deep penetration was left to Rundstedt's southern forces. Once they broke through the French defenses in the Sedan-Dinant sector of the Meuse front, the Germans could go hell-bent for the Channel or turn southward and roll up the French forces behind the Maginot Line.

Hitler's intuition was often mocked during the war, especially when the Germans began to lose. But when Von Manstein presented his plan to "the Austrian corporal" (a sobriquet first given him by Rundstedt incidentally), Germany's Supreme Commander accepted it, and it was written into the operations order. The shift of German weight southward from Army Group B to Army Group A was not a secret. Allied Commander Gamelin and his staff officers knew of it, but they were prisoners of their intellectual convictions. They clung to their plan of a sweep into Belgium by the French and British forces, a sweep that would reduce the reinforcements available to meet a breakthrough in the Ardennes.

These were the plans. What of the opposing forces?

The popular impression at the time in both France and Britain was that the Germans attacked on May 10 with forces that were qualitatively and quantitatively immensely superior to those of the Allies. But the facts are quite different.

On that momentous day the Germans had 136 divisions in the west (it was not yet possible or politic to increase German strength *vis à vis* the Soviet Union). Ten were armored, seven motorized, one was horsed cavalry, and one airborne. The French and British had a total of 104 divisions deployed, 94 French and 10 British. When the

German attack began, 22 Belgian divisions were added to the Allied forces. The French force included three armored divisions, three light mechanized divisions, whose armament despite the appellation "light" was as formidable as that of the German panzer divisions, and ten cavalry divisions.

The ultimate difference lay not in numbers but in quality. That of the French reserve divisions was low for various reasons. I vividly recall talking to a French officer in London after the debacle. He explained that the bulk of General André-Georges Corap's Ninth Army which had failed so miserably in the Ardennes fighting was drawn from reservists from the Red Belt of Paris. During the previous winter their deputies, in one of those grotesque misjudgments to which the French government of the day was prone, had been arrested as Communists and hustled off to prison camps in Algeria. "In effect," the French officer told me, "they were disenfranchised. Why should they fight?"

In armor the balance was much less one-sided. In fact the French army deployed 3,254 tanks compared to the Germans' 2,574. The German tanks had the edge in speed and range, the French in armor and guns. In antitank guns, a weapon whose importance was being recognized belatedly, the French had the advantage.

The decisive element was a novel tactical doctrine of the Germans. Their armored divisions, including motorized infantry, were supported by tactical aircraft, in particular the Ju-52 Stuka. The pilots were trained to co-operate with the panzers. The French tank formations were tied to the infantry and, most important, lacked the air support which was so crucial an element in the German victory.

Even in the air, however, the German superiority has been exaggerated, although those who were unfortunate to be on the receiving end in May and June 1940 find this difficult to accept. Postwar statistics show that the Luftwaffe had 3,226 combat aircraft available: 1,016 fighters, 248 medium-range bombers, 1,120 bombers, 343 Stukas or dive bombers, and 500 reconnaissance aircraft. This was an imposing total. The French, however, had 1,220 modern combat aircraft, including 700 fighters, 140 bombers, and 380 reconnaissance planes. Qualitatively these aircraft were less impressive than those of the RAF's Air Component of the BEF—four fighter squadrons, four bomber squadrons, and five army co-operation squadrons. There was also an Advanced Air Striking Force composed of ten bomber squadrons and two fighter squadrons based on

Reims. In the first week of the battle, the RAF sent an additional ten fighter squadrons to France. Other fighter squadrons operated from southeast England in the closing days of the campaign, and their valor and enterprise contributed to the success of the evacuation from Dunkirk.

But as in the case of the armored formations, the German air divisions were better trained and organized for their role. The Stukas were sitting, or rather flying, ducks in the subsequent Battle of Britain; but in the Battle of France, operating in the closest co-operation with the armored formations against French troops of indifferent morale, they proved highly effective.

No comparison of the prebattle situation should omit the key question of morale. The Germans undoubtedly had greater *élan* and drive than the French. Although the latter were fighting in defense of *la Patrie,* they too often gave the impression that they were interested principally in getting out of the war and going home. A winter of idleness, the strong anti-Communist, pro-Fascist feelings of many in the officer corps—it was in that winter that I first heard the phrase, "Rather Hitler than Blum" (Léon Blum of the French Left) —contributed to the French collapse.

A remarkable aspect of the battle is that although France did not finally capitulate until June 22, the outcome of the battle was decided in the first seven days.

The offensive opened at 4:00 A.M. on the morning of May 10. In its first phase, most of the attention and concern were directed to the victories of Army Group B on the northern sector of the German advance. The German Eighteenth Army forced the capitulation of the Netherlands on May 15. German parachute troops seized the vital Belgian fortress of Eban Emael on the Meuse and with it, the use of three bridges across the river.

Despite British forebodings, the Allied armies had rushed into Belgium and the Netherlands. According to Churchill, the first phase of Plan D was completed by May 12. The French Seventh Army was in the north. The Belgians, who had failed to hold the Albert Canal, had retreated to positions from Antwerp to just north of Louvain. The BEF occupied the sector between Louvain and Wavre, and the French Ninth and Second Armies lay to the south.

The Allied advance into Belgium and the Netherlands did not attract, as might have been expected, continuous and heavy attack by the Luftwaffe. This mystified us at the time. The reason became

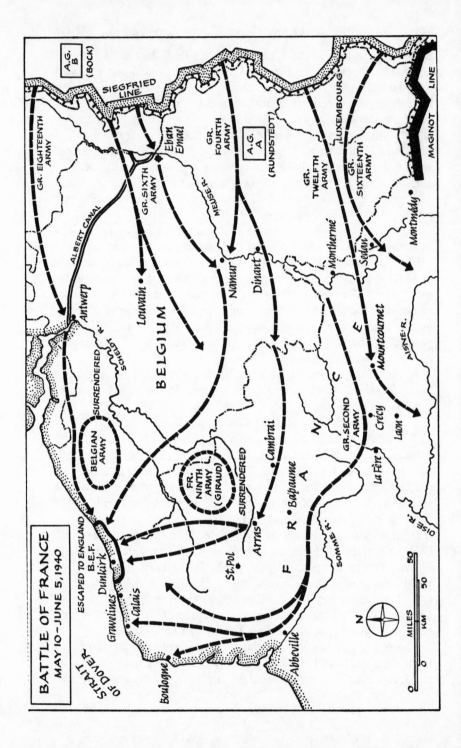

BATTLE OF FRANCE
MAY 10 – JUNE 5, 1940

clear when the main German attack developed through the Ardennes. Nothing could have suited the German high command better than a headlong Allied advance into the Low Countries.

The scale of the German victories in the north, the Dutch capitulation, and the smashing of the Belgian army have obscured the fact that the German advance was not successful everywhere. At Louvain in Belgium, for example, the British Third Division, under a then-unknown commander, Major General Bernard L. Montgomery, threw back two attacks by troops of the German Sixth Army. Accurate and heavy artillery fire and hard fighting by regular infantry units, the Royal Ulster Rifles, the King's Own Scottish Borderers, and the Coldstream Guards broke the German advance. "The Bren guns just swept them back like leaves before a hose," an enthusiastic captain told me that evening.

While Army Group B was sweeping across the inviting terrain of Belgium, Army Group A to the south was moving steadily toward the Meuse through the supposedly "impassable" Ardennes. General Paul L. E. von Kleist's panzer group of three tank corps led the march westward. This was the largest concentration of armor ever seen in war. On Kleist's right lay yet another panzer corps, commanded by General Hermann Hoth and including the Fifth and Seventh Armored Divisions.

The Belgians offered little resistance to the forty-four divisions of Army Group A. The roads through the Ardennes had been mined or blocked, but since the Belgians did not remain to defend the roads, these measures delayed the Germans only temporarily. By the evening of May 12, the leading armored divisions had reached the Meuse at two points, forty-eight hours earlier than planned.

The forcing of the Meuse by the Germans was the key to the Battle of France. There were other equally daring operations in the next five weeks, but none had such a startling impact on events.

General von Kleist's Armored Group had been assigned the task of driving across the Meuse between Sedan and Monthermé. The group included Guderian's three armored divisions. Their commander was so well prepared for the operation that on the night of May 12, he dug out of his files orders that he had written for war games the preceding winter and sent them to his units. "They were perfectly fitted to the reality of the situation," he wrote later.

The attack began at 11 A.M. on May 13. The movement across the river was preceded by attacks in waves of Stukas bombing the

French artillery batteries on the other side of the river. This attack was supplemented by shell fire from Guderian's tanks and from the eighty-eight-millimeter antiaircraft guns employed, not for the first or last time, as supporting artillery.

The effect of this barrage on the French was disastrous. One of their generals wrote: "Five hours of this punishment shattered their nerves. They became incapable of reacting to the approaching enemy infantry."

By 4 P.M. the German commanders decided that the French had been softened to the point where an infantry attack was practical. Elements of a rifle regiment of the First Panzer Division and of the Gross Deutschland Regiment started across the Meuse in rubber boats. Most of the boats got across. The French pillboxes and artillery positions had been silenced by the German air and artillery preparation. The infantry, once ashore, attacked the French positions with flamethrowers and demolition charges. The French retreated. By night the Germans had overrun the Bois de las Marfée, and by midnight they were five miles south of the Meuse.

Neither the Second Panzer Division on the right nor the Tenth Panzer Division on the left did as well, but both had infantry over the Meuse by nightfall. All three penetrations had been made solely by infantry. The Germans had no tanks across the river and, by the standards of 1914–18 under which the French high command still operated, the German bridgeheads were precarious.

But suddenly, panic! The French Fifty-fifth Infantry Division, in the path of the Tenth Panzer Division, broke. It is difficult to understand why; the Germans, we know, had only a few hundred infantry across the Meuse.

The artillery ran first. The rumor ran, as rumors do, that the German tanks were at Boulancourt—that is, in the French rear. The gunners pulled out. The contagion spread to the infantry. By late evening most of two infantry and two artillery regiments were in headlong flight accompanied and, in some cases, preceded by their officers. Parenthetically, it is interesting to note that neither the momentous news that the Germans were across the Meuse or that the Fifty-fifth Division was in flight was sent to General Gamelin, the Supreme Allied Commander.

The French did attempt counterattacks, but these were ineffectual. The troops got to the starting points too late. Or the jump-off time was put back. Or the commanders decided not to attack. In the few instances where attacks were launched, individual units fought well; but in these actions, as elsewhere in the battle, there was an evident lack of dynamism and enterprise among the French commanders. And, of course, the morale of the troops was ebbing. "There's no use trying to fight. There's nothing we can do. We're lost. We've been betrayed." This was the reaction from soldiers to whom a colonel appealed for resistance against the advancing Germans.

French field commanders retained in their minds hazy recollections of how in 1914 France had halted another German offensive by well-timed, well-placed counterattacks. But contemporary German doctrine overcame French dreams. The French Third Armored Division was poised to attack when the First and Second Panzer Divisions were moving to the west. But the opportunity was lost. The attack was called off by the corps commander, and the division was instructed to block the roads and hold defensive positions against German tanks. The Germans, of course, had no intention of using those roads. The Third Division was scattered, and its usefulness as a counterattacking force was destroyed. French commanders could not bring themselves to adopt the doctrine of full-bodied attacks by armored divisions. They still thought of tanks as auxiliaries to infantry.

If the situation of the French Second Army was bad, it was nothing compared to the disasters which now fell upon the Ninth Army to its left. General Corap's army was probably the weakest of those along the whole Allied front. Because the high command did not expect it to be actively engaged—those "impassable Ardennes"—it was given only two active (that is, regular) divisions out of seven, and only one motorized division. But the Ninth Army had the widest front: seventy-five miles from Namur to Sedan. And it had to hold this front against the second German panzer strike delivered by troops whose commanders included Erwin Rommel.

Rommel's infantry from his Seventh Panzer Division were the first to cross the Meuse. As they had done at Sedan, the infantry literally scrambled across the river, using rubber boats and skiffs unaccountably left on the shore by the French.

The bridge at Dinant had been blown by the French. But late on May 12, a German motorcycle patrol found that the lock which linked the island of Houx with both banks of the Meuse was intact. This was three and a half miles north of Dinant.

Sharp French resistance held the island until nightfall. Then a new

German attack drove the French off the island, pushed onto the far shore of the Meuse, and overwhelmed the French.

It was a success, but considering the scale of the battle and events elsewhere, a minor one.

Two miles to the south, Rommel, exhibiting that tigerish energy that marked his career, sought to ferry his Seventh Rifle Regiment across the Meuse on rubber boats. The crossing met heavy fire from the French Sixty-sixth Regiment, and in Rommel's words the situation "was none too pleasant."

He had pushed a rifle company across the river, but the French responded with heavy artillery, machine gun, and rifle fire. The crossings were halted. But Rommel and his staff found more rubber boats. By 10 A.M. the next morning, he had sufficient infantry across the Meuse to take Bouvignes and infiltrate toward the woods beyond. By noon on May 13, the German bridgehead was about three miles wide and two miles deep—not an impressive penetration between equal forces, but the forces were not equal. And nowhere less than in the skill of their commanders. The French prepared but failed to deliver two counterattacks against the bridgehead. Both were postponed until the next day. And by then it was too late.

By dawn on May 14, Rommel's German engineers had completed a pontoon bridge across the river. Just in time, the first armored and artillery units began to cross. The French put in one of their few successful counterattacks, smashing Rommel's motorcycle battalion. The success, however, had little impact on the main battle. General Corap pulled back his forward elements to a new defensive line, and Rommel was free to consolidate and organize the next phase of the offensive.

Corap's order symbolizes the almost indescribable confusion that reigned in the French armies. Orders were issued. New orders canceled them. Units were shifted from place to place for no discernible reason. Generals gave orders to units that had long since dissolved in the disaster. General quarreled with general. When a division did move into position for a counterattack, it was usually too late.

This was the fate of the French First Armored Division, which launched its attack on the morning of May 15. It was engaged by Rommel's Seventh Panzer Division driving in from the north. The French fought well. One regiment lost thirty-three of its thirty-six heavy tanks. Two companies of light tanks were destroyed by German fire.

The First Armored Division stood and fought, but the remainder of the Ninth Army was in retreat toward the French frontier, a disorderly mass. Here and there a few units turned to fight; inevitably they were overrun by the panzers and their supporting infantry. By May 16 the Germans had smashed through into good tank country on a front of fifty miles.

Allied air power's intervention in the battle was a disastrous failure. The main attack against a pontoon bridge at Sedan cost the Allies eighty-five bombers, most of them British. In three days of battle, the RAF lost more than 250 aircraft, most of them to German flak (antiaircraft guns).

The two elements that might have turned the tide, air power and French armor, were no longer available by May 16. Three German armored corps were across the Meuse and smashing through the demoralized troops of the French Ninth Army. Its commander, Corap, had been relieved and replaced by General Henri Giraud. A few days later Giraud was captured. As the panzer divisions sped westward, the bulk of the German infantry with its horsedrawn transport moved across the river to add weight to the German offensive.

If the extent of the disaster was not fully realized by the French high command, or indeed by most of the French government, still less was it understood by the new British government headed by Winston Churchill. But the capitulation of the Dutch government and disturbing reports about the French army from British headquarters led Churchill on May 16 to fly to Paris to consult with Premier Paul Reynaud. It was a fateful meeting. Almost as soon as he saw Premier Reynaud, Edouard Daladier (formerly Premier and now Minister of National Defense), and Commander in Chief Gamelin, Churchill realized that the situation was far worse than he, always buoyant in disaster, had realized: "Utter dejection was written on every face."

Gamelin described what had happened. The Germans had broken through on a front of fifty miles north and south of Sedan. The French forces in their path were destroyed or demoralized. The Germans could drive westward to the Channel coast or they could turn south on Paris. As Churchill described it, Gamelin talked for five minutes.

Then the Prime Minister asked the fateful question, first in English and then in French: "Where is the strategic reserve?" *"Où est la masse de manoeuvre?"*

Gamelin with a shrug said, *"Aucune."* ("There is none.")

This was the political turning point of the battle. Churchill was dumbfounded. He could not understand, then or later, how the great French general staff with all its experience could have failed to assemble a number of divisions to counterattack the invading Germans. He urged a counterattack by the northern armies against the German flank. He was "staggered by the conviction of the French commander in chief and leading ministers that all was lost. . . ."

Gamelin's mordant final comment to Churchill was: "Inferiority of numbers, inferiority of equipment, inferiority of method."

The second phase of the battle opened with the German armies driving westward toward the Channel with the objective of cutting off the northern armies from the French armies in the south and completing their annihilation. The French attempted to halt the rush along the Oise and Aisne Rivers. But they had thrown away their most powerful armored divisions in earlier, misconceived attempts to halt the panzers.

Now a new figure entered history. Colonel Charles de Gaulle on May 11 had been given command of the Fourth Armored Division which, he remarked later, "did not yet exist." He had no tanks and little logistic support. But he was an apostle of armor and, in that time of dissolution, a man who knew what he wanted and what he would do if he got it. By May 17 he had scraped together three battalions of tanks, one heavy and two light, just east of Laon, which was already threatened by the Germans.

De Gaulle's first encounter with the refugees, and "a military rout," aroused in him what he later described as "a terrible fury." It drove him to attack.

His objective was Mountcournet, and the French tanks did well. But after driving through German armored elements, they found that their infantry and artillery elements lagged. Under heavy fire from German guns north of the Serre River and almost continuous bombing by Stukas, De Gaulle was forced to withdraw. The attack had failed for the same basic reasons that other French armored counterattacks had failed—too little and too late.

Two days later De Gaulle returned to the charge. This time his objective was Crécy-sur-Serre and an opportunity to block the Germans driving to La Fère. But an order came from General A. J. Georges for a general withdrawal south of the Aisne. So the efforts of another French armored division had been thrown away by a high command ignorant of its capabilities.

Political considerations now impinge on the military situation—this time from the German side. The German generals were worried about the prospect of a French counterattack by the strategic reserve which, we know from Gamelin's statement, did not exist. But more important, Hitler was nervous about the same possibility, although, except for De Gaulle's brief and unsuccessful attack from Laon, there had been no sign of a French counterstroke. It is odd that, even then, despite the speed and effectiveness of the attack by Army Group A and the success of Army Group B, the German commanders still retained a high respect for the French army.

The debate within the German high command was between those who believed that the French were capable of a massive counterattack—memories of the Marne haunted both sides—and those who, like General Franz Halder, believed that the French were beaten, that they could not maneuver, that their commanders were inept, that they feared taking the offensive.

Whatever their opinion of the French to the south, the German generals had to take into account the Allies' situation in the north. There were three elements in this situation: first the defeatism of King Leopold of Belgium, who five years before had led his country out of an alliance with France and Britain; second the qualitative inferiority of the French forces faced with the German panzers; and third the growing distrust of the other Allies on the part of the British commander, General the Viscount Gort (also known as Lord John Vereker).

It is now known that the Belgian king, early in the battle, formed the idea that his forces should withdraw to the north—that is, *away* from the French and British—if retreat became necessary. His reasons are obscure. Some believe that he saw withdrawal into an entrenched camp at Antwerp, which the Belgians had done in 1914, as a means of saving his army and maintaining a foothold on Belgian soil. Others, more severe, see the move as a preliminary to capitulation. Leopold may have thought, they argue, that with a nearly intact army, he would be in a better position to negotiate with the Germans.

Historian William Shirer raises a question that has disturbed many Belgians: If the country was to be overrun by the Germans and the government to capitulate, how else could it be liberated but by an Allied victory?

This essay in power politics by Leopold had no influence on military events. On the evening of May 20, the Second Panzer Division reached Abbeville at the mouth of the Somme, finally isolating the Allied armies in the north. The stage was set for the victory within a defeat—Dunkirk.

In Paris Premier Reynaud, unmanned by events and hag-ridden by Madame de Portes, his mistress, tried another throw of the dice. He demoted Daladier from the Ministry of Defense to the Ministry of Foreign Affairs but, more ominously, he sought the help of two illustrious leftovers from World War I: General Maxim Weygand, recalled from Syria to replace Gamelin on May 17, and Marshal Henri Philippe Pétain, brought home from the embassy in Madrid to become Vice Premier and Minister of State. Few appointments in France's tangled history have been more disastrous. Into a rapidly moving battle in which new technologies and a new doctrine held the upper hand, France had thrown two old gentlemen. Weygand, the younger, was seventy-three!

The situation of the northern armies was critical but not disastrous. Had they been launched against the right or northern flank of the German forces moving to consolidate the seizure of Abbeville and if the Second and Sixth French Armies had driven north against the left or southern flank, there is a possibility that the German offensive might have been checked. But a paralysis appeared to have overtaken the French First Army in the north, and naturally Weygand was too new at his job to plan an offensive before he familiarized himself with the situation. This took an intolerable time in a battle in which success or failure was measured in hours rather than days.

All these contingencies weighed heavily on the British commander, General Gort. As early as May 19, he told London he was "examining a possible withdrawal toward Dunkirk, if that were forced upon him." The British government took a firmer position. Gort was instructed to move southwestward to join the French in the south. But the commander in chief's doubts were echoed in London. On May 20 Churchill ordered that "as a precautionary measure" the Admiralty should assemble a large number of small vessels "to proceed to ports and inlets on the French coast." This was the genesis of the Battle of Dunkirk.

Meanwhile the German forces that had burst across the Meuse were doing pretty much as they pleased. Small panzer formations roved across the countryside in the general direction of the Channel, shooting at any French formations they found in their way and helping themselves to fuel from gas stations and to other provisions. The British stolidly rebuffed attacks on their front which, during this period, were surprisingly light. The reason later became clear. The panzers were smashing through the Belgians and the French. Why should they rush headlong against the BEF, the only force that fought back?

Gort had two alternatives: to cut his way south toward the French, a task that might be beyond the logistics of the BEF but not beyond its valor; or to retire to Dunkirk.

Churchill made one last try. He flew to Paris again, to confer with Reynaud and Weygand. The Allies decided that the BEF and the French First Army should attack to the southwest, toward Bapaume and Cambrai, with the Belgian cavalry corps on the British right. A new, recently formed French army group, then forming on the line of the Somme, would drive northward to join the British and the rest of the French, thus cutting off the German spearheads farther west.

Like all plans, it looked good on paper. The facts were that the Belgian cavalry corps was not a reliable element; the new French army group lacked weapons, leadership, and morale, and the British were deficient in armor. At any rate, the BEF tried.

On May 20 Gort informed the French that he intended to attack out of Arras with two infantry divisions and an armored brigade, in co-operation with two infantry divisions from the French First Army. But the German pressure was increasing. They had crossed the Scheldt (Escaut) River on May 20 around Oudenaarde, and the three British corps fell back to the defenses they had built during the winter along the Belgian frontier.

On that day, May 20, the BEF went on half-rations.

The only serious attempt to cut the neck of the German offensive now developed. It was launched by the British southward from Arras toward Bapaume on May 21. Again, on paper the force seemed adequate; it consisted of the First Army Tank Brigade, together with the Fifth and Fiftieth Infantry Divisions. On the field, the situation was less encouraging. Both the infantry divisions had other missions in addition to the attack, and the tank brigade's vehicles were in poor shape after constant travel. Their tracks were wearing out. As it turned out, the advance by two mobile columns included only two infantry battalions, one in each column, and the tank brigade could muster only seventy-two tanks, most of them undergunned.

Despite these problems, the attack prospered. The French were to co-operate on the left of the British along the Cambrai–Arras road and, it was expected by the British, French forces south of the German salient would attack northward.

Although there were three panzer and one S.S. divisions in front of them, the British made reasonable gains, taking 400 prisoners. But German counterpressure increased. The armored cars of the Twelfth Lancers reported that Germans were moving in from Saint-Pol and threatening to turn the attacking force's flank. During the night General H. E. Franklyn, who commanded the British, withdrew his forces to the Scarpe River.

The French contribution was even less successful. Initially it included the V Corps of the First Army. When it came to events, the attack was delivered by a single infantry regiment, the 121st, supported by two small armored assault groups. The regiment reached the outskirts of Cambrai on the evening of May 21. It was immediately ordered to withdraw because of the danger of encirclement.

At this point the incompetence of the French command under Weygand began to exert a malign influence on the battle.

Weygand had evolved a plan to cut through the neck of the German advances. In itself the plan was feasible. The fault lay in the absence of forces to implement it and the unreliability of the information reaching French GHQ. At one point Weygand was told that the British had retreated twenty-five miles toward the Channel coast when, in fact, they had withdrawn fifteen miles in another direction. Moreover the French forces south of the German salient had done little and were to do less to attack into the salient.

By May 25 the British position had become desperate. Their counterattack had failed. The Germans had driven them out of Arras. Then, on May 25, came the news that the Belgian front had been smashed and that King Leopold was prepared to capitulate. Once he had done so, the left or northern flank of the BEF would be exposed. Gort in the field and Churchill and Sir John Dill, the Chief of the Imperial General Staff, recognized that their only course was to form a bridgehead around Dunkirk into which the BEF would fight its way.

It should be noted that despite strenuous attempts by some historians to magnify its role, Ultra, the top-secret British intercepts of German high-level messages, played little part in Gort's decision making. But a controversy still surrounds German strategy at this point.

Hitler, according to General Franz Halder, later the Germans' chief of staff, was worried about the fate of his panzer divisions in a countryside laced with canals. He therefore sent a message through General Walther von Brauchitsch, the army commander in chief, to halt the panzers. Halder saw this as a step that cleared the British path to Dunkirk.

Historians have ridiculed Hitler for his fears and for his order to cease the attack. But there was something there. The tanks of 1940 were not the tanks of 1945. Canals and flooding would have rendered many of them unable to attack.

Others lay the blame on Marshal von Rundstedt, who represented to Hitler, according to Rundstedt's diary, that his panzer formations after two weeks' operations and some losses required time to reorganize and re-equip. It may be that Rundstedt feared an Allied counterattack from north and south—in other words, the Weygand Plan. It seems certain that he, like a number of other senior officers, exaggerated the resilience of the French army and its leadership.

The blame is immaterial. The panzers did stop. And now, for the British, every road led to Dunkirk.

A key element in the Dunkirk operation, one often discounted by historians, was the three-day defense of Calais, south of Dunkirk. There a small British force, commanded by Brigadier C. N. Nicholson held out for three days against a vastly superior force of panzers, artillery, Stukas, and infantry. The French garrison fought as bravely as the British. On May 25 the Germans sent a flag of truce demanding a surrender. Brigadier Nicholson's reply was memorable: "The answer is no, as it is the British Army's duty to fight as well as it is the German's."

Nonetheless, on the next evening Churchill and Anthony Eden, then Secretary of State for War, decided to withdraw what remained of the garrison.

The effect of the defense of Calais was very great. Had it not been held, the Germans, as Guderian noted, would have pushed up the coast to Dunkirk before the British could have organized that port's defenses or the evacuation.

With the Belgians out of the war, Gort plugged the gap on his left flank and began his march to the sea, co-ordinating his movements with those of General Georges Blanchard's First French Army. The French had farther to go and moved first. Elements of the British First and Second Corps clung to their positions in the defenses along the Franco-Belgian frontier until the night of May 27–28. But a little before 7 P.M. on May 26, a critical decision had been taken. The Admiralty in London signaled, "Operation Dynamo is to commence." "Dynamo" was the code word for the evacuation of the British and French forces from Dunkirk.

Evacuation would be possible only if the Allies continued to hold the Dunkirk position. They were threatened by the Germans' encircling movement, which sought to cut off four British divisions and the French First Army. The Allies fought successfully for four days around Lille. Then, on Gort's orders, the British withdrew and, because their transport was mechanized, they were able to make the coast in a night. The French followed, but the Fifth Corps was lost largely because its horse transport was slow in starting. All the British divisions had mechanized transport, whereas only the French armored divisions did.

The Germans had not abandoned their efforts to break into the corridor to Dunkirk by driving through the gap left open by the Belgian capitulation, but the British, the majority regular soldiers, held. By the afternoon of May 28, six British divisions had formed a defensive line along Gravelines–Bergues–Furnes–Nieuwpoort. The evacuation could begin.

It is not in the compass of this chapter to describe the harrowing and heroic battles around Dunkirk or the evacuation itself. There are two aspects, however, that had their influence on the future course of the war. Of the 338,226 troops evacuated, the greater part were British regulars who formed the nuclei of armies that went on to fight with distinction in Africa, Italy, and Normandy. The charge is untrue, but the French believe that the British deserted them at Dunkirk, a conviction that scarred Anglo-French relations for the rest of the war. The choice, however, was between escape and destruction.

The Royal Navy suffered heavily during the evacuation. But so did the Luftwaffe. Dunkirk was close enough to southeast England to allow Fighter Command to deploy its Spitfires and Hurricanes over the beaches. Patrols over the beaches bit into the German bomber formations and caused serious losses. Wars, as Churchill was to remind the House of Commons, are not won by evacuations. But the course of reverses like Dunkirk often illuminate the paths to future victories.

It was now the turn of the French. On June 5 the Germans launched their final offensive against a French front consisting of the Second, Third, and Fourth Groups of armies—perhaps 1,500,000 men in 65 divisions. The German attacking force was approximately 124 divisions in three army groups.

The German offensive was almost everywhere successful. It was then, rather than earlier in the battle, that defeatism swept the French. I have two memories that are apposite.

I was quartered in Le Mans, in the home of a prosperous French garage owner. On his wall was a large battle map on which he had traced in pencil the inexorable German advance and the French retreat.

"It is folly," he said. "There is nothing to stop them. Why continue? Poor France."

The next day, during breakfast at a pavement café, I noticed a Paris taxicab draw up across the square. Two women, obviously prostitutes, got out.

"In the Great War," the elderly waiter said, "our taxis carried soldiers to battle. Now they take whores to safety."

In Paris the government was in disarray. Reynaud had dropped Daladier from his cabinet and was under an unremitting barrage of defeatist counsel from Madame de Portes, Pétain, and now from Weygand, whose principal preoccupation appeared to be the salvation of the honor of the French army.

The final phase of the Battle of France was an uneven affair. In their attempt to hold the line of the Somme River, the French Seventh Army repulsed repeated attacks by four panzer divisions. But on June 7 the Seventh Panzer Division—Rommel again—burst south of the river, advancing forty miles to Forges-les-Eaux. By June 8 the Battle of the Somme was lost. The Germans had cleared the way for a pincer attack on Paris. This was carried out by Army Group B (Von Bock) and Army Group A (Von Rundstedt). Moving as they had since May 10 with the greatest speed, the Germans shifted armored formations from flank to flank. Again the French fought bravely on the Aisne River. But by June 10 that battle too was lost. On the next day, Reims fell and the Germans reached Château-Thierry.

By then, the defeatists in the cabinet were alternating between rabid criticism of the British and suggestions for capitulation. The criticism of the British centered largely on Churchill's refusal to commit further RAF fighter squadrons to the battle. Weygand was the spearhead of those advocating capitulation. Paris was abandoned by the government on the night of June 12–13. The government fled southwestward, halting briefly on the Loire and then moving on to Bordeaux. The German armies swept southward as French resistance crumbled.

The last acts were political. Reynaud gave way to Pétain. The Marshal asked the Germans for an armistice. The long Battle of France was over. The Germans now controlled Western Europe from the North Cape in Norway to the Spanish frontier. The military geography of World War II in the area most important to America had been established. It was not to be changed for four years.

Militarily the French were beaten on the Meuse. Politically they were beaten by many factors: popular inertia, wishful thinking, and finally defeatism. It is easy to blame Pétain, Pierre Laval, and the rest of the shoddy crew of collaborators who took power. One point should be made in explanation if not in defense: when they surrendered to the Germans, the French were convinced that Britain would be forced to surrender before autumn.

Indeed, General Charles Huntziger, whom we last saw in the Ardennes, remarked to a colleague after the act of capitulation at Compiègne, "If the British are still fighting by December, we're all traitors."

The British, as we shall see, were fighting then and to some purpose.

VI

So Much Owed by So Many to So Few

THE BATTLE OF BRITAIN

Late in the afternoon of Sept. 15, 1940, Winston Churchill asked Air Vice Marshal Keith Park, "What other reserves have you?" Park told the Prime Minister, "There are none." Four months earlier, at the most critical hour of the Battle of France, Churchill had asked a similar question and received the same answer from General Gamelin.

This time, however, there was a different outcome. The pilots of the Royal Air Force's Fighter Command, many of them inexperienced and incompletely trained, all of them unutterably weary after weeks of combat, held on. By nightfall the climax of the Battle of Britain had passed and the British had won.

Forty years of argument and investigation of the records on both the German and British sides have not altered the basic truth that dawned following the end of the series of daylight air battles which we now call the Battle of Britain. The Luftwaffe, the most powerful air force in the world, the glittering ornament of the seemingly invincible Wehrmacht, had been defeated. The immediate and long-term consequences to the war and to history were of enormous importance.

The German defeat ended Hitler's plans for invading Britain: Operation Sea Lion. This project, planned after the fall of France, depended for success on the elimination of the RAF as a coherent fighting force. To do this, the Luftwaffe had first to defeat the Fighter Command. Only when they had command of the air could the Germans launch an invasion across the English Channel. In a series of battles that began in July and lasted into the third week of September, the British not only retained command of the daylight air over southeastern England, the area chosen for invasion, but they inflicted such heavy losses on the Germans that the Luftwaffe was forced to bomb by night, for which it was neither trained nor, initially, well equipped.

One immediate consequence of the victory was that the Germans, correctly assessing the British inability to take the offensive in Europe, turned their minds to the invasion of the Soviet Union. But ten months later, when the Wehrmacht launched its great offensive into Russia, the Luftwaffe went into battle minus some hundreds of its best pilots and air crew who had been lost in the great aerial duel of the previous summer.

The outcome of the Battle of Britain had a significant effect on the American attitude toward the war. Watchers in Washington, alarmed by the defeatist dispatches of America's Ambassador Joseph P. Kennedy, noted that the British had not only won the battle, contrary to the ambassador's predictions, but that the island and its industrial potential remained largely intact. If the United States were ever to enter the European war, Britain was there, "the unsinkable aircraft carrier," the base for a future invasion of the continent.

The Battle of Britain was the first decisive battle of history to be fought in the air. It was also a battle fought by relatively small numbers. When the pilots and air crews on both sides, the ground staffs and maintenance men, the British radar operators antiaircraft units, and Royal Observer Corps personnel are considered, it is likely that the total was well under 100,000. The Battle of France in May and June had involved approximately 4,000,000.

The incredulous surprise that greeted the British victory in the Western world reflected the view, held by both governments and peoples, of Britain's chances after the fall of France.

The Germans were seen then as all-powerful, all-conquering. They had defeated the French, long considered the foremost military power in Europe. They now occupied the airfields and ports of Western Europe from Norway's North Cape to the Spanish frontier. The railroad and canal systems of the countries from which an invasion of Britain would be launched—France, Belgium, and the Netherlands—had been only marginally damaged in the fighting of May and June. The British Expeditionary Force had returned from Dunkirk without most of its heavy equipment. The conscripted forces on the island were woefully short of modern arms. There seemed to be very little between the Germans and a successful invasion of Britain and the end of the war.

Only a very few realized that it might not be all that easy. One was Carl A. Spaatz, later commander of the American Eighth Air Force but then a major sent to England to report on the RAF. He had noted that when the British Spitfires and Hurricanes had been able to patrol for Dunkirk from their bases in southeastern England, they had fought the Luftwaffe to a standstill. From May 22 onward some 200 fighter sorties (a sortie is one operational flight by one aircraft) had been flown each day over the battle area. By May 24 German General Franz Halder was noting in his diary, "For the first time now, enemy air superiority has been reported by [General] Kleist."

In early July, when the Luftwaffe began its first operations against British shipping in the Channel, the Germans were quantitatively superior in the air. Three *Luftflotten,* or air fleets, had been assigned by Hermann Goering to launch the operations against Britain. Luftflotte II, commanded by General Albert Kesselring, was based in Holland, Belgium, and northeastern France. Luftflotte III, under General Hugo Sperrle, was deployed in north and northwest France; and Luftflotte V, under General Hans-Juergen Stumpff, was in Norway and Denmark. The assets of the three air fleets amounted to approximately 3,500 aircraft. The British reckoned that if seventy-five percent were serviceable, the Luftwaffe could start the battle with 1,000 long-range bombers, 1,000 fighters, and 250 dive bombers. German records show that the Luftwaffe began the battle with 1,102 bombers and 1,025 fighters.

The best bomber in service with the Luftwaffe, and probably the best bomber then in service anywhere, was the twin-engined Junkers Ju-88A. The Ju-88 had a top speed of 287 m.p.h. at 14,000 feet. The best-known bomber was the Ju-87B, the Stuka, a dive bomber which had registered extraordinary success in the Polish and French campaigns. Used against inadequately defended ground targets and raw troops, the Stuka had a terrifying effect. In the Battle of Britain, attempting to elude modern fighters, it was by no means as effective. With a top speed of 232 m.p.h., it was the slowest operational aircraft in the fight.

The Luftwaffe had more Heinkel He-111's than any other bomber. But it was the slowest of the German twin-engined bombers and, although it had been given extra armor and extra machine guns, it was gradually found to be inadequate against determined defenders.

The two other German bomber types were the Dornier Do-17Z and the Dornier Do-217. The former was the famous "Flying Pencil," a name arising from its long, slim fuselage. Both aircraft were relatively slow, and their bomb payloads were small.

If the German bombers other than the Ju-88 had obvious weaknesses, this was not true of the two fighters, the Messerschmitt Me-109 and Me-110. In the early summer of 1940, the pilots of the British Fighter Command held both in high respect.

The Me-109 was a single-engine, single-seat fighter with a speed of 386 m.p.h. It was produced until the end of the war in greater numbers than any other combat fighter of that conflict. By the opening of the battle, it had been armed with a twenty-millimeter cannon instead of machine guns. In combat it was reckoned as better than the British Hurricane and the equal of the Spitfire. These two British aircraft bore the brunt of the battle.

The Me-110 was less spectacular. It was a twin-engined aircraft with a crew of two; at 342 m.p.h. it was slower than the Me-109, with poor acceleration and a wide turning circle. The Me-110 was heavily armed with two cannons and four machine guns. During the battle it did prove effective in providing escorts for the bombers, but it was less effective in one-on-one encounters with British fighters.

Throughout the battle, and indeed almost until the end of the war, the Luftwaffe experienced no shortage of pilots and air crew. The loss of experienced airmen in the Battle of Britain did eventually take its toll, but in 1940 pilots were graduating from training schools at a rate of about 800 a month. Moreover, a high percentage of the first-line pilots in that battle had fought successfully in the French and Polish campaigns. They were more experienced than the British and, in the case of the veterans, more skilled as pilots.

The British Fighter Command that faced this imposing force in July of 1940 included 609 fighters, of which 531 were serviceable. This figure includes twenty-seven Boulton Paul Defiants, which proved almost useless and were soon phased out of the battle. The

Germans at that time had 658 Me-109's and 110 Me-110's in north-west Europe alone.

Even so, the British strength had grown since the end of the fighting in France. On June 4, Air Marshal Sir Hugh Dowding, the chief of Fighter Command, had had only 446 serviceable aircraft, of which 331 were Spitfires and Hurricanes. Even at that early date, fighter-pilot replacement was a problem. The RAF had lost 219 fighter pilots over France and the Low Countries.

The most successful fighter of the battle on the British side was the Supermarine Spitfire, a single-engined, one-seat aircraft with a speed of 355 m.p.h. at 19,000 feet. It was armed with eight machine guns. It was a beautifully structured aircraft, much more so than the Me-109. The Spitfire, like its rival, took off after a short run but the Me-109 could outclimb it.

The Hurricane, which with the Spitfire did most of the fighting, was slower but had the same armament. It was, however, an easy aircraft to maintain and repair. Hurricanes often limped home riddled with bullet holes to be repaired by crews on the airfield and to be ready for operations again in forty-eight hours. The Hurricane Mark I did 316 m.p.h. at 17,500 feet; the Mark II, 342 m.p.h. at 22,000 feet.

The Germans, about to embark on a campaign unique in military history, had to reckon with radar on the British side. The Germans, of course, knew that the British possessed radar, although they underestimated its importance. The Germans had their own radar, but it was used principally for naval operations.

By the opening of the battle, the British had installed two radar chains. The first, Chain Home or CH, monitored aircraft flying below 15,000 feet and provided less accurate coverage of planes flying at 20,000 or more feet. A second network, Chain Home Low or CHL, detected aircraft approaching at lower levels down to about 2,500 feet, the then-effective radar vision limit. The chain of stations along Britain's coasts was formed like a reversed "L." At the top of the "L" were the Shetland Islands. The angle was the bulge of Kent toward France, and the horizontal arm extended westward toward Land's End in Cornwall.

The advantage to the British of radar is incalculable. Without it an effective defense would have been impossible, granted the numer-ical weakness of Fighter Command compared to the three German air fleets. Although there were many technical difficulties, throughout the battle the British knew when the Germans were coming and approximately where.

The Luftwaffe had been planned, equipped, and trained to operate in daylight in the closest co-operation with the army. Its experience in long-range bombing against a determined defense was limited. The three air fleets arrayed against Britain lacked a common strategy, and at the outset the commanders knew so little about British defenses that their tactics were poor.

Fighter Command on the other hand had been built, equipped, and trained for the defense of Britain. Its leaders, particularly Dowding, had devoted a great deal of thought to the tactics of defense. Dowding was a quiet, studious man of outstanding intellect. The shabby treatment given him after he had won the first British victory of the war is a stain on the record of the Churchill government. No title, no awards for Dowding. He passed into history unhonored save by his pilots.

If a German invasion was to be successful, it was the Luftwaffe's task to bring the RAF to battle and defeat it. To lure the British fighters into the air, the Germans had to launch bombing attacks by daylight against shipping, ports, aircraft factories, and communications. They also had to knock out as many of Fighter Command's airfields as possible.

Like boxers feeling each other out in the early rounds, the Battle of Britain began in July with a series of Luftwaffe attacks on British shipping in the Channel. This brought into action Fighter Command's No. 11 Group commanded by Air Vice Marshal Keith Park with headquarters at Uxbridge. No. 11 bore the brunt of the entire battle, for it guarded both the great citadel of London and the most probable area of invasion, southeast England. At the height of the fighting, No. 11 Group deployed fifteen squadrons of Hurricanes, seven of Spitfires, and two of Blenheims, an elderly bomber which could be used as a fighter-bomber.

The second most important formation was No. 12 Group commanded by Air Vice Marshal Trafford Leigh-Mallory. It was charged with the defense of the eastern counties and the midlands. To the north was No. 13 Group, protecting northern England, Scotland, and Northern Ireland.

The Luftwaffe attacks on convoys moving through the Channel served two purposes. They interrupted, marginally, Britain's sea transport, particularly that of coal, and they brought Fighter Com-

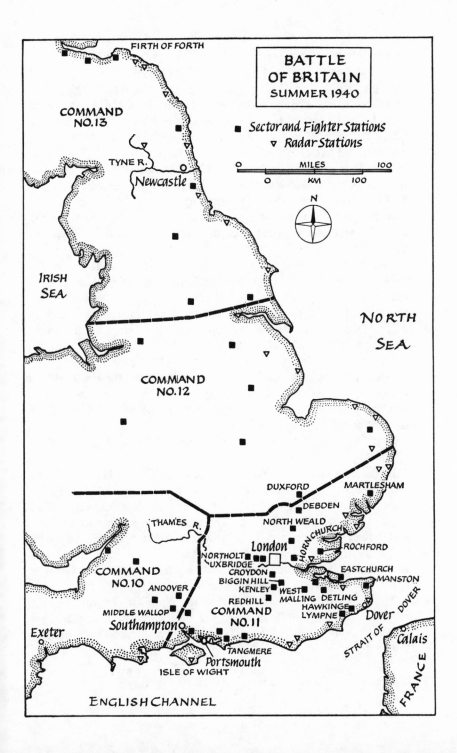

mand to battle. Dowding warned the government that he could not protect the coastal convoys without risking a high percentage of his fighter assets. He was losing pilots at an alarming rate—220 in the first three weeks of July. Eventually pressure from the Air Ministry forced the Admiralty to discontinue the coal convoys through the Channel. The coal was now carried by rail, which had been possible and practical from the start.

The Germans had selected Aug. 13 as *Adlertag* (Eagle Day), the opening of the main air assault. They had attacked heavily on Aug. 8, 11, and 12, with the raids focusing on airfields at Hawkinge, Lympne, and Manston, and on radar stations on the Isle of Wight and in Sussex and Kent counties, but the fighting on those days was overshadowed by that on Aug. 13.

The Germans began early. At 5:30 A.M. radar picked up, at the then-astonishing range of 110 miles, two large formations assembling over Amiens. By 7:00 A.M., 120 RAF fighters were airborne from the Thames estuary to Exeter. German tactics were inconsistent. One force of 80 bombers flew over the Thames estuary without escort. It was badly mauled.

The afternoon saw three other heavy attacks, which included raids on eleven airfields. A heavy cloud cover hampered the bombers, although one squadron bulled through to bomb Detling. Canterbury was the geographical center of the day's fighting which extended on the British right flank about 140 miles to the west. There two squadrons of No. 10 Group came to the support of the hard-pressed fliers of No. 11.

Eagle Day must be accounted a reverse for the Germans. The Luftwaffe flew 1,485 sorties by day and night, compared to Fighter Command's 727. The Germans lost thirty-nine aircraft, the British thirteen planes and seven pilots. There also were evident weaknesses in German intelligence. Of the eleven airfields bombed, only one was a fighter field. Some bomb damage was reported from Southampton and near Detling. But considering the extent of the German effort, *Adlertag* was a disappointment.

That day's fighting began the climactic phase of the battle. From Aug. 13 until the middle of September, the air battle maintained an unprecedented intensity. The Germans knew they had to destroy Fighter Command before they could turn to preinvasion targets. Fighter Command's task was to stay alive as a fighting force until the weather worsened and invasion became too risky.

Both sides exaggerated enemy losses in aircraft and pilots, but this was not as important to the conduct of the battle as the serious misjudgments made by the German commanders on the basis of pilots' reports. For example, Halder wrote in his diary after *Adlertag* that the Luftwaffe had destroyed eight major RAF bases, whereas they had *attacked* eleven bases without destroying any. General Otto Stapf of the Luftwaffe, who a month before had predicted it would take between two and four weeks to smash Fighter Command, now considered the job could be done in a week or ten days. The Germans also miscalculated the British production of fighters and the number of pilots available, in each case setting a figure far lower than the actual one.

Equally important to the next German foray was the belief at Luftwaffe headquarters that the large number of fighters encountered over southern England meant that the north had been denuded of fighter protection. This erroneous view contributed to the setbacks which ensued on Aug. 15.

On that day the Germans threw into the battle not only Luftflotten II and III in France, Belgium, and Holland but Luftflotte V stationed in Norway and Denmark. The attack from the north was to be directed against airfields and the industrial area along the Tyne River. As a feint, forty-five bombers heavily escorted by fighters attacked the airfields at Lympne and Hawkinge in the south to pin down fighters from No. 11 Group.

No. 13 Group, commanded by Air Vice Marshal Richard E. Saul, guarded the north, its pilots, its planes, its radar virtually untested. Shortly after noon the group's Operations Room at Newcastle-on-Tyne reported twenty or more German aircraft approaching about 100 miles east of the Firth of Forth.

Again the Germans had made a feint. The first aircraft monitored were He-115C reconnaissance float planes; the main attack was delivered by more than seventy-five He-111 bombers escorted by Me-110 twin-engined fighters. Possibly because of the extreme range, the German fighters had taken off without their gunners.

Spitfires of No. 72 Squadron met the Germans. Dividing their efforts, one half of the squadron attacked the bombers, the other the Me-110's. Under attack, some of the He-111's jettisoned their bombs. Others turned south, away from the targets. The Me-110's, at a disadvantage because of the lack of a rear gunner, formed a defensive circle with each aircraft's forward firing guns covering the undefended tail of the plane in front.

Meanwhile the RAF had brought in additional squadrons from as far north as Drem in Scotland and from Catterick, Yorkshire, in the south. For once the British were close to parity in numbers. In this single action, the Germans lost fifteen aircraft against a single Spitfire shot down.

Luftflotte V now delivered its second attack. About fifty Ju-88's, flying without escort, flew from Aalborg, Denmark, to the English midlands where they encountered the fighters of No. 12 Group. The Ju-88's were renowned for their speed, which is why the German command sent them off without escort, but they were no match for the Spitfires and Hurricanes. Despite losses, however, the Germans pushed on to bomb the RAF field at Driffield in Yorkshire. But seven Ju-88's were shot down and three more crash-landed on the way home.

The results were disappointing for Luftflotte V. Nearly twenty percent of the raiding force had been lost. It was this air fleet's first and last intervention in the Battle of Britain.

But the day was far from over or won. In the south attacks in great strength developed in the middle of the afternoon. About 100 bombers, well escorted by Me-109's, struck into the air above Kent. The Me's were engaged by British fighters; the bombers pushed on to bomb aircraft factories at Rochester and airfields at Eastchurch. This German success went some way to balancing the reverses of Luftflotte V.

The Luftwaffe added another thrust, this one against targets around Portland. It was delivered by Ju-87 dive bombers. Another attacking force fought through the fighters to bomb Middle Wallop airfield, losing seven of fifteen bombers. At 6 P.M. radar sounded another alarm: German formations headed for No. 11 Group's airfields at Biggin Hill, Kenley, and Redhill with about seventy aircraft.

To meet this final attack, only one British Hurricane squadron, No. 501, was airborne. Air Vice Marshal Park scraped together parts of other squadrons to stiffen the defenses. This reinforcement enabled the British fighters to drive the Germans away from their original targets. But the bombers seriously damaged two aircraft factories at Croydon. This was the last attack of a day that had seen 1,786 German sorties and the most intensive fighting of the battle thus far. The British lost thirty-four aircraft, the Luftwaffe seventy-six.

The day's operations strained Fighter Command's resources, especially pilots. When the 501 Squadron went into action against the German evening attack, the pilots were fighting for the third time that day. Strain, however, was cumulative. It might, or might not, show in the next week's battles. The day was won by the British. Henceforth Luftwaffe pilots referred to it as *der schwarze Donnerstag,* Black Thursday.

The Luftwaffe, too, was feeling the strain of continuous operations. The Reich's Air Marshal Goering, the Luftwaffe's commander in chief, decided that officer casualties were now so high that only one officer should fly in each aircraft. He also ordered that Stukas, Ju-87's, must each have three fighters as protection. Finally, and from the German standpoint most seriously, he told his lieutenants, "It is doubtful whether there is any point in continuing the attacks on radar sites, in view of the fact that not one of those attacked has so far been put out of action." This was the first of the two major tactical mistakes made by the German high command in the battle.

The Luftwaffe maintained pressure. About 1,700 sorties were flown on Aug. 16. As the fighting continued, tactics were adjusted on both sides. The Germans began to time raids on fighter airfields in the period just after a squadron had been in action and the aircraft were being refueled on the ground.

An attack on the airfield at Brize Norton, as writer Len Deighton puts it, "pointed to the ever-present dilemma of the defenses. Aircraft left on the airfields during these attacks were lost by bombing and strafing. Yet if all the aircraft were sent into the air, they would need rearming and refueling at the same time. This would mean undefended sky, and more fighters on the ground vulnerable to follow-up attacks."

Successful British attacks on the German bomber formation also forced a change in the Luftwaffe's tactics. The fighter escorts no longer flew above the bombers, prepared to pounce on attacking fighters, but flew at the same altitude ahead or alongside the bombers. In response, the controllers of Fighter Command altered their tactics, ordering all fighters to attack the bombers rather than sending Spitfires after the fighters and directing the Hurricanes on the bombers.

The second phase of the battle opened in the last week of August with the German raids concentrating on the sector stations which had operational control of the fighter squadrons once the planes were airborne. There were seven such stations in No. 11 Group, located at Tangmere, Debden, Kenley, Biggin Hill, Hornchurch, North Weald, and Northolt. Each station customarily controlled up to three squadrons. These stations and their airfields were the keys to victory or defeat. If they were knocked out, the effectiveness of the Luftwaffe attack would increase. If they remained operational, the British could continue the battle.

The shift in German tactics forced another shift onto the British defenders who, at this period of the war, were much quicker to identify changes in the enemy's tactics and alter their own than were the Germans. Park, on Aug. 19, told his Sector Commanders and Controllers that their first priority was the defense of sector airfields. This meant that German bombers must be intercepted as far from the sector stations as possible while other squadrons would be assigned to protect the airfields rather than meeting the enemy bombers near the coast. These deployments gave no scope for the "big-wing" tactics being pushed by Leigh-Mallory of No. 12 Group. He and his staff advocated the deployment of large formations of fighters rather than the use of single squadrons or half-squadrons. Argument on this point poisoned the British Fighter Command for months.

This next phase of the battle opened on Aug. 24, when just after noon the Germans, after making their customary feints elsewhere, hammered the forward airfield at Manston. Manston, however, was not a sector station, and the damage, although severe, did not seriously hamper the defense. But a successful attack on Hornchurch did. This was followed by an assault on North Weald. There the defenders found it extremely difficult to get through the screen of German fighters and attack the bombers. North Weald continued operation as a sector station—but only just.

The RAF knocked down five bombers and four fighters, but they lost eight fighters (although five of the pilots were unharmed). A loss ratio of nine to eight, if extended through the battle, would have meant defeat for Fighter Command.

Again faulty German intelligence played a role in decision making east of the Channel. A Luftwaffe intelligence report estimated RAF losses at 574 fighters since July and added another 200 lost as a result of ground attacks and accidents. Other German intelligence reports calculated that Dowding's total assets were 430 fighters, of which about 300 were probably serviceable. The true figure was over 700.

Nightfall of Aug. 24 showed the British ahead in the day's tally by 36 to 22. But generally the day had gone against them. In addition to the attacks on Manston, North Weald, and Hornchurch, Luftflotte III made a successful attack on Portsmouth and its dockyard.

The fighting on Aug. 25 was on a reduced scale. But the lone important German attack was successful. Warmwell, an airfield in No. 10 Group's sector, was knocked out by forty-five bombers escorted by over one hundred fighters. There were no operations from Warmwell for eighteen hours.

Pilot replacement developed as a serious problem for Dowding. Since *Adlertag,* he had lost nearly eighty percent of his squadron commanders from death, wounds, or replacement. Other pilots joining the squadrons often had no more than ten hours flying time in single-seat fighters. At the same time the training period in the Operational Training Units was cut from six months to two weeks.

The German pressure was relentless. Sector stations and fighter airfields were attacked again on Aug. 26. The RAF continued to destroy more enemy planes than it lost, but the cumulative weariness of weeks of flying and fighting was beginning to affect the pilots. This was the most critical phase of the battle from the British standpoint.

The Germans were accepting their losses but getting to the vital target: Biggin Hill, the Coastal Command station at Detling, and then Biggin Hill again. On Aug. 30 the Luftwaffe flew 1,345 sorties; Fighter Command flew 1,054, its greatest effort thus far in the battle. The German losses were thirty-six aircraft, the British twenty-six. The next day the sector stations that controlled the defense of London, Croydon, Hornchurch, and Debden were bombed in the morning, Biggin Hill and Hornchurch in the afternoon. The Germans lost forty-one aircraft, the RAF thirty-nine. September began with more punishment for the sector stations, with some of the important targets hit twice in a day.

Between Aug. 29 and Sept. 7, there were thirty-three major German attacks, twenty-three of them on airfields. Park reported "extensive damage" to five forward airfields and to six of seven sector stations. By Sept. 5 the damage was affecting Fighter Command's combat efficiency. Telephone lines were out. Emergency operations rooms operated at reduced effectiveness. The ground organizations were suffering casualties. Above all, Fighter Command was losing pilots, experienced and otherwise. The transfer of pilots from the Bomber and Coastal Commands and the Navy's Fleet Air Arm did not suffice. Pilot strength had been 1,434 at the end of July. At the end of August it was 1,023. The reserve of Spitfires and Hurricanes was down to 125. To the worried men in Whitehall, it seemed that a continuation of German pressure could have but one result: Fighter Command losses to the point where the British could no longer halt the bombing necessary to prepare for invasion.

Now came an unexpected turn in the battle. Bomber Command had been carrying out small raids on the barges collected by the Germans for use in the invasion and on communications in Germany itself. Then in late August, after a few bombs had fallen in the center of London, quite possibly unintentionally, Bomber Command retaliated with a raid on Berlin.

The Germans were enraged. Hitler proclaimed, "If they attack our cities, we will rub out their cities from the map." Goering, an experienced airman who should have known better, agreed to switch the attack from the sector stations and forward airfields to London. He estimated that the RAF had no more than 350 fighters; actually it had 650. Attacks on London, Goering predicted, would force the RAF to use its final reserves. London was to be the next target, and the battle would begin on Sept. 7. The offensive against the British capital was to be the climax of the German air effort in 1940. This was the second and greatest mistake made by the Germans.

The switch in German targeting did not catch the British entirely unaware. The German bombers had been coming closer to London. Dowding and Park both realized that the docks along the Thames, the railway termini, and the aircraft factories to the south and southwest of London were inviting targets. But neither commander could be absolutely sure of a shift in German tactics. The sector stations still had to be protected as well as the new potential targets in London. Park asked for help from No. 10 Group to the west and No. 12 Group north of London. He again ordered his squadron commanders to leave the German fighters alone and concentrate on the bombers. Whenever time permitted, squadrons were to be committed in pairs.

The Luftwaffe's attack developed late in the afternoon of Sept. 7, with 642 fighters escorting 372 bombers. The targets were the docks and oil tanks along the Thames, the Royal Arsenal at Wollwich, and two factories nearby. Fighter Command put twenty-three squadrons into the air, and twenty-one engaged the Germans. But the Germans did extensive damage, dropping over 300 tons of high explosive and thousands of incendiary bombs. They lost forty-one aircraft but the British losses were high: twenty-eight fighters shot down, sixteen badly damaged.

That night the Germans began the bombing of London, inaccurately called "The Blitz." From Sept. 7 until Nov. 3 an average of 250 bombers attacked London every night. But night bombing was far less accurate than daylight attacks, even when these were delivered in the face of British opposition.

The next major daylight attack came on Sept. 9. Park positioned his squadrons forward to meet the two columns of German aircraft approaching London from Dover and Beachy Head. The first was intercepted and forced to drop its bombs on Canterbury. The second was deflected from the docks and engaged over the countryside. Individual German bombers were seen to jettison their loads over the suburbs. The Luftwaffe lost twenty-eight planes, the British nineteen aircraft and fourteen pilots.

The next day the Germans returned with about one hundred bombers fighting through to bomb the docks and the city of London. This time the loss ratio shifted to the Germans' favor: twenty-five Germans lost, twenty-nine British.

Sept. 15 has been selected as the critical day of this critical period. As such it is celebrated as the Battle of Britain Day in the United Kingdom. There were bigger days of battle, but on Sept. 15 the tide turned.

From their fields at Mondidier and Clairmont, Saint-Légerand and Cambrai, from Eindhoven, Brussels, Lille, and Beauvais, the German bombers rose heavy-bellied with bombs. The Me-109's and Me-110's flew from their fields to join the He-111's, Ju-88's, and Dornier 17's. Kesselring, whose air fleet launched the attack, sent 400 fighters to protect approximately 100 bombers.

The British controllers, checking radar reports, noted that it took longer than usual for the Germans to assemble the striking force. Then, as the force swept westward, the pilots of Fighter Command ran to their aircraft; some indeed had been put at a state of "superreadiness." They had spent the early morning hours in their cockpits.

By 11 A.M. Fighter Command had seventeen squadrons in the air, eleven from No. 11 Group, five from No. 12 Group, and one from No. 10 Group. As the German force crossed the coast, it was hit by a cloud of fighters. Two Spitfire squadrons led the attack, and three more joined the battle over Canterbury. Park was not satisfied with his forces. Six more squadrons were deployed.

Two of these hit a German air formation over the Medway River. They were joined by four Hurricane squadrons. Then five squadrons from No. 12 Group entered the battle, the Spitfires engaging the German fighters and the Hurricanes seeking out the bombers.

Despite Goering's orders, the bombers were inadequately protected. Harried by the Hurricanes, they headed for cloud cover. Under pressure heavier than they had encountered thus far in the battle, the bombers began to jettison their loads onto eastern and southeastern London and the suburbs. One bomb exploded in the grounds of Buckingham Palace. The German formations, badly mauled, swung homeward, only to encounter four fresh Hurricane squadrons over Kent.

Cautiously RAF intelligence and operations officers assessed the results of the morning's fighting. The lesson seemed to be that with fighters concentrated and attacks delivered by two or more squadrons, the Germans could not bomb effectively without sustaining heavy losses.

The Luftwaffe developed its second attack in midafternoon. This time the Germans did not try to feint Fighter Command out of position. There was a shorter warning time from the radar stations. But No. 11 Group got twelve squadrons into position while the first German wave was over the Channel. By the time the Germans had crossed the coast, another seven and one-half squadrons had been added by No. 11 Group. No. 12 Group added five squadrons, flying as a single formation, and No. 10 Group sent a single squadron from the west.

The British now had a total of 25½ squadrons in the air to meet three attacking forces. The first of these encountered two Spitfire squadrons. The second ran into a cloud of Hurricanes. In this engagement, part of the German formation turned back toward the sea and safety, jettisoning bombs as it retired. The third force bulled on toward London, beset by fighters. Again some of the bombers turned back, those that remained and their escorts fighting a major battle in the air from over the heart of London to the west. By 3

P.M., ten squadrons from No. 11 Group and a five-squadron wing from No. 12 were in action. This was the peak of the day's fighting.

This was the last major action of the day. At about 6 P.M. a small force of bombers and fighters eluded the squadrons guarding the Hampshire coast and got through to bomb the Southampton area. The force withdrew, harried by five squadrons of fighters.

The day's fighting was over. The Germans had lost fifty-six aircraft to British fighters and four more to antiaircraft guns. The RAF loss was twenty-six planes.

As mentioned before, battles are won and lost in the minds of the opposing commanders. On the morning of Sept. 16, the Luftwaffe high command had to face four facts: First, a major attack on London had cost sixty aircraft and their crews. Second, Fighter Command, which the Luftwaffe had believed to be on the verge of defeat, had massed an unprecedented number of Spitfires and Hurricanes. Third, the bombers that had managed to get through to their targets in London had been so beset by the fighters that the bombing was haphazard. Fourth, since the daylight attacks on London had begun on Sept. 7, the Luftwaffe had lost more than 200 aircraft, over half of them bombers.

In light of these conditions air supremacy, which the Germans regarded as essential to a successful invasion, remained remote if not unattainable.

On Sept. 17 the war diary at German naval headquarters recorded: "The enemy air force is still by no means defeated; on the contrary, it shows increasing activity. The weather situation as a whole does not permit us to expect a period of calm [in the Channel]. The Fuehrer therefore decides to postpone [Operation] 'Sea Lion' indefinitely."

The battle was over. The British had won it. But the war went on.

VII

The Descent of the Rising Sun

MIDWAY

On May 5, 1942, Imperial Headquarters in Tokyo directed Admiral Isoroku Yamamoto to carry out Operation M1: the occupation of Midway Island and the Western Aleutians. The timing of the directive reflects the sublime confidence of the Japanese leadership. The directive was transmitted when the Battle of the Coral Sea had not yet reached a decisive phase, when Japanese intelligence on American fleet dispositions was sketchy, and most important, when few in Imperial Headquarters or the upper ranks of the army and navy had comprehended the impetus that Pearl Harbor and subsequent reverses had given industrial mobilization and national resolution in the United States.

May 1942 marked the high tide of Axis military success in World War II. The German armies in Russia, still qualitatively superior to the Red Army, were about to launch a series of major offensives driving into the industrial and agricultural heartlands of the Soviet Union. The British army in North Africa was fighting a rearguard action against General Rommel's Panzer Corps and its Italian allies. In Cairo and Alexandria, planning began for British withdrawal out of the Nile Delta. In the Battle of the Atlantic, German U-boats held the upper hand. If their pursuit and destruction by the Royal Navy had shown signs of improvement on the northern trade routes, this was more than balanced by the wholesale sinking of merchant ships creeping along the brilliantly lit east coast of the United States. The Allied bomber offensive against Germany was gaining strength, but inflated claims of bomb damage by the air forces could not hide from intelligence that these attacks had not yet had any discernible impact upon German war production.

For the three major allied powers—the United States, Britain, and Russia—it was a time for stubborn defense on the land and sea, and frantic improvisation in military and industrial preparation. Before the year was out, the turn of the tide would be evident in two great Allied victories at Midway and Alamein, and a third would be in the making at Stalingrad.

Midway was the first of these battles. Its prize was a small and desolate island, the westernmost of the Hawaiian chain and, after the fall of Wake Island, also the westernmost United States outpost in the central Pacific Ocean. By Christmas of 1941, Midway had been reinforced by two squadrons of aircraft and a battalion of marines. This reinforcement was defensive in nature. Midway was not, as some senior Japanese officers believed, the base from which Colonel James Doolittle and his bombers had flown to attack Tokyo. The raid had been launched from the aircraft carrier U.S.S. *Hornet*.

If battles were fought on paper, Midway would have been an easy victory for the imperial forces. Yamamoto's Combined Fleet represented the most awesome accumulation of maritime power seen in World War II: eight carriers and more than 400 aircraft of all types, eleven battleships, thirteen heavy cruisers, eleven light cruisers, more than sixty destroyers, and scores of submarines. There can be little doubt, in retrospect, that had Yamamoto struck directly at Midway with this formidable force, far stronger in every category than the United States could muster, Midway would have been taken and the war rolled back to the eastern Pacific. But before the battle began, the Japanese admiral made a startling strategic error. He divided his armada into five major forces, some of which were divided into three or even four subdivisions.

Why did he do it? Yamamoto is dead, shot down by American fighters, and cannot testify. He was Japan's premier admiral—experienced, sagacious, tough. But he made a mistake. Perhaps the reason was faulty intelligence. Perhaps, after six months of war, on the whole successful, he held the Americans cheaply. He might have believed that a victory at Midway and in the Aleutians would bring the Americans to their knees and lead to a negotiated peace.

The Japanese deployment followed established tactics in the Imperial Navy. These emphasized surprise, diversions, and the quick-kill of inferior forces. All these elements in the Japanese plan were weakened by intelligence failures. Yamamoto believed that two American aircraft carriers had been lost in the Coral Sea battle and that Admiral Chester A. Nimitz had no information about Japanese plans and dispositions. He was wrong on both counts.

The two carriers Yamamoto thought sunk had actually survived. More important, *Magic* intelligence, which had broken the Japanese naval code, kept Nimitz informed of the size of the Japanese force, its objective, and the date. This information, naturally, did not arrive completely packaged. Bit by bit the cryptographers of naval intelligence pieced it together. This was supplemented by submarine reports and by analysis of Japanese wireless traffic. The result was that Nimitz was well informed of the Japanese plans. But as has been so often pointed out in histories of intelligence in the Second World War, accurate prebattle information is of little use unless its recipients have the means and the resolution to use it. Nimitz had both. By late May, he had made his first important assessment. The attack was to be directed at Midway and the Aleutians and not, as some senior officers in Washington believed, at Pearl Harbor.

Nevertheless the American situation was precarious. One carrier, the *Lexington,* had been sunk in the Coral Sea fight. Another, the *Yorktown,* was so badly damaged that it was estimated that ninety days of work would be necessary to make her battle-ready. Even so, the workers at the Pearl Harbor Navy Yard did the job in less than two days. This accomplishment, made possible by unstinting labor, hurried but precise improvisation, and perhaps by deep-seated frustration, should have proved to the Japanese, had it been known, that the war had tapped hitherto-unknown resources of American effort.

The Americans also changed the command in a vital area. Vice Admiral William F. Halsey, who commanded Task Force 16, including the two carriers *Enterprise* and *Hornet,* was ill with a skin disease. He was replaced by Rear Admiral Raymond A. Spruance. The new commander was not an aviator as Halsey had been, but he inherited a brilliant chief of staff, Captain Miles Browning, and had great qualities of judgment and a flexible, incisive mind.

The other component of the American defense, Task Force 17,

consisting of the *Yorktown* with its cruisers and destroyer screen, was commanded by Rear Admiral Frank Jack Fletcher.

The first forces to enter the battle were Japanese submarines. The main force scouted Oahu island and then deployed in positions suitable for the interception of American Pacific Fleet units moving toward Midway. Here the intelligence factor made its first appearance. Spruance and Fletcher, as a result of accurate American intelligence, were already past the Japanese submarines on their way to the battle.

The first major surface force, Rear Admiral Kakuji Kakuta's Second Mobile Force, assigned to the Aleutian adventure, left the home islands first. Admiral Chuichi Nagumo's Carrier Striking Force, including the four heavy carriers *Akagi, Kaga, Hiryu,* and *Soryu,* left the Inland Sea of Japan on the late afternoon of May 26. Yamamoto with the main battleship force followed two days later, and the transports of the Midway Occupation Force left Saipan on May 27. Four heavy cruisers and two destroyers of Rear Admiral Takeo Kurita's Close Support Group left Guam on the same day and preceded the transports eastward.

As their dispositions indicate, the admirals of the Imperial Navy were confident. They had the ships, the planes, the guns, the men. However, as we noted earlier, nothing, as Winston Churchill once wrote, is as uncertain as a battle at sea. Admiral Yamamoto, his lieutenants, and Imperial Headquarters were soon to encounter this unpleasant truth of naval war.

At the outset, all went well for the Japanese. The Americans were intent on locating the enemy fleet before it penetrated to within bomber range of Midway. Catalina long-range flying boats probed a sector from the north-northeast to the south-southwest of Midway. Nothing was sighted—for good reason. Clouds covered Nagumo's force, and a fog shrouded the ships—a fog so thick that Nagumo lost contact with his fleet and was forced to break radio silence to order a change of course. Occasionally the officers on the Japanese ships could hear the beat of Catalina engines.

The battle reports from both sides are like the impressions of two blindfolded boxers flailing the air in the same ring. At this point no contact had been made. Task Force 16, centered on *Enterprise* and *Hornet,* sailed from Pearl Harbor on May 28. The *Yorktown* task force departed on the morning of May 30. All now depended on the early location of the Japanese armada. Nimitz's admirals hardly

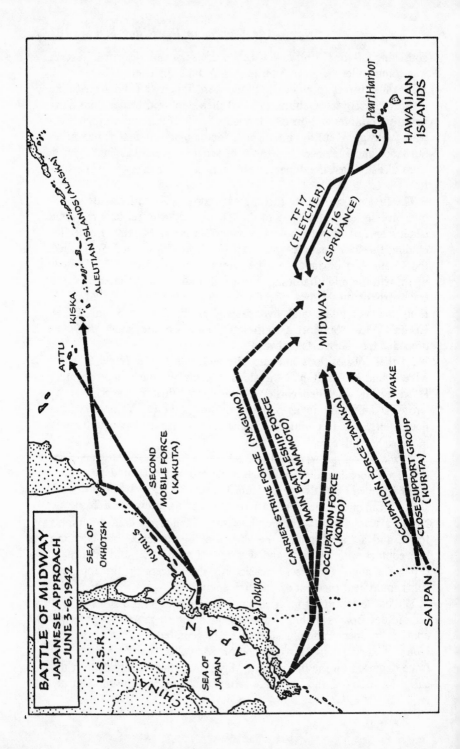

BATTLE OF MIDWAY
JAPANESE APPROACH
JUNE 3-6, 1942

needed a reminder that if the Japanese broke their task forces, Midway would fall and the Pacific coast would be open to attack. The elderly battleships that now formed its first line of defense would be able to do little against triumphant Japanese carrier forces.

Spruance and Fletcher had Nimitz's Letter of Instruction as a guide. They were instructed to "inflict maximum damage on [the] enemy by employing strong attrition tactics." The last two words sound strange to modern ears. But "maximum damage," as Spruance and Fletcher both knew, could be inflicted only by successful attacks on the enemy by their carriers' aircraft.

"In carrying out the task assigned," the letter continued, "you will be governed by the principle of calculated risk, which you shall interpret to mean the avoidance of exposure of your force by superior enemy forces without good prospect of inflicting, as a result of such exposure, greater damage to the enemy." In other words, the enemy is stronger, so don't mix with him unless you can hurt him more than he can hurt you. Hardly a trumpet call to sacrifice and glory, but reflecting the down-to-earth quality of Nimitz's strategic ideas.

It was not until the morning of June 3 that the Americans sighted any Japanese. By 11 A.M. the approach of a group of ships of the Japanese Midway Occupation Force, the transports and seaplane tender groups, was sighted making eastward at nineteen knots.

Midway reacted with a sortie of nine Army Air Corps B-17 Flying Fortress bombers. These located the Japanese ships, made three attacks, and reported hits on battleships or heavy cruisers. We know now that the B-17's made no hits. It was the first of many exaggerated Army Air Corps reports in the Battle of Midway.

In one sense the battle had been joined. In a larger sense it had not. The two fleets still groped for each other in the vast expanses of the central Pacific. The carrier forces were moving toward each other blindly. The Battle of Midway was about to begin in earnest.

Thursday, June 4, the critical day of the battle, brought a soft wind from the southeast, enough for the Americans to launch aircraft against the enemy to the west. The air was cool, and visibility was between thirty-five and forty miles. These were idyllic conditions for an excursion, but hardly those to be approved by the captains of aircraft carriers.

The first word of the presence of Japanese carriers reached the *Enterprise* early that morning. A minute or so later, another message reported that Japanese planes were headed for Midway. A third message located Japanese battleships and carriers 180 miles from the island.

Fletcher's was the first and, possibly, the decisive American action. He ordered Spruance to take his two carriers to the southwest and attack the Japanese carriers "when definitely located." *Yorktown* would follow as soon as its aircraft, then on exercises, had been recovered.

While the American carrier forces were taking the first moves that were to lead to victory, Midway, the objective of the Japanese offensive, was subjected to heavy attack. The Japanese carriers launched seventy-two torpedo planes and bombers escorted by thirty-six fighters against the island. One Marine Corps fighter squadron of twenty-six aircraft went up to meet them. The squadron's effect was negligible. The Japanese blew Midway's ground installations to bits. They were, however, unable to destroy the runways. American casualties were light. So although the powerhouse, oil tanks, seaplane hangar, and storehouses were smashed or set afire, this, the only attack on Midway, must be accounted a failure because the Midway base could still be accounted as usable and was in fact used in the battle. The same could not be said for the fighters that had flown to its defense. Of the twenty-six aircraft deployed, seventeen were destroyed and seven more badly damaged. These were slow, heavy Buffalos and Wildcats. The Americans at Midway had no aircraft capable of fighting on even terms with the Zero Mark 1 Japanese fighter.

Midway struck back. Six Navy torpedo bombers and four Army Air Corps B-26's that had survived the attack swept down on the Japanese carriers. In order to attack, these Midway-based aircraft had to get through the enemy fighter patrols, which shot down at least four American aircraft before they could get into position to bomb. When the attack was delivered, it was a catastrophe; only one of the torpedo bombers and one of the B-26's returned. No damage to the Japanese had been done, although the Army Air Corps claimed three hits on the carriers and the Navy, one. What might be called the command error of the battle now took place.

Nagumo had delivered one successful strike on Midway; he had also reserved ninety-three planes armed with bombs and torpedoes to attack enemy ships. As far as he knew, there were none in his area, but it was better to be safe than sorry. He sent four float planes from his cruisers to locate the Americans. There were no sighting reports. Meanwhile the commander of the force that had attacked Midway told Nagumo that a second attack was necessary.

Note how the dice began to fall to the Americans. Nagumo had no way of knowing the results of the initial raid on Midway. Suddenly the Navy torpedo planes and the B-26's launched their attack. His subordinate must have been right; Midway was still operational. The aircraft armed with torpedoes for attacks on American surface vessels were sent below to clear the flight decks for the landing of the Midway bombers and, what is more important, the torpedo planes were to be rearmed with bombs for a second attack on Midway. This rearmament under the best of conditions would demand a good hour's work by the maintenance crews.

Nagumo, with all his aids, all his ships, all his men, was at this moment dependent on the tenuous information sent to him from one float plane launched from the cruiser *Tone*. Nagumo knew that there were American surface ships at sea; the aircraft from the *Tone* had confirmed this by their sighting of ten vessels. Very well, Nagumo and his ships could deal with them in good time. The aircraft maintenance crews were now ordered to prepare for attacks on American warships, leaving torpedoes on those planes that had not yet been rearmed with bombs.

Then the lonely float plane relayed the most significant message of all. The ten ships, the pilots reported, were accompanied by a carrier. Nagumo's situation was immediately transformed from one of confident victory to possible, immediate vulnerability. His decks were cleared to receive the bomber attack force from Midway. His second wave of attack was caught below deck. He was open to attack from the American carrier.

The attackers, he may have thought, would be as easy to repel as those land-based aircraft from Midway. Sixteen Midway Marine Corps dive bombers, manned by largely inexperienced pilots, had launched one attack. Only eight had returned to the island. The Japanese lost only four sailors, who were machine-gunned on the flight deck of the *Hiryu*. Then fifteen Flying Fortresses targeted on the transport were diverted to attack the carriers. Bombing from 20,000 feet, these B-17's dropped 8,500 tons of bombs and claimed four hits on two Japanese carriers; in fact, Japanese battle reports were that there were a number of near-misses but no hits.

For Nagumo, then, the land-based aircraft were a paper tiger. The morning's fighting had gone in favor of the Japanese. They lost about forty planes, but in return they destroyed most of the aircraft based on Midway and the island's installations were seriously damaged. The Japanese ships had not been hit, and their casualties were almost negligible. A good morning's work. Shortly before 9 A.M. Nagumo's planes began to return from Midway, and he prepared for the final, conclusive attack.

One hundred odd miles away, Spruance's Task Force 16 changed course and increased speed to twenty-five knots. Spruance's original plan was to launch his aircraft at 9 A.M. But he knew he had been sighted by a Japanese seaplane. He had been receiving reports on the enemy's strike on Midway. His Chief of Staff, Miles Browning urged him to attack now in the hope of catching the Japanese aircraft refueling on their carriers. The admiral weighed the arguments, glanced at the charts, and decided. The aircraft roared off *Hornet* and *Enterprise*. The battle was nearing its decisive phase.

Spruance launched all his aircraft, except those necessary for the protection of the carriers—sixty-seven Dauntless dive bombers, twenty-nine Devastator torpedo bombers, and an escort of twenty Wildcat fighters.

Meanwhile Fletcher, on the same course and at the same speed as Spruance, delayed his strike, hoping that reconnaissance would find other Japanese aircraft carriers. Then he, too, sent off his attackers —seventeen dive bombers and twelve torpedo bombers. The planes launched, climbed above the carriers, and sped off toward their prey. There were only a few cumulus clouds in the sky; the sea was calm, the air cool. Ahead, Nagumo's force plowed onward toward Midway, the four carriers in a rectangular formation within their screen of cruisers and destroyers.

The Japanese carriers were busy. The aircraft returning from the Midway strike were homing in on their vessels. Now Nagumo got word from scout planes of the approach of American bombers. The recovery of the scout planes was completed, and the Japanese Striking Force changed course from Midway—in the admiral's words, "to contact and destroy the enemy task force." The change of course was fortune's last smile for Nagumo.

Thirty-five dive bombers from *Hornet* were unable to find the carrier force and, forced either to land at Midway or ditch, were out of the battle.

The Japanese carriers were unscathed, their crews and pilots confident. A few minutes later this confidence was strengthened. The torpedo bombers from *Hornet,* attacking without fighter cover and against heavy antiaircraft fire, were all destroyed. Of thirty air crew in the fifteen planes, only one, Ensign George H. Gay, survived.

The torpedo squadron from *Enterprise* fared little better. Ten of the fourteen aircraft were shot down attacking the *Kaga.* The torpedoes that were launched failed to register a hit. The Japanese fighters were everywhere and, when they were not, the Americans flew into a wall of antiaircraft fire.

Now it was the turn of *Yorktown*'s aircraft. The torpedo squadron headed for *Soryu.* But the Zeke fighters were waiting. The squadron's Wildcat escort was knocked down. Ten of twelve torpedo bombers burst into flames. Only five launched torpedoes and no hits were reported by Americans or Japanese.

The torpedo attacks had been a failure. Only six aircraft of forty-one returned to their ships, and not a single torpedo struck home. Brave men flying obsolete planes had made an unknowing sacrifice, for their attacks had drawn the Japanese Zeke fighters down to "the deck" and prevented the carriers, zig-zagging to evade torpedoes, from launching other aircraft. The stage had been set for the attacks by the next wave of American aircraft—the dive bombers. This was the decisive action of the Battle of Midway.

The dive bombers had taken off without fighter cover, intent on finding the Japanese force. But when Lieutenant Commander Clarence McClusky of *Enterprise* reached the point where he expected to find the Japanese, the sea was empty. By luck he sighted a Japanese destroyer speeding toward the main body. He followed it. Spurred by Browning's frantic radio telephone message—"Attack, attack, attack!"—McClusky found the four Japanese carriers maneuvering to escape the doomed attacks by the American torpedo planes. The rectangular formation had broken up; the carriers were now deployed in a circle with a diameter of about eighty miles.

McClusky commanded thirty-seven Dauntless dive bombers. One squadron was sent off to bomb the *Kaga,* the second to attack *Akagi.* The torpedo bombers' heroic but fruitless attack provided the Americans with a singular advantage. As the dive bombers came in for the assault, the air was clear of fighters. They were still at lower altitudes after their destruction of the torpedo bombers, and they had not had time to climb to intercept the Americans.

The dive bombers peeled off and dived at seventy degrees toward the carriers.

Akagi was the first casualty. She had forty aircraft on deck, and the ship was disorganized after intensive evasive action forced by the torpedo bombers' attack. Her captain, in fact, blamed his inability to dodge the dive bombers on his preoccupation with avoiding torpedoes.

The Japanese saw three bombs dropped from about 1,500 feet. One hit near the elevator amidships and penetrated to the hangar. Another was a near-miss. The third, the most damaging, exploded amid the aircraft on the flight deck. Stored torpedoes exploded, and bombs blasted crewmen off the flight deck. Nagumo stood on the bridge, unwilling to believe that the situation, a few minutes ago so favorable to the Empire, had been reversed.

The admiral still believed the situation was under control. But his staff, showing little of the stoicism often attributed to the Japanese by the West, tried to convince him to shift ships. He had no communication with the other vessels in the squadron save by signal flags and semaphores, hardly adequate for a complicated encounter.

Finally, after repeated entreaties, Nagumo and his staff left *Akagi* for the cruiser *Nagara* from which the admiral attempted to direct the remainder of the battle. Nagumo left *Akagi* at 10:47 A.M. But there is an odd postscript.

The *Akagi* damage-control parties were unable to quench the fires or to raise enough power to enable the ship to head for a home port. In the midst of this frantic and futile labor, a strange little ceremony took place. The portrait of Emperor Hirohito, the shrine that was the focus of the ship's morale, was ceremoniously transferred from *Akagi*. Soon after, all hands abandoned ship and the *Akagi* drifted off to the north where at sunrise on June 5 she was torpedoed and sunk by a Japanese destroyer to prevent her from being captured by the Americans.

The *Kaga* was the next to go. She took four hits from the dive bombers. The most damaging landed just forward of the towering command-and-control center (the "island" as it was known in those days), blew it into rubble, and killed the captain and everyone else on the bridge. The other three bombs burst among the planes on the flight deck or smashed through to the hangar, destroying or setting aflame the aircraft then being refueled. A series of explosions of gasoline and bombs followed. Flames swept through the ship. Again, the Emperor's portrait was solemnly transferred to a destroyer. Most of the officers and men left the ship. A handful remained to fight the fires. They were brave men. So fierce were the fires that the guns of the antiaircraft batteries were firing because of explosions in their magazines and the paint on the upperworks was aflame. At about 7:25 P.M. the *Kaga* sank.

The next blow was delivered by *Yorktown* on *Soryu*. The attack was carried out by seventeen dive bombers, who commenced their assault at 14,500 feet. *Soryu*'s situation, if anything, was worse than that of the other carriers. Aircraft were lined up on deck, ready to take off for the second strike on Midway. The remainder were in the hangar where maintenance crews frantically tried to complete their rearming. Three waves of dive bombers swept in to attack. Three 1,000-pound bombs hit. Here, again, the hits were lethal. The first bomb pierced the flight deck and exploded in the hangar, putting the forward elevator out of operation. The second burst among the planes parked on the flight deck. The third hit near the rear elevator.

The American attack had followed a new pattern. One wave of the squadron attacked from the starboard bow, another from the starboard quarter, and the third from the port quarter. The three hits set *Soryu* aflame, and twenty minutes later the crew abandoned ship. All the dive bombers survived.

Some brave souls went back aboard the carrier to attempt to save it. She was sighted as she fell out of formation by the submarine U.S.S. *Nautilus*, which earlier had made an unsuccessful attack on Japanese cruisers. Her commander now saw *Soryu* making about two knots and under escort by two destroyers. The carrier was a wreck, but the fires appeared to be under control.

From 2,700 yards *Nautilus* fired three torpedoes. All hit and exploded, a rarity at a time when submariners' confidence in their main weapon had been shaken by repeated failures. The Japanese destroyers' depth charges drove *Nautilus* into the deep. When their attacks ended, the submarine got the last view of *Soryu*. She was on fire from end to end. After seven o'clock that evening, the fires got to her gasoline storage. The resulting explosion broke the ship in half, and both halves disappeared beneath the waves.

By midday the Americans could count a victory. Three Japanese carriers were sinking. The Navy's carrier force was undamaged. The toll in aircraft, however, was heavy. *Hornet* had lost all her torpedo bombers and at least eleven fighters. *Enterprise* had sent thirty-seven dive bombers into battle, and fourteen were knocked down. In addition ten of her fourteen torpedo bombers had been destroyed, plus one fighter. *Yorktown*'s toll was all of her torpedo bombers save one, two dive bombers, and three fighters.

Historian Samuel Eliot Morison thought this was "no excessive price for what had been accomplished" and, viewing the battle against the strategic situation of the war at that time, he was correct. Had the Japanese been in the position to renew the battle with other carriers, Spruance and Fletcher might have found the price not only excessive but destructive.

The irony was that the torpedo bombers, whose attacks had been completely unsuccessful, helped create the tactical situation that was the condition for victory. The Japanese fighters, superior to anything the Americans had in the air, were lured down to low altitude to meet the torpedo bombers and, as we have seen, were not in a position to attack the dive bombers when they swept into their attacks. No one planned it that way. It was just luck.

At this juncture the Americans were triumphant. But final victory was to be delayed and the margin reduced. There was one Japanese carrier remaining, the *Hiryu,* which was steaming well ahead of the stricken trio destroyed by the dive bombers. Nagumo transferred his command to Vice Admiral Hiroaki Abe, commanding the cruisers and destroyers of the carrier group. Abe had one undamaged carrier with him. He directed her aircraft against *Yorktown,* already located by reconnaissance planes from a Japanese cruiser. The Japanese had an opportunity to retaliate for the loss of their three carriers. Yamamoto ordered two carriers from the Aleutian strike force, *Ryuho* and *Junyo,* to steam south and join the hunt.

About noon, *Yorktown*'s radar reported more than thirty aircraft approaching from the west-southwest. The ship, therefore, had time to send up covering fighters and to drain fuel lines.

The American fighters did well against the eighteen unescorted bombers. More than half were knocked down or driven off. But eight got through. The cruisers *Astoria* and *Portland* and the attendant destroyers got two more of these with antiaircraft fire.

The remaining six made three hits, two of them serious. One came when one of the attackers, torn apart by antiaircraft fire, broke up over the *Yorktown*'s flight deck. The plane's bombs tumbled out and one exploded on the flight deck, killing and wounding scores and starting a huge fire. Here luck favored the Japanese.

A second bomb exploded in the funnel, disabling two boilers and putting out fires in five more. Twenty minutes after this hit, the carrier was stopped in the water. The third bomb could have been the most destructive of all. It exploded on the fourth deck, started a fire near the ammunition magazines and gasoline storage, and forced their flooding.

Yorktown had been grievously hurt, but she was still alive. By 1:34 her boilers were working, and she regained speed up to eighteen knots. But if the carrier was not finished, neither were the Japanese.

Again radar picked up incoming attackers, forty miles out. *Yorktown* got off eight Wildcat fighters, all with insufficient gas in their tanks. They were not able to handle either the six escorting Zeke fighters or the ten torpedo bombers. *Yorktown* veered to the left into the protection of the antiaircraft fire from the cruisers. Spruance had detached two cruisers and two destroyers to go to Fletcher's aid. Their guns threw up a curtain of steel. But curtains can be penetrated.

The torpedo planes swept in on four tangents, flying at masthead height. Four aircraft got through and released their torpedoes, but not before they had penetrated a curtain of water as well as one of steel. The American cruisers had trained their heavy guns so that the shells hit the sea, sending up huge spouts of water in the path of the oncoming attackers.

Yet the torpedo bombers loosed their weapons at 500 yards or less. It was as gallant an attack as any on that memorable day.

Two torpedoes hit and exploded. They opened the fuel tanks on the port side, jammed the rudder, and cut power connections. With power gone there was no way in which the ship could be flooded, and at 3 P.M. the order was given to abandon ship.

Both Spruance and Fletcher were aware that a fourth Japanese carrier was intact and in operation. But they could not find her. Not until 2:45 P.M. did a patrol sight the carrier *Hiryu* and two battleships, three cruisers, and four destroyers about 110 miles from *Yorktown*.

On receipt of the sighting message, Spruance immediately turned *Enterprise* into the wind and launched fourteen dive bombers for the attack. The dive bombers hit *Hiryu* at about 5 P.M. Four direct hits were scored. The resulting fires could not be controlled. One bomb had blown the forward elevator plant onto the island, destroying all the power lines and communications there. *Hiryu,* like her consorts, was a flaming, inoperable wreck. The carrier was abandoned early the next morning, and although two Japanese destroyers tried to sink her with torpedoes, she drifted on, sheathed in flames until she finally went down.

Now the theater of battle diminished to the battleship *Yamato* carrying Admiral Yamamoto in command of the Combined Fleet. It was there, on the bridge but more specifically in the minds of the Japanese commanders, that the battle was finally and irretrievably lost.

Measured in terms of guns, the Japanese retained superiority. Yamamoto ordered a screening group from the Aleutian force and Admiral Nobutake Kondo's Second Fleet to join his main force the next day. Much had been lost, but much could still be retrieved. But the Japanese admirals did not yet realize how much had been lost. By evening they learned that four carriers had been knocked out. Nagumo was more realistic than Yamamoto, whose message that the American fleet had been "practically destroyed" weighed little with him. Nagumo realized that the battle had gone against the imperial forces and, like so many commanders in similar circumstances, he now overestimated the strength of the force opposing him.

Yamamoto was told that there were still four American carriers but that "none of our carriers is operational." Nagumo's information drained Yamamoto's aggressiveness. His course was set eastward to fight a night battle. But with four—actually only two—American carriers operating, he saw that the night encounter, which he could expect with some reason to win, could turn into an attack at first light on his unprotected ships by carrier-based aircraft. Just before 3 A.M. on June 5, Yamamoto ordered a general retirement. He had lost four carriers—and the naval war in the Pacific.

The remainder of the battle was devoted to picking up the spoils of victory. The cruisers *Mogami* and *Mikuma* had collided when they began the retreat ninety miles east of Midway. They were observed by a submarine which could not attack. Flying Fortresses were sent from Midway, but they could not find their targets. Finally torpedo bombers and glide bombers from the marine wing at Midway found the ships and attacked. Again, no luck: six near-misses and one plane crashing into the afterturret of *Mikuma*. The attackers had encountered antiaircraft fire so fierce they were unable to make accurate attacks.

As Yamamoto's main striking force headed east, the two colliding cruisers had the unenviable role of being the main targets for the

Americans. *Enterprise*'s scout planes picked them up early on June 6. *Hornet* attacked with two groups, *Enterprise* with one. The cruisers, without air escort, were textbook targets. *Mogami* took two hits which killed many. But she remained in action and made the island of Truk for repairs. *Mikuma*'s fate was less happy. She was hit by two bombs, one of which detonated the torpedoes on her decks; she was swept by fires and went down during the night.

Of the major combatants on the American side, only *Yorktown* was still at risk. Morison in his somewhat florid style says that her loss "is the one blot on an otherwise golden scroll of victory." Great efforts were made to save her. She had floated for a day without help after the crew had abandoned ship. Salvage crews were put aboard and she was taken in tow. But the sea was rising, the sea that until now had been an ever-present if quiescent factor in the battle.

Nagumo was looking for *Yorktown,* and on the morning of June 5 his scout planes found her. A submarine, *I-168,* which had shelled Midway harmlessly was directed to *Yorktown*'s position. The submarine wasted twenty-four hours trying to find the carrier. When she did, she evaded the American escorts and fired four torpedoes. Two hit the *Yorktown.* One hit and tore apart the escorting destroyer *Hammann.* At 6 A.M. on the morning of June 7, *Yorktown* rolled over and sank. The Battle of Midway was over.

There was no doubt that the Japanese had been whipped. There was some doubt, and it continued for a long time, about who had done the whipping.

The Army Air Corps, which exhibited throughout the war a highly developed sense of the importance of public relations (through an adroit use of interviews) and of eyewitness accounts, gave the public the impression that its bombers had done most of the damage to the Japanese fleet.

Army pilots claimed hits on three carriers, one battleship or cruiser, a cruiser, a destroyer, and a large transport. The Air Corps brass then contributed weighty statements to the effect that their pilots' performance had proved the effectiveness of high-level bombing of ships at sea.

In fact both the Japanese and American records fail to show a single hit by Air Corps bombers during the battle. The victory had been won by the Navy fliers. And what a victory it was!

Midway was the first serious check to Japanese war planes. Imperial Headquarters' projects for seizing Fiji, New Caledonia, and New

Zealand were forgotten. Instead the Japanese leaders now turned to the uncongenial task of fighting a defensive war at sea.

The battle also initiated the era of aircraft-carrier supremacy in the United States Navy. The carrier and its bombers were a weapons system whose effect on sea warfare was as revolutionary as the introduction of the tank had been to land war. So rapidly has warfare changed in this century, however, that forty years later the combat effectiveness of both the carrier and tank are under severe challenge from the remotely piloted missiles developed in the sixties and seventies.

VIII

Stalin Leads, Mother Russia Triumphs

STALINGRAD

They fought in the tormented city with sharpened spades, with grenades, with knives, with pistols. They fought in the darkness and the brief daylight, in cellars and blasted alleys, in rooms and in alcoves. They fought for a room, a floor, a house. These were won and lost and won again. Flames, smoke, ash; the detonation of bombs, shells, and grenades were the background of their combat. Cold, hunger, thirst, and of course fear were their companions.

Beyond the stricken city another battle was being fought. This was a battle of maneuver employing thousands of guns and tanks, and hundreds of thousands of men. There men died in the open, caught in bivouac, shot down in the snow, roasted in tanks, blasted by bombs. Such death at long range was more impersonal, but it was just as final as in the stricken city. These two combats together were the Battle of Stalingrad, the decisive battle on the eastern front of World War II. When it began, the German Wehrmacht was on the offensive. When it was over, the masses of brave and willing Russian soldiers commanded by a new generation of generals gradually assumed the offensive which, despite local reverses and staggering casualties, they were to maintain until they reached Berlin.

The tide of the war turned in 1942. The American carriers at Midway parried the last Japanese thrust at the Hawaiian Islands.

And while the Russians and Germans were locked in combat in the sewers, homes, and streets of Stalingrad, the British Eighth Army broke the back of the Afrika Korps at El Alamein, Egypt, sending it reeling in retreat, harried by bombers and fighters, westward across North Africa. After these three battles, it was clear that the Axis could not win the war. Nevertheless how it was to be won by the Allies was still obscure.

As the winter of 1941–42 neared its end, the Russian and German armies faced each other across a front that was relatively stable. It extended from west of Murmansk in the north, past the heroic soldiers and civilians of stubborn Leningrad, southeastward to battle lines west of Moscow, now due south to Kursk and the Ukraine, from there to the Donets River east of Kharkov, and finally to the Azov Sea near Rostov on the Don.

This enormous front was stable in the sense that as the winter ebbed there were no major battles. The last significant operation had been the Soviet offensive that had driven the Germans west and away from the gates of Moscow. The front *was* stable . . . but this did not preclude thousands of isolated actions involving a platoon, a company, and a battalion in which men died in the snow and the cold.

The Germans, still superior in tanks and in the air, had the option. They could not, of course, stand still. They were impelled by the inexorable laws of conquest to resume the offensive, just as Napoleon had been driven forward by the same furies a century and a quarter earlier.

The Nazi high command decided to strike in the south. The primary objective was the opening of a corridor across the Don and Volga Rivers toward the Baku oil fields. In the sense that these oil fields were necessary to the German war machine, the strategic motivation was largely economic. The plan also had a larger geopolitical motivation. Beyond the Caucasus Mountains lay the back door to the Middle East. A successful German thrust from the north into that area could be expected to divert British forces from the defense of Egypt and the Suez Canal and to lead to their final destruction at the hands of superior Axis forces.

There were—there always are—beaten generals who after defeat stress that had their counsel been taken, disaster might have been avoided and victory won. But in the Germany of 1942, dominated as it was by Adolf Hitler, their counsel, if given, was disregarded.

Hitler's strategy, supported by "toadies" like Keitel, Chief of the General Staff, prevailed.

The Fuehrer's Directive No. 41 of April 5, 1942, laid out the overall plan: a breakthrough to the Baku oil fields after a drive to the Don and the Volga. At that point German planners apparently considered Stalingrad little more than a city on the Volga that had to be taken or, at least, neutralized so that the major offensive into the Caucasus could flow eastward unhindered by attacks upon its northern flank.

The resources assembled for the southern thrust by the Germans were impressive even by eastern front standards. The German high command assigned sixty-seven infantry divisions and seven panzer divisions to Field Marshal Von Bock's Army Group South. Von Bock's German forces included the First and Fourth Panzer Armies and the Sixth, Eleventh, and Seventeenth Armies. These forces were supported by one Italian, one Hungarian, and two Rumanian armies. The total Axis strength was about one million men, supported by about 1,500 aircraft of the Fourth Air Fleet.

The brawn was there. So was the brain. The German armies were commanded by the most renowned leaders of the day. They had not only defeated Russian armies but had conquered, or so it seemed then, the logistical problem of maintaining armies a thousand miles from their homeland. And for those who secretly doubted the wisdom of the whole affair, there was always the (so-far) proven genius of Adolf Hitler.

In every battle, in every campaign, there are points where the historian can glimpse the initial steps toward victory and defeat. In the case of Stalingrad one of these must be Hitler's decision, in Directive No. 45 issued on July 23, to give the capture of Stalingrad operational parity with the drive, then prospering, into the Caucasus. The northern Army group was ordered to take Stalingrad and then to swing southward toward the Caspian Sea at Astrakhan. The southern force was to drive from the lower Don to the Caucasus.

Did Hitler at this point make the grave mistake of dividing his forces in the face of a superior enemy? There are no grounds for believing that Hitler or his generals had guessed the size of the reserve armies which Stalin had been collecting over the winter. Nor is there anything in Hitler's character or in the arrogant confidence of most of his generals that would lead us to believe that, had they had reliable information about these reserves, any drastic changes in operational plans would have been made.

Nevertheless the reserve armies were there. Walter Kerr, who is the leading authority on this aspect of Russian strategy, asserts they "were unknown to the German High Command, unknown to Churchill and Roosevelt, unknown to each other so far as I can determine, and, what is still more astonishing, unknown to some members of Stavka's staff." *Stavka* was the Russian term for the Soviet high command.

Kerr estimates that there were ten reserve armies, all of which were subsequently activated; the First Reserve, for example, became the Sixty-fourth Army; the Seventh Reserve, the Sixty-second Army. His estimate that each army included six or seven divisions with between 5,000 and 8,000 men to a division plus armored, artillery, engineer, and rocket units and that the ten armies totaled about 800,000 men seems a little high.

Nevertheless these armies, plus a number of other reserve forces such as the Third and Fifth Tank Armies, four independent tank corps, and two Guards rifle corps contributed impressively to the Stalingrad battle and to subsequent operations.

The Russian triumph at Stalingrad was all the more extraordinary because it followed a period of severe reverses for Russian arms. Army Group B opened its offensive on June 28 and broke through for gains of up to fifty miles on a wide front to the north. The Germans were approaching Boronezh by July 2. This first German attack was followed by a massive offensive by Army Group A starting east of Kharkov in the Donets River basin. By early July the Russian forces in the eastern Ukraine were in full retreat, broken and harried by swarms of German tanks that rumbled almost unhindered over the open plains.

The psychological effect of the two German offensives on a Russian army that had suffered grave reverses in the preceding year was serious. Morale fell, and generals and political commissars began to trade charges of incompetence. Whispers of treachery were heard. Stalin's remedy then was not the wholesale introduction of the reserve armies but drastic changes in operational command. Names that were to shine so brightly in the next three years appeared. Alexander M. Vasilevsky, the army chief of staff, took over operations on the Boronezh front. On Aug. 28 General Georgi K. Zhukov, the most notable of Soviet field commanders, reached Stalingrad to confer with Vasilevsky.

The front was reorganized into the Stalingrad Front and, for the first time, Stalin fed into the new front three of the reserve armies— the Sixty-second, Sixty-third, and Sixty-fourth. The front was placed under the command of General V. N. Gordov, a veteran of World War I and the Finnish War. His line ran in a long arc from the upper Don to the west of Stalingrad and then south across the plains to the Caspian Sea.

Gordov, incidentally, was poorly treated by Soviet historians in the immediate postwar period, possibly because he was imprudent enough to quarrel with Nikita S. Khrushchev, the political commissar on the front. Khrushchev, then and later, considered his own military views superior to those of professionals, and there is little doubt in light of subsequent Russian writings that he tried to undermine Gordov and replace him with one of his favorites. Fortunately for the Russians, he failed.

No juggling of fronts or commanders, however, could stop the Germans. By August their Army Group B had raced down the valley of the Don toward the great bend where the river turns southwest. Army Group A had punched through the Russians in the Donets basin and driven them out of Rostov and over the lower Don into the north Caucasus. Marshal Rodion Y. Malinovksy, the local commander, was sacked and his forces placed under the command of Marshal Semyen M. Budyenny, a cavalryman more at home at the head of a squadron than before a staff map. Budyenny was no more successful than his predecessor. By the middle of the month, the Germans were at the mouths of the passes through the Caucasus Mountains.

There they were halted, partly by stiffening Soviet resistance but, more important, by the first tactical effects of Hitler's decision to make a maximum effort to take Stalingrad. Tank and infantry divisions were diverted from the Caucasus to Stalingrad. The drive for the oil fields which, had it been successful, would have made a significant difference to the German economy, ground to a halt.

By that time the fight for Stalingrad had entered its first phase. On Aug. 15 the German Sixth Army, commanded by General Friedrich Paulus, attacked the Soviet Fourth Tank Army in the small loop of the Don River. This Russian army was in pitiful shape. Some of its infantry divisions were reduced to 200 effectives. Tank divisions could deploy only a handful of tanks. The Germans smashed across the Don in the Trekhostrovskaya-Gerasimov sector and at Perepolnyi-Luchenskii. These two drives created a critical situation on the right flank of the Soviet Sixty-second Army.

The Sixteenth Panzer Division smashed into the Sixty-second Army. That same day, Aug. 23, Stalingrad received its heaviest blow from the air. The German Fourth Air Fleet flew 4,000 sorties, its bombs destroying the administrative and residential sectors, setting afire oil tanks and docks. That afternoon the workers in the factories in the northern sector of the city were issued rifles and ammunition and told to prepare for a German attack from the north.

Slowly the Russian resistance stiffened. The Germans' headlong assaults were slowed. Despite their superiority in armor and in the air, it took the Germans from Aug. 21 to Sept. 2 to cover the few miles from their crossings of the Don to the center of Stalingrad. One reason was that Russian morale had recovered. Another was that there was more confidence among the soldiers in the new commanders. The third, and probably dominant, reason was that the Germans were beginning to suffer from the strain on their long line of communications. At the same time they were feeling the results of the pressure on their left flank along the Don from General Gordov.

Zhukov had instructed Gordov to attack the flank with his understrength forces—one tank *army* had only four tanks operational—and to maintain the attacks regardless of cost. The result was the continual diversion of forces from the main German thrust to deal with these Soviet attacks.

Soviet resistance in a city which he had regarded as an easy prize provoked Hitler to order a full-scale attack by the Sixth Army and the Fourth Panzer Army, which had been summoned north from its successful campaign in the Caucasus.

Hitler was not the only civilian mastermind at work. Joseph Stalin in Moscow was giving orders to "mobilize an armored train" for deployment on the circular railway around Stalingrad and to "use plenty of smoke screens to confuse the enemy." One Stalin *ukase* ends, "The most important thing is not to let panic take hold; do not be afraid of the enemy threats and keep your faith in our ultimate success." The Russians needed such faith. The two German armies, the Sixth to the north and the Fourth Panzer to the south, smashed into the ruined center of the city, and by the middle of September Russian footholds in the city were small and precarious.

Stalingrad straggles along the western bank of the river for almost thirty miles. Nowhere in 1942 was its width from the river westward more than 4,000 yards; in some places it was only 1,800. To the north lay three large factories, a tractor plant, the Barricades plant, and the Red October plant. By Sept. 13 German shells and bombs had knocked out the telephones and the lighting. The sewage system was smashed. The water supply ended. In little groups women and children made their way to the river bank to be evacuated in small boats. When larger craft were brought over to ferry the refugees, they were sunk by German guns. Over a thousand civilians were drowned when the steamer *Joseph Stalin* was sunk by gunfire.

The Russian defense was now under General Vasili Chuikov, who had taken command of the Sixty-second Army on Sept. 12. A veteran of World War I and the Finnish War, Chuikov had been recalled to active service from his post as military attaché in China. His selection to hold the few square miles of rubble and shattered buildings on the west bank of the Volga which was all that remained of Stalingrad was one of the most successful of Stalin's appointments. Chuikov proved resolute, ingenious, and flexible. He was ruthless with the faint-hearted.

Now in the middle of September the fate of the battle, perhaps the fate of the Soviet Union, rested with the battered Sixty-second Army. The war of maneuver, of brilliant tank attacks and counterattacks, had degenerated into a dogged and bloody defense by the Russians of buildings and floors in buildings and finally rooms on floors. There were no large units engaged. Hand-to-hand combat, a rarity in World War II (despite Hollywood), became customary here. In ruined, often burning buildings, Germans and Russians sought each other in the swirling smoke.

German tactics followed a familiar, hitherto-successful pattern. The Luftwaffe bombed and strafed Soviet positions. Then tanks and infantry attacked the Russians who had survived. The Russians, frequently driven out of their burrows by furious German attacks, customarily counterattacked by night. It was a battle in which the sniper became as important as the tank commander, in which personal courage by commanders as well as by their men was essential. Chuikov repeatedly turned up where the fighting was heaviest, encouraging the brave, berating the laggard. His army headquarters moved under fire from sewer to damaged house to trenches cut into the ravines that ran through the city. These ravines were used by both sides as avenues of approach, and often bloody battles were fought to seize a few yards of ravine that would open a better field of fire.

Some of the fiercest fighting centered around a low-hill feature, Mamayev Kurgan, in the center of the city. On Sept. 13 Chuikov's headquarters on the hill was smashed by German fire. By late that afternoon all communications between headquarters and the army it commanded had been lost. Chuikov shifted his headquarters that night.

Bitter and prolonged fighting raged around the salient which the Germans had driven to the Volga and near the Red October and Barricades factories. Casualties were very heavy. The nights were longer and colder.

Chuikov in his memoirs cites Oct. 14–16 as the critical period of the battle. But it was clear to the Russians at that time that the German attacks were not as frequent or as fierce as they had been, that the intervals between attacks were longer. German morale was beginning to reflect fifteen months of successful but inconclusive war.

The defenders, however, were in desperate straits. Each of the Sixty-second Army's six divisions reported strengths of a regiment or less. Soldiers and officers were exhausted, mentally and physically. Some, including a few relatively senior officers, simply disappeared. Those that were left, however, were the skilled, the professionals, the ingenious. They were ready when called upon for night attacks, for sudden sallies against an isolated German division. They had learned to live with the bombs, the shells, the stench, the bad water, and lack of sleep.

Reinforcements, sadly needed, were slow to arrive. General Andre Yeremenko on the east bank of the Volga did his best to organize supplies and to give the Sixty-second Army artillery cover from his batteries. Yeremenko was often in Stalingrad and, like Chuikov, was wounded there.

Because of the Germans' almost undisputed command of the air, moving reinforcements was difficult and costly. By Sept. 14 the Thirteenth Guards Division had arrived on the east bank. It crossed the river on the next day and marched straight into action on the Mamayev Kurgan. After a week's fighting, the division's strength was that of a regiment. Now, one by one, eight more fresh divisions were thrown into the battle line. This, in fact, consisted of a string of rifle pits, posts in shattered buildings, and street barricades.

Chuikov's selection of the period, Oct. 14–16, as critical is supported by the events of Oct. 14, when three German infantry divisions and two armored regiments attacked along a 2½-mile front toward the tractor and Barricades factories. The attack was preceded, as usual, by a massive bombardment of the Soviet positions by the Luftwaffe and by German guns and mortars. This preliminary barrage was so heavy that the waiting Russian infantry reported visibility down to almost 0 feet. The soldiers could hear, behind the curtain of yellow smoke and dust particles, the German tanks clanking ponderously to the attack.

Behind the tanks, German infantry dashed into the inferno to be met by rifle and machine-gun fire from the remnants of two Russian divisions, the Thirty-seventh and the Ninety-fourth. The German attack disintegrated into the type of fighting with which this part of the battle is associated. Buildings between the two factories were taken and lost, then taken again. The pattern of combat reproduced that in the southern sectors of the city—a battle for a room, a war for a floor. Perhaps this century's only parallel is the fighting between French and German at Douamont in the Verdun battle of World War I.

The Germans fed their attack. Tanks and infantry battered through the tattered lines of the Thirty-seventh Division, reaching the tractor plant and turning the flank of the 112th Division. Unchallenged by Soviet fighters, the Luftwaffe covered the narrow front, bombing divisional and army headquarters. Soviet communications, always tenuous, were broken repeatedly. German tank groups methodically eliminated Soviet strongpoints that were armed with little more than machine guns, Molotov cocktails, and grenades.

By the dawn of the fifteenth, the Germans had established positions on three sides of the tractor factory. Small groups of infantrymen broke into the building to fight the defenders in isolated, savage actions that are part of the epic of Stalingrad. On the approach to the factory, the German and Russian dead and dying lay untended. That night the Russians had ferried 3,500 wounded across the Volga. This was the largest number evacuated during the battle.

The German storm intensified in the morning of the fifteenth. Tanks smashed into the tractor plant itself, followed by assault groups armed with submachine guns and grenades. Sweeping through the plant and the narrow streets of the workers' tenements around it, the invaders reached the Volga along a stretch of about 2,000 yards. Chuikov's right flank now was isolated from the rest of the army. The Thirty-seventh Guards Division had been smashed by the German advance, the 112th Division, three rifle brigades, and a motorized rifle brigade constituted the Soviet defense. The Guards Division had the Volga at its back and was under continual pressure from the north and west. *Division* and *brigade* are courtesy titles here, since most units had lost half or more of their effectives. But small groups continued to fight throughout Oct. 15, when the Germans mounted new attacks against soldiers of the Guards Division still firing from isolated positions in the tractor plant.

The possession of the plant was vital. Chuikov was determined to hold it, even though the German reinforcement placed the rest of his army in jeopardy. Eremenko crossed the river early on the morning of the sixteenth for a conference with the army commander and then departed, promising ammunition and weapons. But time is needed to fulfill promises, and dawn brought another massive German attack.

This time the axis of attack was southward from the tractor factory to the Barricades plant. Again the assault was preceded by Stuka dive bombers and heavy artillery preparation. This time the initial advance was checked.

The Russians had dug in their T-34 tanks of the Eighty-fourth armored brigade along the road running south. Their fire stopped the leading German tanks, a fusillade of machine-gun and rifle fire checked the infantry, and a salvo of Katyusha rockets and gunfire from the east bank stalled the entire advance.

The Germans persevered. More infantry was thrown into the battle. The attack was renewed. The Soviet forces were in a desperate plight; of the 114th Guards Division only eighty-four men survived; in the 117th, there were thirty men.

For the next three days these meager forces, supported by guns from the opposite bank and a few tanks, managed to hold the invaders in check, but by a narrow margin. By Oct. 19 the Russian bridgehead on the west bank of the Volga was reduced to about 1,000 yards. The Red October and Barricades plants were under constant attack. On the twentieth the Germans smashed into the central and southwestern sections of the Barricades plant while on the north and northwest fronts of the factory, Russian infantry and the factory militia were holding off another German attack.

Again the familiar Stalingrad pattern took shape. Bayonets, sharpened spades, pistols, and grenades were the weapons. Men groped for enemies in the smoke and gloom broken only by German flares. The only ones who rested were the dead.

Churchill's tribute to the Germans—"they are a very brave race" —can be applied to both sides at Stalingrad. At Stalingrad we see the outcome settled in the minds of boys from the Rhineland and the Ukraine, minds—and wills—which forced them forward hour after hour, day after day into the fiercest, most unremitting battle of World War II.

Reinforcements were sent to the Sixty-second Army. But, granted the strength of the Soviet reserve armies, the reinforcements were on a niggardly scale. The reason for this parsimony was that Stavka was now planning the massive counteroffensive which is the other half of the Battle of Stalingrad.

Many generals claimed the credit for devising the plan for this counterstroke. From what is now known of the rather unreliable Russian writings, it appears certain that the plan originated with the General Staff and was approved by Stavka. For "Stavka," at this stage of the war, read "Stalin."

The planners hoped to take advantage of Hitler's preoccupation with the capture of Stalingrad. By mid-October the Germans, on Hitler's personal orders, had concentrated close to 350,000 men in the Stalingrad area; the German Sixth Army, the Fourth Panzer Army, and two Rumanian armies, the Third and the Fourth. Two panzer and twelve German infantry divisions were swallowed in the tremendous battle within the city limits. The flanks on the north and south had been denuded of German formations and were held by Rumanian and Italian formations of dubious reliability.

Russian military writers have acclaimed the counteroffensive as a stroke of genius. To the historian, it may seem something less. The Soviets understood from the fury of the German attacks in Stalingrad and from the identification of prisoners that the invaders had concentrated maximum forces for the capture of the city. They knew, too, that the flanks were held by troops of indifferent quality. Given these conditions, a counteroffensive that would cut off the German forces in the Stalingrad salient was not only attractive but was militarily mandatory.

German ignorance helped. Leaving aside Hitler's demonic mania about Stalingrad, it is fairly clear today that the German commanders were ignorant of the number of reserve divisions which the

Russians had husbanded throughout the frightful battles in the city. The reserves were present and virtually intact. They would be needed for the counteroffensive which Stavka called "Operation Uranus," which was on a giant, truly Russian scale.

There were to be two breakthroughs on the flanks—one against the Fourth Rumanian Army south of Stalingrad, the other against the Third Rumanian Army northwest of Stalingrad. There Gordov's troops held a bridgehead across the Don at Serafimovich.

The operational objective was then a meeting of the converging forces at Kalach on the Don. The general staff and Stavka recognized that this juncture was only the first step on the road to success. After it had occurred, the Sixth Army and the Fourth Panzer Army in Stalingrad would have to be defeated and the lines of encirclement held against the inevitable German counterattacks.

The assets which the Russians concentrated for the counterstroke cannot be measured by a simple enumeration of the number of divisions. It has since been estimated, on the basis of Soviet writings, that twenty-five percent of the Red Army's infantry and air strength and sixty percent of its armored and mechanized formations were concentrated for the offensive. In the critical sectors the Soviets enjoyed a two-to-one superiority in men and machine guns, a three-to-one superiority in mortars, and a four-to-one superiority in antitank guns over the luckless Rumanian armies.

Although the movement of forces to jump-off points was carried out at night and in the strictest secrecy, the German commanders were not blind to the opportunities offered the Russians by Hitler's Stalingrad mania. Aerial observation and ground reconnaissance soon reported heavy troop movement into attack positions opposite the weak flanks. But the intelligence service, instead of choosing the most obvious Soviet course, presented the high command with a list of options, of which the encircling movement was obviously one.

Command of the whole operation was concentrated in a triumvirate of Vasilevsky, Zhukov, and General Nikolai N. Vornov. The luckless Gordov was relieved and demoted. (He disappeared in 1946 after some accurate but imprudent criticisms of political interference in military operations.) While these forces were being assembled, the fighting in Stalingrad continued, although the pitch and tempo of the German attacks was clearly reduced. Chuikov's Sixty-second Army was able to hold the German assaults. But it was holding, not advancing. But by late October, an increase in the number of guns on the Volga's east bank and improved communications between the hard-pressed infantry and the artillery made it possible to bring a withering fire to bear on German attacks as they developed. By the evening of Oct. 29, the German offensive was grinding to a halt. The tank crews, the infantrymen, the gunners, and the engineers had given their best. But down the rubble-strewn alley, across a ruined row of tenements, "Ivan" still held on.

Winter comes early in Russia. Nov. 19, the day chosen for the opening of the counteroffensive, was bitterly cold. The massed artillery opened on the Rumanian positions around Serafimovich on the Don at about 7:30 in the morning. The infantry of the Fifth Tank and Twenty-first Armies attacked twenty minutes later. The Fifth Tank Army was one of the reserve forces which had been formed late in the previous spring.

The Russian infantry, clad in white overalls, swarmed through the fog that shrouded the Rumanian positions. The infantry broke into the Rumanian positions after brief but heavy fighting. The armor entered the fight around noon. The IV and V Rumanian Corps disintegrated under the impact of three Russian armored corps, and by early on Nov. 20 the Russians were twenty miles deep into the Rumanian sector.

The Germans, as always, reacted with remarkable speed and vigor. A German panzer division was sent to counterattack, and very heavy fighting ensued. But the Russians were superior in manpower. With the German attack contained, the main Soviet tank forces wheeled to the east and plunged on toward Kalach.

Now the pincers began to close. The southern drive had started a day earlier than the northern one. The first fighting on that front was confused, largely because some of the Russian infantry attacked before the artillery barrage had begun. In any event the Soviet infantry were unstoppable. They broke the lines of the Fourth Rumanian Army in three areas and cleared a path for three corps, one tank and two mechanized, which sped north toward Kalach. As they went, they brushed against the reserve formations of the Fourth Panzer Army in the outskirts of Stalingrad on their right.

The short, cold afternoon of Nov. 22 was one of the most memorable of the war. The IV Tank Corps from the northern arm of the counteroffensive was moving warily southeast of the great bend in the Don. Then, suddenly across the snow, the forward formations sighted tanks and white overalls moving toward them across the icy plain. This was a patrol of the IV Mechanized Corps advancing from the south. The initial objective, encirclement, was achieved. In the trap were twenty German divisions, an antiaircraft corps, two mortar regiments, two Rumanian divisions, and a Croatian regiment.

The battle, however, was far from over. Individual Soviet units were vulnerable to hasty but fierce German attacks. Communications were rudimentary. The best German divisions, those in the Stalingrad battle, were still relatively strong and of a far higher quality than the Rumanian units through which the Russians had smashed. Those German and Rumanian units that had not been destroyed made their way eastward to the forces in Stalingrad. Transport aircraft began to bring in German reinforcements, and the German infantry began to rebuild the old Soviet positions facing westward.

The Russians now had two missions. The line around Stalingrad had to be strengthened and moved westward to meet attacks from the forces within Stalingrad and from fresh troops that might be brought in from other fronts. The Fifth Tank Army and the First Guards Army were ordered into the line to secure it against attacks from the west. The armies on the south were ordered to increase pressure on the German Sixth Army now encircled in Stalingrad. Progress was slow. The Russians now were fighting Germans, not Rumanians. But the Soviet high command determined on an all-out offensive against the Stalingrad salient.

The Germans beat them to the punch. On Nov. 27 they bit deep into General Konstantin K. Rokossovsky's forces, bringing his offensive to an abrupt halt. Then the Germans struck against what they considered the weakest link in the chain forged around them, the area around Kotelnikovo on the Stalingrad–Rostov railroad. This was a major attack directed by General Erich von Manstein, one of the ablest German senior commanders, and carried out by 35,000 men and 300 tanks. These forces were drawn from the Army Group Don, which included part of the Fourth Panzer Army.

For some days, relief of the encircled forces in Stalingrad was in sight. Three panzer divisions broke through a Russian army and a cavalry corps. The forces in Stalingrad could hear the roar of the German guns. General Hermann Hoth, the armored commander, sent a message: "Hold on. We're coming." They never arrived.

The Russians demonstrated that they, too, could react speedily. The Second Guards Army was thrown into the battle. More and

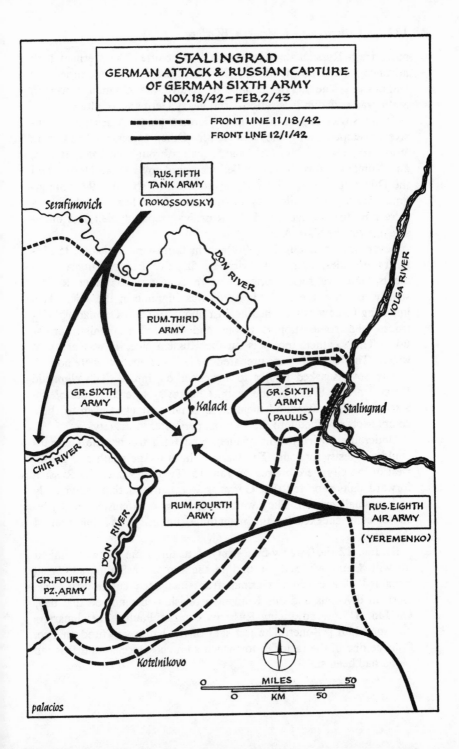

STALINGRAD
GERMAN ATTACK & RUSSIAN CAPTURE
OF GERMAN SIXTH ARMY
NOV.18/42 – FEB.2/43

FRONT LINE 11/18/42
FRONT LINE 12/1/42

Serafimovich

RUS. FIFTH TANK ARMY
(ROKOSSOVSKY)

DON RIVER

VOLGA RIVER

RUM. THIRD ARMY

GR. SIXTH ARMY

Kalach

GR. SIXTH ARMY
(PAULUS)

Stalingrad

CHIR RIVER

RUM. FOURTH ARMY

DON RIVER

RUS. EIGHTH AIR ARMY
(YEREMENKO)

GR. FOURTH PZ. ARMY

Kotelnikovo

N

MILES
0   50
0   50
KM

palacios

more fresh Russian divisions entered the battle. The German tank advance slowed down, halted. On Christmas Eve, Hoth ordered a withdrawal. The major attempt to relieve the German forces in Stalingrad ended in frustration—and heavy German casualties.

Other Soviet attacks now upset German plans. A Russian offensive developed along the Chir River. Other forces attacked from Voronezh, reached the Chir and, driving through German, Italian, and Rumanian formations, spilled westward toward the Donets and the Donets Basin. Rostov was recaptured on Feb. 14, 1943. Stalingrad now lay 200 miles beyond the main front line. The besiegers were now the besieged, and the Russians prepared their last offensive against the Sixth Army.

Seven armies, about 280,000 men in thirty-nine divisions, ten infantry brigades, four tank brigades, fifty-five heavy artillery regiments, and five rocket brigades were concentrated under Rokossovsky. By now the Red Air Force was supreme in the skies. This imposing force was launched against about 190,000 German fighting troops plus some support troops and battered Rumanian formations. The weather, too, was on the Russian side. It was a severe winter. The Russians were prepared for it. Their enemies were not.

The Soviets asked Paulus to surrender on Jan. 8. The climactic Russian attack began on the tenth. Chuikov's battered forces of the Sixty-second Army found themselves heavily attacked even as their compatriots smashed into the German perimeter in the city.

Under the Soviet weight of metal and fresh troops, the Germans could not resist for long. The German lines to the south and southwest of the city were broken on Jan. 15. Two days later the Russian forward units reported that Germans were surrendering individually and in small groups. They were cold, hungry, exhausted, and psychologically shocked by the magnitude, intensity, and duration of the battle.

By Jan. 22 the Twenty-first Army, thrusting from the west, linked up with Chuikov's Sixty-second in the center of Stalingrad. What remained of a coherent German front had been cut in two. Two German divisions and one Rumanian division surrendered that day. On Jan. 31, the advancing Russians overran Paulus's headquarters and took him prisoner. The last shot of the battle was fired on Feb. 2 inside one of the factories for which so much German and Russian blood had been shed.

As we know, after Stalingrad the Red Army, despite desperate battles and temporary reverses, remained on the offensive until the fall of Berlin in 1945. The victory at Stalingrad, coming after so many defeats, bought with such an abundant outpouring of blood and treasure, was a psychological stimulus whose effect on the army and the Russian people cannot be overestimated. The defeats of 1941 and early 1942, if not forgotten, were avenged. Stalingrad also was the test-bed for Soviet tactics, weapons, and commanders that served the Soviet Union well in the rest of the war.

Not all that was learned at Stalingrad remained in the Red Army's doctrine. But the essentials—improved liaison between armor and infantry, the effectiveness of the Katyusha rockets, the necessity for modernized communications, the fallibility of the political commissars who interfered with the professional command—remained. The world, of course, was slow in learning all this, for the Russians of World War II were even more secretive than their successors. What the world did learn was the bravery and the hardihood of the Russian soldier and that the victory belongs to him.

But, on balance, the impact of the battle, physically and mentally, was even greater on the German side. After nearly 3½ years of war, almost universally successful, 330,000 men with all their weapons and equipment had been destroyed in battle. The myth of German invincibility on the ground was destroyed. The eastern front, which a year before had seemed only another in the long series of Wehrmacht triumphs, now assumed a sinister significance to the German soldier. Here was an enemy, more numerous and equally tenacious than he and his comrades. Here was a great, unconquered land mass from which who knew what new armies, what frightful weapons, would spring. It was clear that the mobilization of Soviet resources had only begun, that Russian armies would be better equipped and better led as the war went on.

Stalingrad will remain in history, however, not simply as a decisive turning point of World War II but as one of the fiercest, most unremitting battles ever fought. That war saw many sanguinary fights—Guadalcanal, Montecassino, Saint-Lô, Arnhem. But in none of these was the scale and duration of Stalingrad matched or even approached. Nor, save perhaps at Montecassino, was the fighting as close or as bitter.

Stalingrad has one more significance. After it, the Soviet Union's path toward the mastery of Eastern Europe and the status of a superpower was open. For this and future generations, this may be the greatest significance of the battle in the shattered city on the Volga.

IX

The Last Victory
of the British Empire

EL ALAMEIN

The night of Oct. 23, 1942, in the Western Desert was exceptionally fine with a bright moon. That same night, a thousand miles and more to the north, the Red Army was grudgingly giving ground to Hitler's panzers around Stalingrad. In the Pacific the lull that had existed since the Battle of Midway was about to be broken by the American shift to the offensive. Here, in the desert, the decisive battle for the control of the Middle East was about to begin.

Alamein is attractive to historians because of its strategic consequences and to tacticians because it was the first enduring marriage on the Allied side of air and land power. To the social historian it has another attraction. It was the last battle of the British Empire, won by English, Scots, Indians, Australians, New Zealanders, and South Africans on the ground, supported in the air by pilots drawn from every corner of the Empire.

The battle was a faint but clear echo of the great engagements of World War I. Those battles had been headlong smashes by infantry and, later, by tanks against strongly prepared positions with no hope of turning a flank. Churchill saw it as "the same kind of trial of strength as was presented at Cambrai at the end of 1917 and in many of the battles of 1918. . . ." Now the right flank of the German Afrika Korps and the Italian expeditionary force rested on the

Qattara Depression in the south which was impassable to armored or wheeled vehicles. The left flank in the north was anchored on the Mediterranean Sea. The Axis forces were protected by literally hundreds of thousands of mines, miles of barbed wire, and abundant, well-sited artillery.

The desert war had been going on since the successful, first British advance into Italian Libya early in 1941. The fortunes of war had swung first to the British, then to the Italians and Germans, then to the British, and finally in the critical summer of 1942 back to the Germans. The Germans had better tanks and antitank guns, and were able to support their forces by seaborne reinforcements across the Mediterranean which had never been seriously interrupted. In addition the Germans and Italians had in Erwin Rommel a tactical commander of great ability. Indeed, Rommel's success in Africa seems to justify Field Marshal Rundstedt's characterization of him as a great corps commander but not an army commander. But now, on Oct. 23, Field Marshal Rommel was far away in Germany with his beloved Lucie and his son Manfred, recovering from a serious illness.

Rommel's success had been accelerated by repeated changes in the British high command. Archibald Wavell, N. M. Ritchie, Alan Cunningham, Claude Auchinlech—all had tried their skills against Rommel and his Afrika Korps. All had failed to a greater or lesser degree.

However, across the front another commander was about to enter history. He was a short, cock sparrow of a man with strong views on training and morale, especially the morale of officers who are veterans of defeats in the desert war. His name was Bernard Law Montgomery. He was to win at Alamein and join that group of individualistic self-confident commanders of which there was no shortage in World War II—Douglas MacArthur, George S. Patton, Guderian, Rommel, Halsey, William Joseph Slim, Lord Louis Mountbatten were all dominant personalities and, in their separate ways, masters of the art of war.

Credit, long overdue, should also be paid to Montgomery's superior, General Sir Harold Alexander, the commander in chief for the Middle East. Alexander was a great soldier—and a modest man. Because of his modesty, it is difficult to discern how great his role was in overseeing Montgomery's victory. Certainly Churchill, no admirer of generals at that juncture, paid Alexander high honor:

Alamein, according to the Prime Minister's dispatches to the front, "has been launched by you and General Montgomery." There are some indeed, who credit Alexander's suggestions at the crisis of the battle as the decisive movements on the British side. In the end there was glory enough for both men.

They were a balanced team for another reason. Montgomery had been wounded early in World War I and spent most of that war in staff jobs, irksome but inevitable. Alexander, on the other hand, had been a combat commander with a few brief respites. It is arguable that only a commander who had not endured the dreadful bloodletting of the British offensives in World War I—that is, someone like Montgomery—could have planned and carried out a battle that could have produced comparable losses.

Major General J. F. C. Fuller, one of the most acute and astringent of British military historians, pointed out that Montgomery was "pre-eminently a general of materiel." Montgomery liked, as he always said, to have "everything tidied up"; and at Alamein, and thereafter, he was loath to attack until he was confident he had superiority in men and weapons.

Montgomery had one advantage not enjoyed by his predecessors in the First World War—a quantitively and qualitatively superior air force totaling over 1,100 combat aircraft. The Royal Air Force was able to hammer the German and Italian ground forces and simultaneously to attack successfully for the first time the Axis tankers and freighters moving across the Mediterranean with oil, ammunition, and food for the embattled armies in the desert. While Rommel's lifeline between Italy and the North African ports was under ceaseless attack, Montgomery was receiving from Britain and the United States the weapons required for a successful offensive: hundreds of new Sherman and Grant tanks from the United States, and more powerful antitank guns and two infantry divisions, the Forty-fourth and Fifty-first, from Britain.

The course of battle was influenced by Rommel's last attempt to turn one of the British flanks. This took place at Alam-el-Halfa on Aug. 31. Three Axis thrusts were directed at the British positions on the Alamein line: a feint attack in the north, a holding attack in the center, and the principal push in the south carried out by the Afrika Korps, the Fifteenth and Twenty-first Panzer Divisions and the Ninetieth Light Division, and by the Italian XX Corps, the Ariete, and Littorio Armored Divisions.

This powerful force made its way through the British minefields north of the Qattara Depression and then swung north against the Alam-el-Halfa ridge on the left or southern flank of the British line. Had Rommel broken through, the bulk of the British forces to the north would have been cut off.

The attack was Rommel's last offensive. It failed. British tanks and antitank guns halted the German thrust to the north, and Rommel's armor spent the night under heavy shelling and bombing. On the morning of Sept. 1, the Axis forces resumed the offensive, this time attacking the center of the British line where they met the tanks and guns of the Tenth Armored Division. The heavy sand impeded the movement of the German and Italian tanks. In addition to the tanks lost to British guns, there was bad news from the Mediterranean. Three tankers carrying fuel for the panzers had been sunk by the British.

Rommel took up defensive positions on Sept. 3. A year before the British armor would have dashed out, to be shot to bits by the German antitank guns. More prudent than his predecessors, Montgomery held back his armor in the central sector and sent the Seventh Armored Division, the "Desert Rats," to attack the Ninetieth Light and Italian Trieste Motorized Divisions on the right of the German line. The Axis forces, fighting bitterly, began their withdrawal after serious losses in tanks and trucks.

Montgomery saw Alam-el-Halfa as "a vital action, because, had we lost it, we might well have lost Egypt." But it was a defensive victory. The offense that would break the Germans was yet to come.

The British commander used the period between Alam-el-Halfa and the opening of "Lightfoot," the code name for the Alamein attack, to push through the reforms he believed were needed.

The free-and-easy command arrangements of the Eighth Army were outlawed. There were to be no more "Jock" columns, operating independently—that is, no more impromptu formations of artillery, tanks, and infantry. Divisions were to be fought as divisions and not broken up under the stress of battle. Officers who had been found wanting in earlier battles were sent back to Britain. The arrangements for supply were strengthened. Two newly arrived divisions, the Forty-fourth and the Fifty-first Infantry, underwent rigorous desert training. The headquarters of the Eighth Army and the Western Desert Air Force were established side by side.

Meanwhile, Rommel flew back to Germany on Sept. 23 for medical care and recuperation. He was replaced by General Georg Stumme, a corpulent, easygoing panzer veteran from the Russian front.

The original British plan of attack was based on the experience of the desert war. In a dozen battles victory had gone to the side that first destroyed the enemy's armored forces. The primary British objective under that plan was to destroy the four armored divisions, two German and two Italian, that had fought at Alam-el-Halfa. Once the armor was out of the way, the remaining formations of infantry and artillery could be driven westward or neutralized on the battlefield.

Under this plan Montgomery envisaged blasting two gaps in the Axis line. Once these were opened, his pursuit force, the X Corps of the First, Eighth, and Tenth Armored Divisions and the Second New Zealand Division, would pass through the gaps to establish themselves on the Axis lines of retreat. The Germans and Italians then would be forced to launch a counterattack under conditions almost as unfavorable as those they faced at Alam-el-Halfa; they would have to face unshaken Allied infantry and massed antitank guns.

At the same phase of the battle, another larger gap was to be opened on the northern or right flank of the British position by General Oliver Leese's XXX Corps of four infantry divisions. General Brian Horrocks's XIII Corps was then to attack in the south with two divisions, in the expectation that the attack would tie down Axis reserves in that area.

This first battle plan, as we see, was complex, depending on the most delicate timing and the closest air-ground co-operation. Doubts multiplied when it was explained to the unit commanders. The tank officers doubted whether the artillery and infantry could open the gaps in the Axis line. The infantry, in turn, asked whether the armor could move fast enough to make the planned breakthroughs. Finally, Montgomery, the perfectionist, was worried about the army's level of training.

As a result the plan was changed. How much Alexander had to do with the original plan is not known. But Montgomery *did* change it and took the credit. He wrote, "My modified plan now was to hold off or contain the enemy armor, while we carried out a methodical destruction of the infantry divisions holding the defensive systems"— that is, the minefields, barbed wire, and forward gun sites.

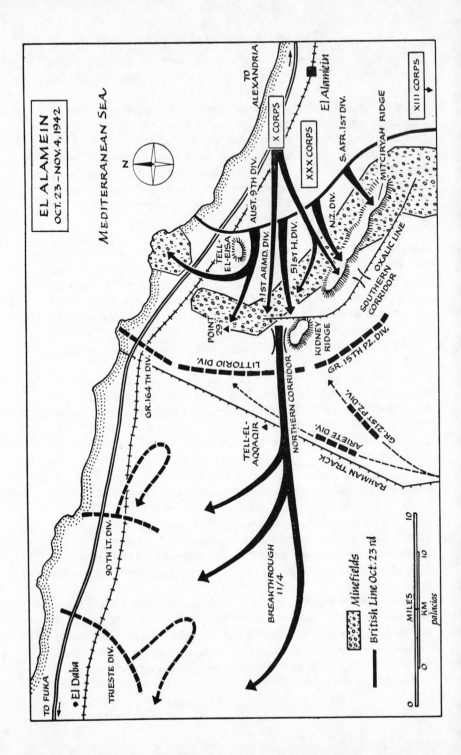

EL ALAMEIN
OCT. 23 – NOV. 4, 1942

MEDITERRANEAN SEA

X CORPS
XXX CORPS
XIII CORPS

TO ALEXANDRIA

El Alamein

S. AFR. 1ST DIV.

MT. CIRYAH RIDGE

OXALIC LINE

SOUTHERN CORRIDOR

GR. 15TH PZ. DIV.

KIDNEY RIDGE

GR. 21ST PZ. DIV.

ARIETE DIV.

RAHMAN TRACK

LITTORIO DIV.

NORTHERN CORRIDOR

TELL-EL-AQQAQIR

GR. 164 TH DIV.

90TH LT. DIV.

TRIESTE DIV.

TO FUKA

El Daba

BREAKTHROUGH 11/4

AUST. 9TH DIV.

TELL-EL-EISA

1ST ARMD. DIV.

51 ST H. DIV.

N.Z. DIV.

POINT 29

Minefields
British Line Oct. 23rd

MILES
KM
palacios
0   10
0   10

British intelligence reported that these defenses were far more elaborate than had been assumed originally. But the Axis forces were increasingly short of fuel and spare parts. The shortage of fuel forced Stumme to alter his plans.

The tank forces no longer were to be concentrated in the rear for counterattacks against the British. Instead they were to be deployed in mixed groups close behind the defense system in order to be available to intervene and block a British penetration before it developed into a major breakthrough. By thus reducing the distance Axis tanks would travel to counterattack, fuel expenditure would be reduced.

In the north the Fifteenth Panzer and the Littorio formed three battle groups; in the south the Twenty-first Panzer and the remainder of the Littorio set up three more.

Alamein was a set-piece battle. All the players were in place. The southern flank of the British rested on the Qattara Depression, the northern on the Mediterranean. The same conditions held true for the Axis. The pieces were all in place. The problem for the attacker, Montgomery, was to put them in motion toward the sectors where the enemy could be confused and weakened.

Deception played a major role in his preparations. By the movement of dummy trucks and tanks and a spate of fake wireless messages, the British sought to convince the Germans that the main attack would develop in the south about the end of November. At first Stumme and his staff bought this deception, but by Oct. 20 the German commander was warning his units that a British offensive was imminent.

Alamein began as battles on the western front had begun twenty-five years earlier. At 9:40 P.M. on Oct. 23, British bombers and artillery attacked all identified Axis gun positions. The attack lasted fifteen minutes. There was a pause. The British infantry emerged from the slit trenches in which they had been hidden and assembled for the attack. The guns, targeted on the Axis front line, sounded again at 10 P.M., and the line went forward.

XXX Corps's four divisions swept through the first belt of mines and the enemy outposts. Then the delays inevitable in any operation began. Axis resistance strengthened. The attackers' momentum dwindled. By dawn most of the infantry were on or near the phase line, Oxalic, running behind the Axis outpost line.

On the X Corps front, progress was slower. The British had introduced a new machine to penetrate minefields. This was the Scorpion tank, which pushed a roller in front of it. Weighted chains were attached to the roller and their impact exploded the mines ahead. The infantry moved in the wake of the Scorpions supported by artillery fire.

As it turned out, many of the Scorpions broke down. The engineers' electronic mine detectors failed. The "sappers," as the British army calls engineers, had to finish the job by the slow, laborious, and dangerous job of prodding through the sand for the mines. By dawn the First Armored Division was only halfway through the northern corridor, with some of the tank squadrons still hung up in the minefields. In the southern corridor the Tenth Armored Division had been slightly more successful, due to the engineers' success. Four routes had been cleared up to the base of Mitciryah Ridge, a major terrain feature before them. When the tanks plunged down over the forward slope of the ridge they encountered another minefield and heavy fire from massed Axis antitank guns. They pulled back and bumped into the New Zealand infantry.

On the whole, the "break-in," as Montgomery dubbed this phase of the battle, had not been significantly effective. Montgomery, however, decided to continue the fight for another twenty-four hours before he opened the "crumbling" process of smashing the enemy infantry.

The Germans and Italians had little chance for reorganization. Throughout the daylight hours of Oct. 25, they were hammered by the RAF, which flew over a thousand sorties, and the United States Army Air Force, which contributed 170 sorties. The armored formations in the rear of the German line, especially the Fifteenth Panzer/Littorio group, were badly mauled by the air attack.

This was not the only Axis problem. General Stumme, in the best traditions of the German officer corps, had gone forward to survey the battle from close range. He died of a heart attack. General Ritter von Thoma, commanding the Afrika Korps, succeeded him. Von Thoma brought forward more antitank weapons and told Berlin he had contained the attack. At the moment he was right. Montgomery was learning that the Axis minefields were too deep to be breached by a single attack. He had to improvise, which meant continuing with greater strength, where this was possible, along the original lines of attack. But things went badly.

In the south the XIII Corps, struggling to find paths through minefields laid by the British in past campaigns, failed to get through the second belt of mines and was ordered to halt. On the X Corps front, the First Armored Division attacked, supported by the Fifty-first Highland Division and the Australians. After severe losses, the armor reached the Oxalic Line but could make no further progress.

The Tenth Armored Division in the southern corridor had little luck. Engineers had filtered forward at dusk to clear the minefield on the near slope of Mitciryah Ridge. The mission consumed time. The tank crews sat fuming in their assembly area. By chance a lone Axis airman—they were now a rarity—bombed the cluster of vehicles. The fires attracted the attention of every Axis gunner in the area. This combined aerial and artillery attack disorganized the British. Alec Gatehouse, divisional commander, concluded that his force might be caught at daylight in a minefield, which afforded no room for maneuver, under heavy fire from Axis antitank and other artillery.

Now there occurred an important psychological turning point. Gatehouse told Lieutenant General Herbert Lumsden, the corps commander, of the gravity of the situation. Lumsden agreed that the situation was, indeed, perilous. Years later in Moscow, Alec Gatehouse told me, "No one can imagine what it's like. Here's a division you've fought with and trained. It's almost an extension of yourself. Now you find it, soldiers and officers you know as well as you know your family, out there exposed. And at the moment there appears to be no way out."

Lumsden took his own and Gatehouse's fears to General Francis de Guignand, Montgomery's chief of staff. That coldly analytical soldier recognized the problem's importance. He summoned Lumsden and Leese for a meeting with Montgomery.

The Eighth Army commander, like Joffre in World War I, hated having his sleep disturbed. Impassively he listened to his corps commanders' conclusion that the battle had not developed as the British had hoped, that casualties were high and would become higher, and that the Eighth Army should disengage before it became too late.

The history of the desert war and memories of 1914–18 were on the side of the plaintiffs; high casualties of World War I proportions were to be avoided. Montgomery, however, had given his orders; the armor was to smash through to the line. If commanders felt they could not carry out the orders, he would find others that could. At this early juncture in the battle, Montgomery established his will over some of his most experienced and popular commanders. Henceforward, the Eighth Army was Monty's army. If the rank and file didn't know it yet, the generals did.

Fate naturally answered Montgomery's *hubris*. The Tenth Armored managed to fight its way out of the minefield only to come under heavy antitank gunfire when dawn broke on the battle's second morning. Montgomery had asserted his leadership, but the first phase of his battle had not gone according to plan. The "Dogfight," as he called it, to destroy the Axis infantry would have to begin with armored and infantry divisions intermingled, an awkward attacking position.

The offensive had gone slowly. In London Churchill was asking Sir Alan Brooke, Chief of the Imperial General Staff, if there was not a single general who could win one single battle? On the other side of the lines, the familiar figure of Field Marshal Rommel, whisked back from his recuperation at Hitler's orders, had returned to command. He found a good deal to grumble at when he considered Stumme's tactics—the dead general had forbidden artillery bombardment as a needless expenditure of ammunition—and even less encouragement in the general Axis situation.

Montgomery's penchant for dramatic descriptions of his tactics produced both the "Dogfight" and "the crumbling process" for the next phase of the battle, which lasted from Oct. 25 to 31. The object was to chew up the Axis infantry. The New Zealand Division was to attack to the southwest from the Mitciryah Ridge, while the First Armored Division felt its way forward from the northern corridor to fight Axis armor around Kidney Ridge.

These were the battle plans. Forget them and consider the men. The tank crews were fighting their own ship-to-ship duel at range against Axis tanks. The New Zealanders, cramped and tired in their trenches, damned the tanks for drawing Axis fire. Beyond the ridge, artillery batteries and supply columns were jostling for positions to enter the narrow tracks through the minefields. Little could be expected from the attack in the southern corridor, and Montgomery, after talking once more with his field commanders, accepted the check.

Fortunately the attack in the northern corridor had prospered. The Australians had driven northward from their sector toward Point 29, a terrain feature west of Tell-el-Eisa which provided the Eighth

Army with a sally point against the Axis units in the rear. Now Montgomery made a second battlefield decision, one as important as his insistence that the armor must continue the battle after the losses of Oct. 24. The army commander called off operations by the New Zealanders in the south and switched the weight of the attack to the north, where the Australians were to seize Point 29 with the First Armored and the Fifty-first Divisions, expanding their attacks in the Kidney Ridge sector.

Napoleon asked for lucky generals; Montgomery, that day, was one. An Australian patrol captured a German regimental commander and a battalion commander. The latter carried a map showing the minefields around Point 29. Lieutenant General Sir Leslie Morshead, the Australian commander, needed no further luck. He mounted his infantry on armored troop carriers. They threaded through the minefields and took Point 29. By dawn the position was consolidated. The balance was beginning to swing in favor of the British, although this change was hidden from the long-enduring infantry and the exhausted tank crews.

For both sides Oct. 26, the battle's third day, was critical. Rommel learned from Von Thoma that the Axis positions were being "crumbled," as Montgomery would have put it, by accurate and heavy artillery shelling, the seemingly incessant attentions of the Royal Air Force, and—a new factor for the Germans—the long-range shelling of the British tanks.

Some Axis units had suffered severely, notably the German 164th Infantry Division, the Italian Trento Division, and the armored group made up of the Fifteenth Panzer and Littorio Tank Divisions. Rommel's immediate reaction was to order an attack to recapture Point 29 and to use antitank guns rather than tanks to answer the British armor. Pessimistic though he might have been in his letters to his wife, the field marshal was the eternal optimist in the field. His thoughts and his will were fixed on organizing a major counterattack against the Eighth Army.

But Montgomery was also an optimist, one who held the high cards of men and guns. The Tenth Corps, his chosen pursuit unit, had been committed. But there were tens of thousands of additional men, hundreds of tanks. The RAF controlled the skies. He would form another corps, out of the Seventh and Tenth Armored Divisions and the New Zealand Infantry Division. Meanwhile the Australians were to attack north from Point 29 to clear the coast road, and the Highland (Fifty-first) Division was to strike out of the northern corridor.

The first German attempt to retake Point 29 broke down under heavy fire from the Australians' guns and equally heavy bombing. Undaunted by this reverse, Rommel assembled his old reliables. The Twenty-first Panzer moved up from the south, incautiously leaving the defense of the southern sector to the Ariete Division. The Ninetieth Light and the Trieste Division were brought forward from around El Daba, where they had been stationed to deal with British armored breakthroughs. The plan was to hit the British around Point 29 and Kidney Ridge, with the Ninetieth Light attacking from the northwest and the Twenty-first Panzer from the southwest. Field Marshal Albert Kesselring, the German commander in chief for the south, promised that every available Luftwaffe aircraft would support the counterattack.

This must be considered the crux of the battle. Rommel was there with his veteran units. The Luftwaffe was there to recreate the conditions of the Blitzkrieg—dive bombing and the remorseless assault by armor. All was in order. As had happened so many times in the past, Rommel reversed the tide of battle, and German arms won another sensational victory.

But this time there was a difference. It lay in the caliber of the men and the officers who were the object of the German attack. The victory in the encounter lay with them. It was a soldier's battle.

The Ninetieth Light came on "like the hammers of hell," as an Irish tank sergeant described it, against Point 29. Once again the sweating Australian gunners broke up the attack and, when the momentum lessened, the RAF, which had punished the Luftwaffe in air encounters, hammered the German ground troops.

The Twenty-first Panzer Division, triumphant survivor of so many battles, attacked in the early evening, taking advantage of the sun which shone full in the eyes of the British gunners. The panzers made some progress preceded by dive-bomber attacks, but the First Armored Division stood its ground.

"Five times they attacked with all available tanks," Alexander reported to Churchill, "but gained no ground and suffered heavy and, worse still, disproportionate casualties, for our tanks fighting on the defensive suffered lightly."

Laurels also go to the Second Battalion, the Rifle Brigade, and the 239th Antitank battery. The fire of the battery's six-pounder guns, the stolid courage of the riflemen, and the shells of the First Armored broke up the attack. The Twenty-first Panzer, which earlier had won the two battles of Sidi Rezegh, stopped, recoiled, and retreated. Rommel's major counterattack had failed.

The failure of the German attack forced Rommel onto the defensive all along the Axis front. Considering his losses in tanks, the RAF's mastery of the skies, and the apparently endless British resources, Rommel concluded that the only course open to him was to ensure that if the Axis could not win, neither could the British.

"We were, therefore, going to make one more attempt, by the tenacity and stubbornness of our defense, to persuade the enemy to call off his attack," the German field marshal wrote.

For Montgomery, the "crumbling" process was not going well. The Australians, attacking northward on the night of Oct. 28–29, had an early success against the Ninetieth Light but were halted well short of the coast road. Churchill fumed in London. Why, he asked the long-suffering Brooke, did Montgomery tell us he would be through in seven days, "if all he intended to do was to fight a half-hearted battle?" In Cairo, Alexander and Chief of Staff General Richard McCreery were equally concerned. The battle had devoured tons of ammunition and fuel, although the British casualties thus far had been relatively light. The message traffic from London reflected Churchill's dissatisfaction.

Montgomery's answer was Operation Supercharge, an all-out attack that would accomplish the breakthrough the Eighth Army needed. But Alexander and McCreery were worried by the direction of the attack. They believed that once launched in the north, it would encounter the bulk of Rommel's forces. Alexander, however, was not prepared to interfere with Montgomery's tactical handling of the battle, although his doubts about the line of attack "got through" to the Eighth Army Commander, De Guignand said years later.

On De Guignand's advice, Montgomery made another vital decision. The Operation Supercharge attack was moved southward because the northern sector was too strongly held by the Axis. This demonstrated a flexibility-in-command decision not often shown by Montgomery.

Supercharge was a replay of earlier attacks. An infantry division, Lieutenant General Bernard C. Freyberg's New Zealanders, was to tear a hole in the Axis forces on a two-mile front. The division was to be accompanied by two British brigades, one from the Fiftieth and the other from the Fifty-first Division. The infantry's mission was to push 5,000 yards through the Axis forces, again opening the way for the tanks. These were to be provided by the Ninth Armored Brigade, which was ordered to smash through to the Rahman track. The hole having been opened, the First Armored Division was to pass through, take on the remaining Afrika Korps tanks, and then wheel northward to cut the coast road.

The attack was scheduled for Oct. 31, but the burden on the lines of communication forced a postponement for twenty-four hours. Meanwhile Morshead's Australians launched another attack in the north. They cut the coast road and railway. But the attack had another dividend. Rommel concluded that this was the main British attack and threw in most of his reinforcements. The Australians suffered heavily but held their ground in one of the fiercest engagements of the desert war.

The Supercharge attack was preceded by a raid on the Axis forces communications by one hundred RAF bombers. The two British infantry brigades in the van reached their objectives by midnight. But the pace slowed when the Ninth Armored Brigade moved through. Some of the tanks reached the Rahman track where German antitank guns were encountered. The British met not the weaker Italian units they had expected but their old enemies the Fifteenth Panzer, with the Twenty-first Panzer in close support. The armored brigade, in the view of the official Australian historian, paid their battle debts to the New Zealanders "dearly and liberally that morning in heroism and blood."

Although the British naturally did not know it, Rommel already was preparing to retreat. He was considering a general retirement to Fuka in the west, where he believed he could take up positions that Montgomery could not penetrate. Already certain chosen commanders, all of them German, were being warned that a retirement might be found necessary.

The British were still delayed by the congestion in the rear. Freyberg urged the First Armored Division forward to support the embattled Ninth Armored Brigade. The division moved up to positions on the flanks of the brigade.

Rommel remained convinced that the main British attack would come from the Australians in the north. General Von Thoma was told to attack in the direction of Point 29. The field marshal realized his mistake when the British attack developed, and switched the attack to the New Zealand division which had established itself in the Tell-el-Aqqaqir sector of the Rahman track. Von Thoma threw in two attacks, but the First Armored Division held the front, destroying 117 Axis tanks. What is worse, from Rommel's standpoint, two armored-car squadrons of the Royal Dragoons slipped through a gap in the Axis defenses to harry the German and Italian supply lines.

By daylight on Nov. 2 Rommel realized that his infantry and armor were outfought. There were scores of British tanks maimed or destroyed in the minefields, but behind them he could see hundreds more moving toward the attack. The German and Italian infantry, subjected to heavy artillery fire and bombing, were outnumbered. Reports arrived of British armored cars operating in the Axis rear areas, shooting up supply columns, destroying ammunition dumps.

The break in German resistance came at 11 A.M. with a telephone call to the field marshal. British "tank masses" had broken through and were advancing westward. Rommel's diary adds, "Afrika Korps estimates 400 enemy tanks here. Our own panzer strength only meager after counterattacks. According to reports of artillery observers, there are about 400–500 more tanks standing by beyond the mine boxes [fields] J and K."

The British XXX Corps launched its attack late on Nov. 2, sweeping through its initial objectives and capturing large numbers of Italians from the dispirited Ariete and Trieste Divisions. The X Corps met more resolute resistance, but the Germans too were tiring. Von Thoma had no more than thirty-five tanks, and these were outgunned by the British Shermans, which could open fire at ranges of 1,000 yards. Casualties had been high. Most units were down by one third of their strength. Von Thoma unequivocally advised retirement to the Fuka position.

Von Thoma's report confirmed Rommel's belief that if the panzer army was to be saved, it must get out of the present fight. The field marshal's decision must have been strengthened by reports that the RAF had sunk one Italian tanker at sea and American bombers had destroyed another in the harbor of Tobruk.

Rommel reported his view to Berlin. Then early on Nov. 3 the Axis forces began to thin out with some of the less mobile units directed back to Fuka. The remaining armor was switched to the north to protect the retirement along the coast road, but all along the front the British noted a slackening of Axis resistance during the day. Nonetheless the Afrika Korps retained its old bite. Any British advance unprepared by artillery and bombing was costly.

But a crisis in command was developing in the Axis camp. Hitler ordered Rommel to hold on. Help was being rushed to him. "Despite his superiority," the message ends, "the enemy must also have exhausted his strength. It would not be the first time in history that the stronger will has triumphed over the enemy's stronger battalions. You can show your troops no other road to victory or death.— *Adolf Hitler.*"

The message, like so many of Hitler's to his embattled commanders, sets the teeth on edge. Rommel tried, but there was little he could do. The morale of the Italians was shattered. The Afrika Korps had lost fight after fight to superior forces. All the Axis troops suffered from the shock of continuing bombardment and accurate and effective shelling; after the war many German veterans of the battle gave credit for the victory to the mobility and accuracy of the British artillery.

The XXX and X Corps continued to apply pressure to the Axis lines. At about noon on Nov. 4 the Axis battle line disintegrated.

A British tank commander recalled, "One minute we were in a ding-dong battle with a Mark IV and an antitank gun. The next, the action fell apart. The tank made off—we got her with a long shot—and the antitank gun disappeared to the west. No, we didn't know then we had won. We just knew that on our bit of the front there wasn't any fighting."

By evening, with the British infantry and armor pouring through the Axis positions, Rommel realized that the battle was lost and ordered a general retirement to Fuka. Von Thoma had been captured fighting futilely with his personal escort to check the X Corps advance. The panzers streamed west, accompanied by the truck-borne German infantry. The Italians were left to be rounded up by the British, who were bone-weary but invigorated by victory. Some units of the Trento and Bologna Divisions got away, but most of the remainder surrendered. The greatest victory of the desert war was moving toward its conclusion.

Most critics of Montgomery's handling of the battle concentrate more on his failure to exploit his victory than the manner in which he won it, although there has been some criticism of that as well. But the failure of the pursuit remains the focus of military criticism.

The field marshal's explanation is that "heavy rains interfered with my plans." He had planned to cut off the retreating Axis forces by swinging northward to cut the coast road at Fuka and Mersa Matruh. On Nov. 5 he regrouped for the pursuit with X Corps, the First and Seventh Armored and Second New Zealand Division named to lead the chase. By nightfall on Nov. 6, the forward elements were nearing Matruh when the rains came. XXX Corps was deployed between Mersa Matruh and Alamein. Rain undoubtedly was an element in the British failure to bring the defeated Axis forces to battle. But there were other reasons.

British staff officers were unaccustomed to the novel task of organizing the pursuit of a beaten enemy. In justice to the staff planners, it should be noted that they had been hard at work since mid-September. There was a shortage of fuel because until the pursuit began, ammunition was the principal requirement of the Eighth Army. Now the emphasis had to be switched to fuel, with delays and confusion resulting. Finally, the German rear guards fought tenaciously whenever the British approached. They were driven out of their positions by flanking movements of British tanks and armored cars, but their actions bought precious time.

Another view is given by Field Marshal Lord Carver, who served as an armored commander during the battle: "It would have been hard enough if all had been under the command of the same corps; with two different corps who were not on the best of terms anyway, both trying to carry out the same task in the same area, it was chaotic. There is no other word to describe the incredible confusion of that dark night in a sea of dust. Vehicles of every formation were traveling in every direction on every conceivable track, looming up in front of each other from unexpected directions out of the thick stifling pall of dust."

So Rommel got away to begin his 1,500-mile trek across the North African littoral to Tunisia. He left behind 30,000 prisoners, 20,000 casualties, 1,000 guns, and 480 tanks. This was defeat.

Rommel had been beaten, not destroyed, but the significance of the British victory was recognized in both Axis and Allied capitals. The blinding strategic result was that the Middle East, the road to the other war in Asia, was now safe. There never again was a serious threat to the Allied position in Egypt, Syria, and Palestine.

A second result, particularly for the British, was that a British—or, as Churchill liked to call it, an "Imperial Army"—had whipped one of Germany's best generals and his forces. The psychological benefit of this to the British army was to be demonstrated in later campaigns in Sicily, Italy, and northwest Europe.

Alamein powerfully influenced the remainder of the war in Africa. New American and British forces landed in Algeria and Morocco on Nov. 8. Although they suffered some setbacks in the fighting that winter, there was never a realistic chance that they could be held by the Germans. Not with Montgomery's veterans advancing from the east.

From the standpoint of military tactics, Alamein demonstrated that the British finally had mastered the effective co-operation of air and land power. Throughout the battle, and never more than in its attacks on the tankers and transports crossing the Mediterranean from Italy with supplies for Rommel, the RAF showed that it could both support troops attacking in the field and harass enemy communications both in the immediate rear of the battle and hundreds of miles away.

The air attacks on Rommel's supply line across the Mediterranean and on the rear areas of the Axis forces did not begin with the Alamein campaign. By the time that the Allied and Axis forces gathered for the campaign, however, the Allied air forces were much stronger in numbers, with General Lewis Bereton's American bombers adding to the overall strength.

Under the direction of Air Marshal Sir Arthur Tedder, the Allied air operations were directed at three principal objectives. The first was the supply line across the Mediterranean Sea. The RAF, working in productive harmony with the Royal Navy, virtually throttled this vital artery, sinking tankers and supply ships by the score from early 1942 onward.

At the same time, light bombers escorted by fighters who commanded the skies ranged far behind the Axis front lines to bomb and strafe supply depots, communications lines, and Axis airfields.

Finally in the battle itself, British fighters and bombers worked closely with the attacking Allied troops, eliminating Axis strongpoints and harrying the retreating Germans and Italians. These operations were carried out by the Desert Air Force commanded by Air Marshal Sir Arthur Coningham.

The British, quite naturally, were prone to exaggerate Alamein's effect. But in retrospect it must be considered with Stalingrad and Midway as one of the battles that turned the tide in World War II. Churchill's description, then, is not an exaggeration: "Before Alamein we never had a victory. After Alamein we never had a defeat."

X

The Unknown Battle

IMPHAL-KOHIMA

Imphal-Kohima was the fourth of the great battles that reversed the tide of Axis success in the Second World War and established a global strategic situation that allowed the Allies to go over to the offensive. Most Americans have never heard of Imphal-Kohima. Yet in northeastern India and northwestern Burma early in 1944, British and Indian troops destroyed the Japanese Fifteenth Army, in a battle which in the considered judgment of Western and Japanese historians was the greatest defeat suffered on land in Japan's history. The Japanese began their offensive with approximately 100,000 men. Of these, they lost 53,000, killed or missing.

The victory had an important psychological effect. It ended the myth of Japanese superiority in jungle fighting. British, Indians, and West Africans proved themselves as resourceful, innovative, and brave as their foes. In doing so, they broke the back of an offensive aimed ultimately at the invasion of India and so sapped Japanese strength that the reconquest of Burma occurred with a speed that would have been unthinkable in 1943.

Tactically the battle was a landmark in the development of air transport to support troops deprived of normal land-supply lines. Under heavy fire British and American airmen threaded their way down narrow, mist-filled valleys to drop ammunition and food to encircled units, or airlifted entire brigades and divisions and their equipment and animals from one sector of the battlefield to another. At the same time, Allied fighters kept the sky clear of Japanese aircraft, and their fighter-bombers mercilessly harassed the Japanese columns. This was a demonstration of what all-around air support, logistical as well as tactical, could do.

Imphal-Kohima went almost unnoticed at the time; there were more spectacular actions in the Pacific and Western Europe to titillate Allied publics. But the day-to-day fighting was as hard and bloody as any in World War II. The battle also produced a new hero, an unlikely one. He was General William Joseph Slim, then commanding the Fourteenth Army and later to become a field marshal. He was a quiet, modest, undemonstrative ex–Ghurka officer who combined in his generalship remarkable flexibility with an ability to concentrate on a single aspect of the battle when this proved necessary.

For the Western Allies, the winter of 1943–44 was a season in which ambitious strategic options were not matched by military resources necessary to sustain them. Political and military leaders in Washington and London, surveying the results of Midway, Stalingrad, and Alamein, were conscious of their coalition's growing strength and the perceptible weakening of the Axis. The American "arsenal of democracy" was working at full blast, British industry was performing prodigies of production after four years of war, and the Russians were sending large numbers of tanks and aircraft to their fronts; but resources still fell well behind planning.

Roosevelt and Churchill realized that the invasion of northwest Europe could not be delayed much longer in view of the rising Russian clamor for a second front. This operation and the American-supported landing in southern France were to absorb a high proportion of the Allied shipping and air resources. The campaign in Italy had to be maintained and, if possible, strengthened. The bombing of Germany by the Eighth Air Force and the Royal Air Force's Bomber Command devoured huge amounts of materiel, and even more important, thousands of men. In the western Pacific, the American navy, marine corps, and army, and the Australian forces were making progress toward eliminating the Japanese from the outermost ring of their island-fortress system. In these circumstances the American and British leaders and the Combined Chiefs of Staff were unlikely to devote much attention or resources to fighting in Burma and Assam, India.

However, Roosevelt and his advisors were attracted, almost obsessed, with the idea of supporting Chiang Kai-shek's armies by opening a road from Ledo in Assam to China. Even if the road were completed in time to "replenish the Chinese armies," Churchill wrote sourly, "it would make little difference in their fighting capacity." The primary reason for building the road, however, was to strengthen the American air bases in China for the coming holocaust by the air force against Japan.

Lord Louis Mountbatten, the newly named Supreme Allied Commander in Southeast Asia, although cognizant of the Allied priorities in Europe, nevertheless had seven different offensives planned for his area. One of these, a seaborne assault on the Andaman Islands, Operation Buccaneer, was canceled because of the shipping shortage. An advance by Chiang's troops in Yunnan toward Bhamo and Lashio in Burma also was deferred because of a shortage of resources—thus, as Basil Collier points out, providing the Generalissimo with an excellent excuse for inaction.

From the British standpoint, the most promising of the proposed offensives appeared to be an advance by the XV Corps of the Fourteenth Army in Arakan in western Burma northwestward toward Akyab. The fighting there was important because, tactically, it provided a classroom for the Imphal-Kohima battle.

Burma is a tumult of land. One of the few breaks in its monotonous parade of mountains, deep valleys, swamps, and rivers is the Imphal plain. Imphal was the capital of the Indian State of Manipur on the eastern borders of Assam with Burma. The capital lies about 400 miles northeast of Calcutta. The plain, 700 square miles, is fertile and healthy. Around it on all sides are mountains heavy with vegetation rising to 8,000 feet. Kohima, the capital of Nagaland, lies approximately 90 miles to the north.

The plain's military importance is evident. It was the only area in the frontier region suitable for the assembly of troops and supplies, the construction of airfields, maintenance shops, depots, and hospitals. Any enemy planning the invasion of northeast India must have possession of the Imphal plain. Conversely, any force attempting to bar the road to India must use the plain as its main supply base.

Japanese strategy in Burma in 1943 showed a curious indecision. The conquest of Burma in 1942 had been much swifter than they had expected, but their troops were tired and their supplies were running low. The conventional generals advocated consolidation and reorganizing and resupplying their armies. There were other generals who advocated a new advance on India before the British could reorganize. In the end, the conventional generals won, largely because the terrain and climate of northern Burma present such hideous problems of supply and such a grave risk of disease for any attacking army.

The Japanese generals here displayed a streak of prudence, so alien to the stereotype of "go-for-broke" improvisers that characterized many of their operations during the war. They settled down to reorganize south of the Chindwin River. At Imphal the British set about building forces for the reconquest of Burma.

The catalyst who broke this stalemate was Orde Wingate. This general, an odd mixture of fanatic and careful planner, drove successfully (if at great cost) into Burma on foot, with his Chindits, did a great deal of damage (although not, perhaps, as much as was claimed at the time), and altered Japanese thinking about the feasibility of campaigning in the inhospitable terrain to the north. The Chindits were infantry columns operating as the commandos did in the west.

Lieutenant General Masakuzu Kawabe, a commander of the Japanese Burma Army, prodded by Lieutenant General Renya Mutaguchi of the Fifteenth Army, began to plan a campaign that would encompass the whole Burma front. The planning was accelerated because the Japanese realized, after Wingate's success, that the construction of airfields around Imphal and the stockpiling of ammunition, fuel, and other stores indicated that the British were about to move to the offensive.

Imperial General Headquarters in Tokyo approved Kawabe's campaign plan on Jan. 7, 1944, stipulating that the offensive, to be led by Mutaguchi, was to start "at the opportune time." The first step was to march the first regiment of the Fifteenth Division 700 miles from Siam to reinforce the Fifteenth Army.

The plan for the offensive as conceived by Kawabe started with a holding operation by the Fifty-sixth Division on the Burma-China front. Chiang Kai-shek's forces in Yunnan, which had no intention of attacking in any case, were to be held on the line of the Salween River. Any Allied attack from the Ledo area would be parried by the Eighteenth Division in the Hukawng valley area.

These were subsidiary operations. The main thrust was to be delivered by the Fifteenth Army, with the Fifteenth, Thirty-first, and Thirty-third Divisions, advancing in two groups. The main objectives were Kohima and Imphal. The Fifteenth and Thirty-third Divisions were to cross the Chindwin, and the Thirty-third Division and the First Division of the Indian National Army were to advance directly on the objectives. The Indian National Army division was made up of Indian soldiers captured in Burma and Malaya in the initial Japanese offensives. It played an unimportant role in the fighting.

An important element in the Japanese plan was a diversionary attack in Arakan by the Fifty-fifth Division. This attack, it was hoped, would divert British forces from the Imphal plain.

If the Japanese had been prudent in the previous year, they were taking high risks now. Mutaguchi's Thirty-third and Indian divisions would be supplied from Kalewa on roads which intelligence told the general were now all-weather highways. They were not. Some of the Fifteenth Division would be sustained by a track from Tamu to Ukhrul, but the remainder of the division and the troops of the Thirty-first would depend completely on the supplies they carried with them. Mutaguchi estimated that they would be in this condition for three weeks.

Another weakness in the Japanese position was the slow arrival of the remainder of the Fifteenth Division. The command realized that this unit would not be able to participate in the main attack until the middle of March and then with only two thirds of its strength. But the main offensive could not be postponed. Kawabe wanted the Fifteenth Army to advance and consolidate its gains before the coming of the monsoon. The result was that Mutaguchi began the offensive without all the troops assigned to him and before the British had been affected by the diversionary attack in Arakan. The most important effect of the Arakan attack was tactical. The Japanese planned to send a column of infantry and engineers about 5,000 strong through the Seventh Indian Division's positions and block its communications in the area of the Ngakyedauk Pass. Then two battalions were to attack from the south.

Enter Slim, the army commander. That cool brain, after studying earlier battles with the Japanese, had concluded that it was futile to meet enemy thrusts by forming continuous fronts. These, he reasoned, were always countered by flanking movements or by infiltration. He ordered his forward units and all formations that found themselves cut off to stand fast unless they received orders to retire. At the same time his administrative staff was ordered to be prepared to supply such units by air. The forward units would become, in his words, "an anvil against which reserves could destroy the enemy forces in their rear."

The Japanese attack prospered at the outset. But the Fifth and Seventh Indian Divisions held on. Their supplies arrived despite the difficulty of depositing them in small areas ringed by high hills and heavy antiaircraft fire. After some heavy initial losses, a combination of night drops and day flights over carefully chosen avenues of approach supported by strong fighter forces succeeded.

The Japanese, however, got no supplies by air. Constantly engaged by the two British-Indian divisions they, the attackers, were running short of food and ammunition while the defenders were receiving daily supplies of those essential commodities as well as mail, cigarettes, rum, and newspapers. The Japanese withdrew on Feb. 23 in the face of a heavy counterattack and the next day the short-lived offensive was canceled.

The lesson of the battle was that the Japanese tactics of deep infiltration could be countered by well-trained forces as long as those forces could be supplied by air and adequate reserves were available. Success in the Kohima-Imphal battles was to rest on those two factors. On March 6 the British forces in Arakan went over to the offensive.

The focus of the Japanese attack in Imphal and Kohima was on the IV Corps commanded by Lieutenant General Sir G. A. P. Scoones and comprising the Seventeenth, Twentieth, and Twenty-third Indian Infantry Divisions. Three hundred miles to the southwest in Arakan was the XV Corps, the Fifth and Seventh Indian Infantry Divisions and the Eighty-first West African Division, under Lieutenant General Sir Philip Christison. An impossible terrain lay between the two corps, forbidding lateral communication by land. Any reinforcement of one by the other meant a three-week journey by road and rail back into Indian territory and then forward again.

Scoones had been preparing for a limited advance toward the Chindwin River. But by March 9 the signs of a coming Japanese offensive were so clear that he decided to withdraw from his forward positions and prepare for the defense of the Imphal plain as Slim had instructed. At that point his two forward divisions were widely dispersed. The Seventeenth was at Tiddim, 160 miles south of Imphal, and the Twentieth was 80 miles due east of Imphal. The former's main communication with the principal base was a road over the mountains which was deep in mud in the monsoon season and often closed by landslides. The Twentieth Division was better served. There was a road that could bear heavy tanks and trucks and enough supplies to support an advance to the Chindwin. Between the two divisions regular patrols and local forces officered by the British protected the flanks of the two divisions.

The Twenty-third Division, less one brigade, corps headquarters, and all the supplies of fuel, ammunition, and food were concentrated in and around the Imphal plain where the main airfields were situated. The newly arrived Fiftieth Parachute Brigade was at Kohima undergoing training in jungle warfare.

Mutaguchi's plan for Operation Ha-Go, as the Japanese called their offensive, began with a series of heavy attacks on the Seventeenth Division. These were intended to involve Scoones's reserves. On March 8, part of the Japanese Thirty-third Division, commanded by Lieutenant General Yanagida, was to launch an attack from the Kabaw Valley and cut the Seventeenth Division's withdrawal route to Imphal at Tongzang, forty miles north of Tiddim. Another thrust was to be made to Milestone 100 where the Japanese would consolidate to meet any British counterattack seeking to relieve the Seventeenth Division. At the same time a strong column of infantry supported by tanks under Major General Yamamoto was to drive on Tamu from the Kabaw Valley.

The Japanese expected that within a week Scoones would be deeply involved in rescuing the Seventeenth Division. The second half of the operation would then begin. The Fifteenth and Thirty-first Japanese Divisions, commanded by Lieutenant General Tamon-Yamauchi and Lieutenant General Ukinori Sato, would then thrust across the Chindwin between Homalin and Thaungdit. The Fifteenth, which had been moved from Thailand, was shy of most of one regiment and some artillery because Allied bombers had interrupted communications. This understrength division was to cut the Imphal–Kohima road north of Imphal and then attack the British base, while the Thirty-first was to take Kohima and prevent any reinforcement of the British around Imphal.

The fatal flaw in the Japanese plan was that all depended on speed. Imphal and Kohima and their supplies had to be captured if the Japanese were to eat. The infantry's scanty supplies of rice and the food taken from villagers along the way would not suffice for more than a month. Mutaguchi believed he would have Imphal by then and his forces could consolidate for the monsoon season.

The Japanese came very close to success in those opening days. One reason was the tardiness of the Seventeenth Division in carrying out Scoones's plan for withdrawal. The divisional commander, who must have been aware of the overall plan to destroy the Japanese on the Imphal plain, did not begin his withdrawal until four hours after the order had been issued on March 23. Neither he nor some of his subordinate commanders appeared to understand the urgency of the situation. Men and officers had fought long and hard to reach their present positions. Was all that blood and sweat to be only the preliminary to another retirement?

As it turned out, twenty-four hours were lost. The Seventeenth now had to cope with strong Japanese formations and to fight its way to the rear. So grave was the situation that Scoones had to send the whole of his corps reserve, two brigades, to help extricate the division.

This alarmed Slim. The IV Corps now had committed all its reserves. He asked Mountbatten for more transport aircraft to expedite the movement of the Fifth Indian Division from Arakan to Imphal.

Now the scene shifted from the steaming jungles of the front to the cool and quiet headquarters in Delhi where Mountbatten reigned and then westward to the orderly military bureaucracies in Washington and London.

Mountbatten responded at once, transferring thirty Dakotas, the U.S. C-47 transport plane, from the Air Transport Command to Slim. The transfer was duly reported to the Joint Chiefs of Staff and created a minor firestorm even though Lord Louis had informed the Joint Chiefs that he saw an opportunity to win a victory larger than that just achieved in Arakan. From Washington came a cable agreeing to the transfer, but informing Mountbatten that he had no right to make such transfers without first consulting the Joint Chiefs.

The cable did not satisfy Lord Louis. He wanted the freedom to make his own decisions on the use of the Air Transport Command to meet tactical situations which the Joint Chiefs were unable to judge.

The Dakotas were a lifesaver, literally. Between March 19 and

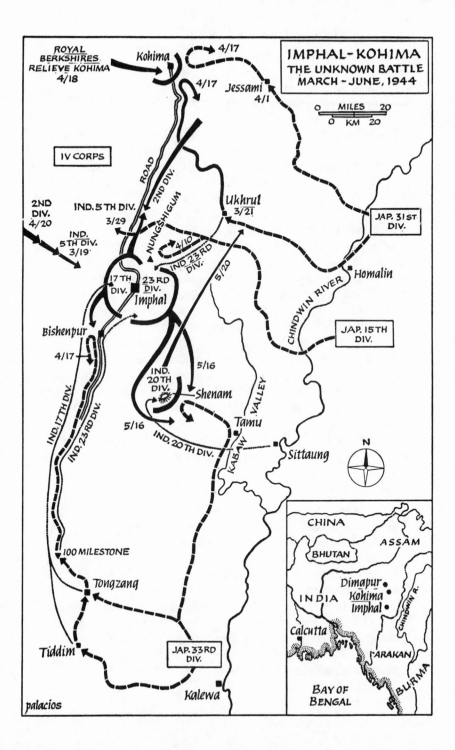

29, forty-five transports flew the Fifth Indian Division with all its guns, mules, and jeeps from Arakan to the Imphal plain to join the other three divisions of IV Corps. It was a notable logistics victory. Subsequently President Roosevelt approved the transfer of the aircraft.

The Fifth Division's arrival was timely. The corps learned on the night of March 15–16 that the Japanese had crossed the Chindwin.

The Seventeenth Division, after its slow start, fought successfully. The Japanese could not encircle it and took losses so heavy that General Yanagida urged headquarters to call off the offensive. But to Mataguchi, in his headquarters at Maymyo 200 miles to the rear, the offensive still appeared ripe with promise.

Admittedly, the Fifteenth and Thirty-first Japanese Divisions had encountered bitter resistance around Ukhrul and Jessami, but by the end of March they had cut the Imphal–Kohima–Dimapur road north of Imphal and on both sides of Kohima. The effect was to cut off Kohima with its resolute but outnumbered garrison until April 18, and the 150,000 British and Indian troops in the Imphal plain were isolated from their supply bases in India.

The defense of Kohima must be accounted one of the most notable of the war, ranking in intensity if not in numbers with that of Stalingrad. Three battalions withstood almost incessant Japanese attacks in superior numbers for sixteen days in an ever-dwindling perimeter.

The defenders frequently counterattacked. Here is an account of one such effort written by Arthur Campbell of the Royal West Kent regiment:

> When Lance-Corporal Harman saw the threat from these two guns, he told Mathews to move his Bren a little over to the left to give him covering fire while he assaulted the position. Mathews brought his gun to bear and saw Harman climb calmly out of his slit trench and walk toward the machine guns. The Japanese soon saw him coming and brought fire to bear and Mathews saw the bullets clipping up the ground at Harman's feet. But he went on, quite casually, and as he walked he took two grenades from his belt and pulled out the firing pins with his teeth. When he was only 30 yards from the building, he put his rifle on the ground and lobbed the two grenades inside. The machine guns were silent for a moment and Mathews saw Har-

man pick up his rifle and run forward quickly until he was under the shelter of the wall. Then he disappeared round a corner and an agonized screaming came from the building and two single shots. Then Harman walked out, carrying one of the machine guns across his shoulders.

The first relief for the Kohima force came from a brigade of the Fifth Division. But that brigade and the original defenders had to fight on until April 20, when units of the newly arrived Second British Division provided reinforcements. Only then did General Sato abandon his attempts to take the town.

To return to the overall situation, by April 4 Scoones and Slim had redeployed their forces in and around the Imphal plain. The Indian and British troops held a front of nearly one hundred miles of a horseshoe shape. Starting at Kanglatongbe in the north, the front ran through Nungshigum, Kameng, Shenam, and Shungau on the Tiddim road. That day General Sato launched the first of the many, unsuccessful attacks on the Kohima garrison.

Imphal was secure. Supplies came in by air in a steady stream. The picture was far different on the Japanese side. The Thirty-first Division had received no supplies from the rear. The Thirty-third got some over roads that could bear light traffic. The Fifteenth was supported by reinforcements and supplies. But these were petty compared to the cornucopia of military wealth opened on the Imphal plain by the British and American air forces.

The arrival of the Second Division, the concentration of IV Corps, and the steadiness of the airborne supply line convinced Slim that the moment had come to turn to a counteroffensive. The Fourteenth Army commander probably did not know that cracks were beginning to appear in the Japanese command. On April 25 General Sato, under heavy attack by the Second Division, refused to send a regiment to help out the hard-pressed Fifteenth Division.

Slim ordered Scoones to pin down the Thirty-third Division at the southern edge of the Imphal plain and to destroy the Fifteenth Division to the north and east of Imphal. A force was to strike toward Ukhrul in order to cut communications with the Chindwin. Then the British would turn on and destroy the Thirty-third Division. Sato's Thirty-first Division was to be assaulted by the Seventh Division with the mission of opening the Kohima–Imphal road.

Six weeks remained before the monsoon broke. The Japanese desperately tried to smash the Seventeenth Division's positions around Bishenpur and those of the Twentieth at Shenam. British historians claim that in and around Shenam more casualties were suffered by both sides, considering the size of the battlefield and the number of troops involved, than in any other engagement of the Second World War.

The Japanese mounted their gravest threat to Imphal on April 10. Infantry of the Fifteenth Division captured a hill feature at Nungshigum six miles east of Imphal. The only defenders between the hill and Imphal were what the British call "odds and sods" collected from the line of communications troops and administrative units in the Imphal plain. The Japanese attacked with their customary valor, heedless of casualties. Three days passed before tanks and infantry, supported by fighters and a heavy concentration of artillery, swept the Japanese from Nungshigum. That hill was the closest the Japanese came to Imphal in a battle that lasted four months.

On defense the Japanese fought as hard and as cleverly as they had on offense. It was a battle of sudden moves through the jungle ending in fierce fire fights. Often the British and Indians took positions only to find that the Japanese had died to the last man. On one occasion they captured a Japanese field hospital to find that all the patients and orderlies had been shot by the officers, who had then committed suicide. The balance in the battle may have been swung by the British command of the air. Hard-pressed infantry could be sure that sooner or later the fighters would sweep in to rake the Japanese positions. The artillery provided additional support—often firing at the Japanese over open sights, so close was the fighting.

Relief now came to Kohima. A battalion of the Royal Berkshire Regiment reached the battered garrison. Again, according to Arthur Campbell: "They looked fresh, these men, and eager for the fray, and they took over with great efficiency, filing in orderly fashion into our posts while our men crept out in small groups . . . ready to leave."

There is an inscription over the graves of those who died at Kohima that says it all:

> When you go home
> Tell them of us and say
> For their tomorrow
> We gave our today.

The Berkshires and the other newly arrived battalions could not expect an early breakthrough. The Japanese fought tenaciously for every yard. But the logistic balance was shifting in favor of the British. Nevertheless, while the Air Transport Command was reorganizing the supply system for Imphal, the IV Corps rations were cut by a third. But there was a break in the weather, and the rations were built up and fifteen days' reserve accumulated.

Slim was convinced that the Imphal "box" would hold. Messages from Mountbatten in New Delhi and from far-off London counseled an immediate breakthrough. Slim's tactics were based on the simple equation that the more men the Japanese lost in their frantic attacks on Imphal, the fewer would remain to oppose his planned offensive into Burma. The IV Corps, therefore, would hold the plain. He also reckoned that the communications of the enemy's Fifteenth and Thirty-first Divisions would break down when the rains came and both would suffer severe shortages of food and ammunition. Meanwhile the XXXIII Corps under Lieutenant General M. G. N. Stopford would continue its attack to reopen the Kohima–Imphal road.

Stopford was hammering Sato's division. Now the British got a gift from fortune. Sato had ordered a regiment to attack Imphal from the north. The orders for this attack and Sato's other plans for future operations fell into British hands. Stopford increased his pressure on the Fifteenth Division, and Sato, as we have seen, canceled the order for the regiment's diversion.

It was now the last half of April; Mutaguchi saw that his force was well behind schedule. The Thirty-third Division on the southern half of the front launched attack after attack to no avail. Lieutenant General Shinichi Tanaka relieved Lieutenant General Yanagida of this command. It made no difference. The Japanese, harried from the air, short of food, could not break through. Now the monsoon added to their problems. The streams became torrents. Mist shrouded the mountains. The conditions, naturally, were no better for the British and Indians, but they could count on the constant supply of rations and medicines and the reasonably rapid removal of the wounded.

Slim maintained the pressure. Sato began pulling out for a retreat, that soon approximated a rout, toward the Chindwin. By June 22, the first sunny day in weeks, the tanks and infantry of the Second Division had pushed from Kohima to a point eight miles north of Imphal after hard fighting against Sato's rear guards and over a road sown with mines. At 11 A.M. that day, the Fifth Indian and Second British Divisions joined up after three months of fighting. The first convoy of trucks drove into Imphal that night.

The British situation was not all sunlight. The troops, after months of heavy fighting, were very tired. Disease was increasing with the monsoon, especially scrub typhus whose only cure, the doctors said, was careful nursing. Men died in isolated positions in the rain. Blankets had long been discarded, and as Sir Geoffrey Evans writes, "officers and men, their skins often covered with irritating sores, lay down in their saturated clothes to be bitten by leeches."

And then there was the country, always the hostile, unforgiving country. What the North Atlantic was to the seamen of the Battle of the Atlantic, the terrain of Imphal-Kohima was to the British and Indian soldiers who now pressed forward against the retreating Japanese.

The advance called for ascents and descents of mountains up to 4,000 feet high. The way ahead led along narrow mountain tracks hidden by mist. A false step meant death. On the mountains it was intensely cold. The valleys were often unbearably hot, the tracks filled with mud of the consistency of pudding. The rivers fed by the monsoon ran fast and free, and engineers sweated for days to restore damaged bridges or build new ones. For the advanced units there was no supply by land. What they needed to fight and eat was dropped by air—when the pilots could get through.

That the infantry went forward is a tribute to the bonds of confidence and co-operation built by unknown Indians and Britons in 200 years of battles in Asia and Europe. None of the battles in which they had fought together in the past approached this in severity. But they went on—Ghurkas and Englishmen, Sikhs and Scots, Dogras and Welsh.

Slim, although he recognized the state of his command, believed that their *esprit de corps* was capable of one final effort. So the retreating Fifteenth and Thirty-first Japanese Divisions, now very weak in men and ammunition, were harried out of India and into Burma. The Twentieth Indian Division repaid old debts at Ukhrul where the remains of the Fifteenth Division were caught. The Seventh Division hung on Sato's heels, thrusting forward from Kohima and forcing that belligerent general to turn and fight the Twentieth at Ukhrul. The Twenty-third Long-Range Penetration Group of Wingate's forces thrust around the retreating Thirty-first Division.

At the same time, the Seventeenth Division hammered Tanaka's Thirty-third Division at Bishenpur and the Twenty-third Division progressed to the encirclement of Yamamoto at Shenam.

The Japanese, the conquerors of two short years before, were now in a pitiable condition—pitiable that is for anyone who had not seen the bayonetted, wounded, or mutilated corpses in Burmese villages. As the British pushed forward along the Tiddim road and the tracks to the Chindwin, they found all the debris of defeat: corpses without boots and clothing, skeletons lying in the mud, transport columns bombed on the move, burned-out tanks. Rifles, ammunition, and equipment had been thrown away by soldiers too tired, too feeble to carry them. The few prisoners that were taken were either badly wounded or suffering from dysentery, beriberi, or malaria. Despite this, some shook off the terrible effects of the retreat and when the pursuing units came too close, turned and fought with desperate gallantry.

Mutaguchi tried to halt the retreat. Orders streamed out of his headquarters to officers who were dead or to units that no longer existed. Tokyo had been warned. In the middle of May, a staff officer from Imperial General Headquarters, after visiting the Burma front, had started his report with the comment, "The Imphal operations stand little chance of success."

This may have impressed the headquarters. It did not impress Mutaguchi, who even then was goading the Thirty-third Division to smash into Imphal from the south. It failed.

Finally, Mutaguchi and his nominal superior Kawabe concluded that there was no other option but withdrawal to the Chindwin, a conclusion that lesser Japanese officers had reached weeks before. The orders for withdrawal came late. Most of the Japanese divisions by then were in headlong retreat.

Mutaguchi and Kawabe were relieved of their commands, the immemorial penalty for military failure. Pondering that failure, the historian must conclude that fate was against them. Their plans were bold, and in keeping with the *élan* of the Japanese fighting man. They ran risks, but since Pearl Harbor the Japanese had run risks and often won. Imphal-Kohima, like Stalingrad, was a soldiers' battle. The Japanese here encountered for the first time in Southeast Asia a general and troops who were not afraid of them and who had devised tactics that could defeat them.

The price was high. The IV and XXXIII Corps had 12,000 casualties at Imphal and 4,000 at Kohima. The losses on the advance for the British and Indians were smaller but took their toll of combat strength. The saving factor on the Allied side was the superiority of medical care and the rapidity with which the seriously wounded were evacuated by air.

Imphal-Kohima was a battle fought in a far-off corner of the world, unknown to most Americans and familiar to only a few British. The forces engaged, although large for the war in Asia, were small compared to those involved in Stalingrad or the Battle of France. Japanese casualties were inordinately high. Their defeat was close to total.

Like all victories, Imphal-Kohima's importance lay in its impact on the remainder of the campaign. Slim and his subordinates had believed from the start that Burma could be reconquered only after the Japanese were defeated north of the Chindwin and then given no time to reorganize for the defense of the country. The virtual destruction of the Fifteenth Army fulfilled this condition. There were formidable obstacles in his way: the tumultuous character of the country together with the drain of other theaters of operations on his reinforcements and supplies. But the back of Japanese resistance had been broken. The Fourteenth Army crossed the Chindwin against only desultory opposition. Japanese defenses did not stiffen until the British reached the line of the Irrawaddy River.

I had occasion to talk to an elderly Buddhist monk in Mandalay on my way down from Maymyo early in 1967, an amiable prelate who had studied at Chicago University. He had served the Arakan Buddha throughout the war and was still doing business at the old stand in that clamorous and beguiling pagoda. I asked him what he remembered of the battle.

Very little, he said—only that when the remnants of the Fifteenth Army returned, wearied, emaciated, and beaten, they had only two words of explanation. These were "Imphal" and "Kohima." And, he said, whenever the survivors heard the sound of an aircraft or the rumble of a truck, they dove for cover.

XI

"Once More unto the Breach, Dear Friends"

NORMANDY

There was a congenial little dinner party at Rommel's headquarters on the night of June 5, 1944. The field marshal himself was absent. The most uxorious of men, he had halted in Paris to buy shoes for his beloved Lucie and then flown on to Germany. His Chief of Staff, General Hans Speidel, acted as host. The writer Ernst Jünger, Consul General Pfeiffer, who had recently returned from internment in the United States, a Colonel Eric List who had been with the high command, the war correspondent Ritter von Schramm, Speidel's brother-in-law Dr. Horst, and Admiral Friedrich Ruge, Rommel's naval adviser, made up the party.

Ruge recalls that a "highly animated discussion" touched on Italy, Russia, French politics, and "the insufficient development of Hitler's future plans." The cognac was passed. War experiences were exchanged. The atmosphere was one of reasoned confidence.

At about the time they were lighting their cigars, the greatest amphibious operation in the history of war was under way across the Channel. Allied infantrymen retched as their landing craft hit the waves. Pilots and their crews swung themselves into aircraft, hoping that the briefing officers' report that Luftwaffe opposition was likely to be light was accurate. On board the battleships, cruisers, destroyers, and fast-attack craft, bridge officers marked the bomb falls along the coast and readied their weapons for their fire-support role.

At German headquarters, the diners strolled through the park and then continued their talk. Colonel List regaled them with stories about German Field Marshal August von Mackensen of World War I and more contemporary figures like Halder and Field Marshal Walther von Brauchitsch. Pfeiffer and Jünger left about midnight. So did a liaison officer from the Fifteenth Army.

The end of that and many other dinner parties, of four years of largely tranquil occupation, came at 0135 on the morning of June 6, when the German Seventh Army reported parachute drops on the east coast of the Cotentin Peninsula. Then the Fifteenth Army reported other drops from east of Caen to Deauville. Radar signaled the approach of large bomber formations.

The landing in Normandy on June 6 was the second of three acts that together constitute the single most decisive battle in Western Europe. Considered together, the buildup, the landing, and the breakout are the greatest achievement of the American and British forces in the Second World War. After the victory in Normandy, it was obvious that the Germans—no matter how successful their local offensives, such as that in the Ardennes in December; or how stubborn their defensive actions, such as those against the Allies at Arnhem and Nijmegen—could not win or even impose a peace.

Historians of military tactics accord the Normandy landing a special place. The victory was the consequence of the closest co-operation of sea, air and land forces that history records. The organization of the invading units and the planning for their deployment was a triumph in which science, delicate resource management, and deception, never to be underestimated, played significant roles.

Years after the war, General Speidel said, "No other allies could have done it. We would not have listened to the Italians. The French of 1940 believed they were the masters of all military science. The Russians are both too proud and too stupid to learn techniques and tactics from others. But you Americans and the British. You learn from each other. There is a special chemistry there."

ACT ONE—THE BUILDUP

During the third week of June 1940, British infantry splashed onto the French coast from whaleboats. They killed some German sentries, shot up transportation facilities, set fire to a depot, and departed. Thus early in the war and against the greatest odds, the British established the principle of eventual return to the continent from which they had been driven in May and June of that year.

Winston Churchill's inspired establishment of the Combined Operations Command gave the British the means to mount attacks against the German-held coastline. The strength of these assaults increased, but their tactical consequences varied. Bruneval and Saint-Nazaire must be accounted successes. Dieppe, although it wrote lessons in blood, was a failure. Psychologically, the commando operations imposed a heavy burden on the Germans and their French and Belgian collaborators. For four years they could never be certain that the night might not explode into an inferno of naval shells, aerial bombardment, and swarms of black-faced warriors.

By the summer of 1943, the war had swung far enough to the Allied side to begin preparations for a landing in northwest Europe. Since America's entrance into the war, the United States chiefs of staff had believed that only by such a landing and a subsequent campaign to destroy the German armies in the west could the war be won. Their British opposite numbers, reviewing their dwindling manpower resources and recalling the losses of 1914–18, took a less aggressive view. This attitude was supported by an addition, understandable in the historical circumstances, to littoral warfare, to sudden descents on bits of poorly defended coastline where the maximum damage could be done with the minimum of casualties. It had worked against Napoleon, and they had been foolish to abandon it in 1914.

The Americans won the argument. The first planning began in London under General Sir Frederick Morgan, who was designated Chief of Staff Supreme Allied Commander, a title which gave his headquarters the acronym COSSAC. That headquarters could draw on experiences in amphibious warfare in the Mediterranean and the earlier commando assaults on the Atlantic coast of France; what it could not draw on was an ample supply of landing craft.

Morgan's initial plan submitted to General Dwight D. Eisenhower, the Supreme Allied Commander, was written under the restraints imposed on the supply of landing craft. It envisaged a landing by three divisions, two British and one American, on the Normandy coast between Caen and Carentan. Two more divisions were to comprise the follow-up force. The operation was limited in geographical scope and numbers because Morgan had been informed that he could count only on a landing-craft lift for five divisions.

The plan appalled Eisenhower, General Omar N. Bradley, the newly designated commander of the American First Army, and, of course, Montgomery, who was to command the Allied ground forces in the initial attack. Eisenhower insisted that the initial landing must be carried out by five divisions and that his forces must receive the landing craft and other equipment required for an operation of this scope even if this entailed a postponement of the landing and a diversion of landing craft from the Pacific and other theaters. In the end, Eisenhower won. The initial invading force was increased to five divisions, and it was agreed that three airborne divisions would precede the seaborne forces—two American, to be dropped on the extreme right of the landing to secure the exits from Utah Beach, the westernmost landing; and one British, to grab the bridges across the Orne River to the east of the British and Canadian forces.

The logistical preparations for the invasion, from late 1943 until June 1944, were on a scale never before or since seen in warfare. Hundreds of thousands of soldiers with their tanks, guns, trucks, and other equipment had to be concentrated in south and southwest England, some of them transferred out of the Mediterranean theater of operations. At the same time hundreds of thousands of tons of supplies, ammunition, fuel, food, medicines, bandages, and such recondite apparatus as bridging equipment and devices for building airfields had to be assembled in the same area.

In the sense that the equipment was assembled in the quantity and variety demanded, the preparation or buildup for D-Day is unique in history. But this was only part of the preparation.

The descent on the Normandy coast had been planned originally for May. Postponement, because of the landing-craft shortage and the time required to assemble stores, worked in favor of the Allies. As Eisenhower points out, it gave the Allied air forces the month of May, when the weather was good if not superlative, in which to hammer the German communications lines to Normandy.

The air assault was complicated by two problems. Churchill and some of his advisors were concerned that an intensive attack on the French communications center would entail heavy casualties. As it happened, French casualties proved less than had been anticipated. And the damage to the railroads, highways, and bridges that the

Germans would use to reinforce their formations in Normandy was extensive. To a great degree the Allied air forces succeeded in isolating the battlefield.

The second problem was deception.

By late 1943 the Germans had assembled approximately sixty divisions in the Netherlands, Belgium, and France. From the enemy camp, "the other side of the hill," the most likely point for the Anglo-American invasion was in the Pas-de-Calais, roughly twenty miles from the British coast. The construction of obstacles along the beaches, the emplacement of guns, the building of blockhouses, and the flow of German reinforcements to this area indicated that the German high command had decided that the Pas-de-Calais was indeed the probable invasion area. If the strong Fifteenth Army was to be held in that region and not sent to the support of the Seventh Army in Normandy, that German decision would have to be reinforced by Allied deception.

Parenthetically, it is interesting to note that Hitler always believed, despite the professional advice he received from his generals, that the invasion would occur in Normandy. But the generals were convinced that the Allies would land in the area nearest Paris. Their conviction was enhanced by their intelligence reports of the formation of a buildup of a separate army in England to be commanded by General George S. Patton. The artificers of deception excelled themselves. The Germans intercepted voluminous radio traffic dealing with Patton's "invasion forces." Their reconnaissance planes sighted tanks and trucks, all dummies, concentrating for a trans-Channel assault. Shipping to carry the new invasion force was assembled. "Leaks" to German intelligence in the Netherlands, Belgium, and France reflected the preparation of a massive assault. Allied bombers hit the approach to the Pas-de-Calais as hard as they hit those into Normandy.

The German overall preparations to meet the invasion had been invigorated by the appointment of Field Marshal Rommel to command the forces that would counter the Allied landing. Field Marshal Gerd von Rundstedt was appointed Supreme Commander in the west. Although his opinion of Rommel as a strategist was not high —he considered him a good corps commander and no more— Rundstedt left the business of meeting the invasion to Rommel.

The latter was active, imaginative, and confident. At one point he told Hitler, "In my view the enemy is not going to succeed in setting foot on dry ground in these sectors." Having made this prediction, he asked that all armored and mechanized forces in the west be placed under his command. This request was refused him.

Rommel, by his tigerish energy, had already succeeded in improving the coastal defenses by strewing approaches to the beaches with steel obstacles, many of them fitted with mines. The minefields on the beaches had been extended. The number of concrete gun emplacements was increased. But in one essential Rommel failed. He could not persuade Hitler to deploy the German panzer divisions to points where they would be in position to launch immediate attacks against the invading forces. This must be reckoned one of Hitler's major tactical misjudgments of the war.

On both sides of the sea, the long, arduous process of preparation was finished. Eisenhower had not received all he thought he needed —no general ever does—but he had enough. Rommel, as always, was supremely confident, although he would have liked those armored divisions farther forward. Now a new element, the weather, intervened.

Act Two—THE LANDING

June 5 had been selected as D-Day. But when Eisenhower and his staff assembled on the morning of June 4, the outlook was forbidding. The waves and the winds were high. The clouds were low. This meant that naval gunfire would be ineffective, air support sporadic at best, and the movement of the smaller landing craft to the beaches extremely difficult. There was a difference of opinion in the Allied command. Montgomery opted for proceeding with the landing. Admiral Sir Bertram Ramsay, the naval commander, believed that the problems caused by the weather could be overcome. Air Marshal Tedder, Eisenhower's deputy, disagreed.

The decision was Eisenhower's. After a worried weighing of the factors involved, he decided that the invasion should be delayed. The landing craft at sea, the warships assembled for their support, the thousands of aircraft in Britain, were condemned to a twenty-four-hour wait. Such delays in war, especially in the launching of a major operation to which hearts and minds have been directed for months, can have a serious psychological impact.

Meanwhile the wind and the rain were rising at Eisenhower's advance headquarters on the south coast. In a gloomy mood the brass assembled for another conference at 3:30 A.M. on the morning of June 5. The oracle was Group Captain J. M. Stagg of the RAF, who appeared this once, and to what effect, in history. His report was that the weather on the French coast would be so bad that day that an invasion could have ended in disaster. That was enough to confirm Eisenhower's wisdom in canceling the operation. But Stagg had more to say.

By the morning of June 6, a period of relatively good weather would follow, lasting for perhaps thirty-six hours. The long-term prediction was not good. But Stagg was confident there would be this short period of good weather between the end of the present storm and the advent of the next bad-weather period.

These are the moments when command is a lonely place. Eisenhower had to consider the danger of leaving the first landing wave open to heavy German counterattack without the means of reinforcement because of bad weather. Against this, he had to weigh the effect of the postponement of the whole vast enterprise until the next period in which the tides would be favorable.

To the Supreme Commander, delay was the greater risk. At 4:15 in the morning of June 5, he announced the decision to go ahead with the operation on June 6. His subordinates filed out into the misty morning to send the messages that would unleash the soldiers, sailors, and airmen.

Men and officers alike welcomed the "Go" signal. This was the end of training, of instruction—above all, of waiting. The paratroops clambered into their aircraft. The antisubmarine forces redoubled their watch against U-boats at the eastern and western limits of the invasion area. The pilots checked their bomb racks and their guns.

Across the Channel, the Germans spent a quiet day on June 5. The commander in chief of Army Group B was back in Germany. Von Rundstedt was closeted in his headquarters. The wind and the rain beat against the barracks and rattled the shutters of the cafés in the little towns along the coast.

"The Tommies won't come in this," a German sergeant said to a French policeman in Arromanches. At Rommel's headquarters they concluded that this was not the sort of weather that would encourage Americans to fight battles. Except for those Germans who had been in North Africa and Sicily, they had a low opinion of the American fighting man.

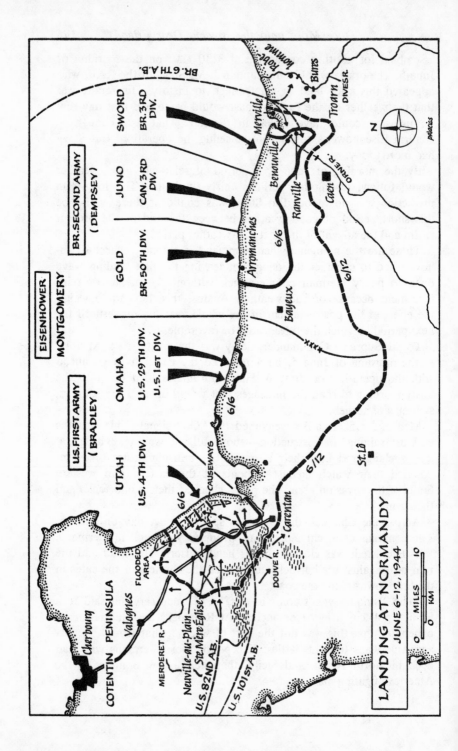

LANDING AT NORMANDY
JUNE 6–12, 1944

See the battlefield from the left, or eastern, Allied flank to the right, or western. See it as the paratroopers' planes crossed it in the first strike of the invasion. Strips of beach of varying width. Here the beach merges into green fields. There it is confronted by a bluff or a succession of knolls. Nestling into the coastline are the blockhouses. Little knots of houses huddle in the landscape, often along the coast, sometimes farther inland. See the battlefield as they saw it from the landing craft creeping toward the coast. A long shadow in the quickening light, along which there are pinpoints of sharp light and here and there enormous bursts of yellow and red followed by pillars of smoke.

If we follow the first action from the left to the right, it begins with the British Sixth Airborne Division, which had three missions: to seize the bridges over the Orne River between Caen and the sea, to deny the Germans the use of the country between the Orne and the Dives Rivers, and to destroy a German artillery battery at Merville which commanded the left flank of the British landings.

These missions were entrusted to two brigades of the division. The division was commanded by Major General Richard N. Gale, inevitably known to his troops as "Windy," a powerful, red-faced man whose *"pukka Sahib"* looks covered a sharp mind and a taste for military adventure.

The affair went well. The bridges at Benouville and Ranville, over the Orne, were taken. Elsewhere there was confusion in the darkness. Some gliders were landed in the wrong areas. Some paratroopers went astray. But the bridges over the Orne had been captured, and roadblocks on both sides were established. The three bridges over the Dives at Troarn, Bures, and Robehomme had been cut.

The battery at Merville was a tougher proposition. Only half the strength of the three companies to be used dropped within a mile of the rendezvous. They had no mine detectors, marking tapes, or other equipment. In the darkness ahead lay the four-gun battery in steel-doored, concrete emplacements six inches thick, surrounded by barbed wire, mines, and an antitank ditch. These were the British of 1944. They marched off, all 150 of them, with their personal weapons and one Vickers machine gun.

A reconnaissance party cut gaps in the wire, found paths through the minefields, and neutralized the inevitable booby traps. The original force, now reinforced by troops from two more gliders which had been towed virtually into the battle, joined those fighting the Germans in the outer defenses. The main gate was rushed successfully. The garrison was overcome, the guns put out of action. At 4:45 A.M. the success signal was fired and a weary signals officer took a ruffled pigeon from his pocket and sent it off to England with the news.

Simultaneously the United States Eighty-second and 101st Airborne Divisions were engaged on the far right of the Allied line in a more ambitious, and in some respects more demanding, operation. Twice as many troops would be dropped. The countryside was not the relatively open terrain east of the Orne but the small fields encompassed by hedgerows which characterize the *bocage* of Normandy. There were more Germans in the area, and they had been instructed to expect an airborne attack.

The divisions' mission was part of the overall American plan. The 101st was ordered to secure the western exits of the flooded area behind Utah Beach and the line of the Douve River to the north of Carentan, to capture that town and link with the troops emerging from Omaha Beach. The Eighty-second was to drop farther inland astride the Merderet River and seize Sainte-Mère-Eglise and the bridgeheads over the river, thus helping the forces landed at Utah Beach to drive across the neck of the Cotentin Peninsula.

Just about everything that could go wrong did go wrong for the Eighty-second and the 101st. Their aircraft took a more intricate route than those carrying the Sixth Division. These had flown straight from England. After the American transports turned east near the Channel Islands and crossed the west coast of the Cotentin Peninsula, they met heavy antiaircraft fire and thick clouds. The tightly knit formations of the 432 carriers of the 101st broke up. As they neared their drop zones, more flak forced further dispersal.

General Maxwell Taylor, commanding the 101st, had 6,600 paratroopers under his command. Most were scattered in small groups, well behind the causeways they had come to seize. About sixty planeloads had been dropped from eight to twenty miles beyond their drop zones. Still others were strewn in the lagoons behind Utah Beach. The manner in which the 101st sorted itself out, then attacked sharply toward the causeways that led from Utah, and then struck toward Carentan to seal off the town and block German reinforcements speaks highly for the division's leadership and combat morale.

General Matthew Ridgway's Eighty-second encountered comparable difficulties. The plan called for the deployment of two thirds of the divisions eight miles inland on the Merderet River where it parallels Utah Beach. The other third was to be dropped east of the river astride the main road from Cherbourg with its German garrison on the beaches.

The Eighty-second's luck was as bad as that of the 101st. Most of the elements were scattered in the drop. Consequently, the better part of the first day was occupied in assembling combat units. The Eighty-second, however, was able to establish a force at Sainte-Mère-Église. The presence of the unit there and some brisk fighting at Neuville-au-Plain served to halt elements of the Ninety-first German Division which was advancing on Sainte-Mère-Église on the Cherbourg–Carentan road. The airborne assault in history's perspective did not do all that was planned. But it did disorganize the German defenders and check their first move to the beaches.

At the time the British call "first light," those beaches were the center of the invasion. The vanguard of 4,000 ships was nearing the Normandy coast. The German defenses on and behind the beaches were being pounded by the first hundreds of tons of bombs dropped by the 14,600 sorties made that day by the Allied air forces. Beyond the minesweepers clearing lanes in the minefields and the destroyers providing close gun support, the guns of battleships shook the air. Their names conjure up memories of long-forgotten sea fights across the world—*Texas* and *Warspite, Nevada* and *Black Prince, Montcalm* and *Valiant*. Their thunderous, accurate pounding of the German shore positions was a mighty requiem for the battleships, a dying breed.

The submarine branch of the German navy may be said to have suffered its most important tactical defeat on D-Day. Grouped off the coast of Normandy was the greatest target a U-boat captain could wish for. But a submarine attack never had a hope due to the work of Ultra, the British system which enabled them and their American allies to read the German message traffic. By the middle of May, Eisenhower's headquarters, through Ultra, knew the details of the German naval plan to attack the thousands of warships and landing craft involved in the invasion.

About forty U-boats were ordered to assail the invasion force. The whole of the threatened area was blanketed by ten naval attack groups covering the western approaches to the Channel. The coverage included surveillance by aircraft of every square mile of the sea area every thirty minutes, day and night. By July 6, a month after D-Day, eighteen of the forty-three submarines sent against the Allied armada had been sunk.

Now, as the landing craft lurched ashore, came the decisive moment. From the British Sword Beach on the extreme left to the American Utah Beach on the right, the infantry struggled ashore. Thousands of aircraft and hundreds of warships were involved. But D-Day was an infantryman's fight and an infantryman's victory.

Initial success varied with the beach. The constant was the tenacity of the German defense. Sword Beach offered the greatest prize— the city of Caen. But the Third British Division, although it plunged inland, was halted when it ran into the Twenty-first Panzer Division. Thus early in the battle, the Germans established their determination to hold Caen, and the road to Paris, with armor. Had Rommel known it, this was exactly what the Allies hoped their enemy would do.

The Canadian Third Division, on the British right landing at Juno Beach, smashed inland for seven miles to within sight of the road to Caen. But by evening, it had been halted by a combination of stiffening German resistance and its own weariness.

The most dramatic but, in the end, least important tactical advance was made by the British Fiftieth Division. This veteran unit landed on Gold Beach, met heavy opposition, but ground forward and took Arromanches and Bayeux.

The British had made it. But like everyone else on the Allied side, they were not complacent. "If Rommel can throw in a couple of panzer divisions," a tired British infantry officer said, "we'll have hell's own time holding them."

The British position, uncertain though it may have seemed to the men on the ground, was a great deal superior to that of the American troops on Omaha Beach. There the First and Twenty-ninth Divisions had landed in discouraging disorder. Only the bravery and the efficiency of company and battalion officers restored the situation and led the infantry forward from the death-strewn sands.

Omaha was the critical point of the invasion. A repulse there would have cut off the American Fourth Division on Utah Beach from the British beaches to the east. But the soldiers responded to galvanizing leadership, and by nightfall the two divisions had a firm, if vulnerable beachhead ashore.

The Fourth Division on Utah Beach encountered stiff German opposition. But after some hours of confused fighting—and it is well to remember that in an attack *all* fighting is confused—the Fourth managed to link up with the Eighty-second and 101st Airborne Divisions and establish a beachhead four miles wide and nine miles deep.

"Stiff opposition." What does a phrase like that mean more than a third of a century later? It means that the German blockhouses, despite the bombing and the naval shelling, still spouted fire. It means that well behind the forward line of defense, the German artillery was zeroing in on the Allied infantry despite the attentions paid the guns by the bombers. It means that here and there inland from the beaches the German infantry, *Landser Fritz* and his comrades, were picking off the first figures to storm off the beaches.

Look at it now—so many thousands of air sorties, so many thousands of bombs, so many rounds of naval shells, intricate deception plans, and the assistance of French guerrilla forces. It all seems preordained. But on the night of June 6, when Rommel had returned to his headquarters after a hurried trip from Germany, it did not look like victory for the Allies.

Yet victory it was. In the next six days the Allies hammered their way inland and established a beachhead eighty miles long and ten miles deep. Into this, they poured eight more combat divisions. The Allied air forces continued to bomb German positions and to strafe every unit that had the temerity to advance along the roads in daylight. The battleships out at sea directed their fire at one German stronghold after another. Their shells traveling overhead sounded like railroad trains.

The losses were far less than had been anticipated—11,000 casualties, including 2,500 dead. The First and Twenty-ninth suffered about 3,000 killed, wounded, and missing on D-Day at Omaha Beach.

Could the outcome have been different? Rommel's idolators believe so. Had the field marshal been there on the morning of the invasion instead of back in Germany with his beloved Lucie, he would have hurled the three panzer divisions available at the invading forces and defeated them on the beaches. That is their story.

But would he have done this? Rommel, like all the German commanders with the single exception of Hitler who, by a streak of prescience, believed that Normandy and not the Pas-de-Calais was the

Allied objective, was convinced that the main attack would come against the Fifteenth Army guarding that coastline. So Rommel, when he telephoned General Alfred Jodl his impression "that the enemy is going to make another invasion focal point elsewhere" was, for once, taking the orthodox German military position.

Rommel's defenders and those German historians who have dealt with the campaign appear to miss the one decisive element in any plans for a German counterattack by a panzer company or a panzer corps. As long as the Allies ruled the air, no concentrations of troops and armor could be made without inviting heavy air attack.

The German alignment after seven days of battle played into the hands of Montgomery, who then commanded all the ground forces, and General Omar Bradley, commanding the United States First Army. The British had been assigned in the overall plan the spectacularly unrewarding job—as far as international attention was concerned—of attacking and attacking and attacking at Caen. The object was to pin down the German armor. After the fall of Cherbourg to the Americans, the time was ripe for a breakout. As Bradley notes, "The basic strategy for this attack out of the lodgement had been written into the basic OVERLORD plan . . . while Montgomery held the pivot at Caen, the whole Allied line was to wheel eastward."

On the extreme right, the American First Army was to smash south out of the Cotentin Peninsula past Avranches and cut the neck of the Brittany Peninsula. Once the deep-water ports of Brittany had been secured—it is surprising in retrospect to see how easy a task this then was considered—the Americans were to turn east. Anchoring their right flank on the Loire River and protected by ubiquitous Allied fighters and bombers, they would drive east to the Seine-Orleans Gap south of Paris.

ACT THREE—THE BREAKOUT

On the maps and in the confident atmosphere of headquarters, the whole operation looked like what the RAF would have called, "a piece of cake." But the commanders, especially Bradley, were beginning to see the problems. The turn in the axis of attack from south out of the beachheads to the east was essential. But it was equally important to this and future offensives that the ports be captured. Cherbourg, stoutly held and extensively mined and booby-trapped by the Germans, had been taken and was being readied for Allied transports. But the support of the multiplying thousands of soldiers, tanks, jeeps, and trucks and of the airfields blossoming within the lodgement would depend on the use of more and better ports.

On their side the Allies had mobility and firepower expressed as much by the air forces as by artillery. Montgomery was concentrating them both on the stubborn German defense of Caen. The most ambitious of commanders, he relegated himself and his army to the most unrewarding but, in some ways, the most important part of the Allied plan.

Bradley was searching for a breakthrough point beyond which he could exploit his superior mobility. His troops were grinding forward a few hundred yards a day through the *bocage* country against determined German resistance. He had to find a soft spot in the enemy defenses beyond the Carentan marshes while avoiding the German strongpoints.

The first attempt to break out of the bridgehead was unsuccessful. Bradley sent General Troy Middleton and his VIII Corps into an attack that had as its axis the west-coast road on the Cotentin Peninsula from La-Haye-du-Puits to Coutances. Bradley's idea was that if his forces broke into Coutances from the west-coast road, the Germans, fearful of an enveloping attack from Saint-Lô, would be forced to pull back, allowing the First Army to reach the Saint-Lô–Coutances road from which the main attack would be launched.

VIII Corps attacked on July 3. By July 14 the operation was called off. The corps had made about 12,000 yards, advancing through minefields against heavy German opposition. The Americans had to find another way out.

Montgomery still was in nominal command of the Allied ground forces. Bradley recorded that the Briton exercised his authority "with wisdom, tolerance, and restraint," noting that he could not have had "a more tolerant or judicious commander."

The British attacks toward Caen were having the desired effect. Seven of the eight panzer divisions on the Normandy front had been drawn to the British sector. Meanwhile Bradley and his staff were searching for the means to break out of the American position. Clearly attracting the German panzers to the British front served little purpose unless the Americans could profit by it and were loosed to exploit their mobility and armored strength.

By July 10 the final operational plan was in its first stages. They

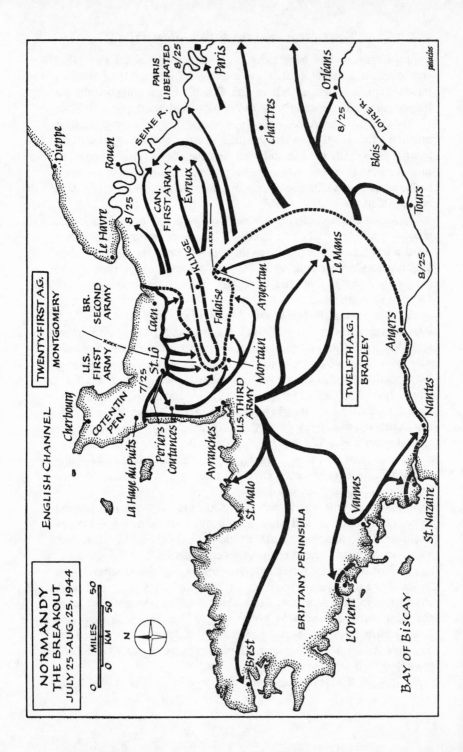

NORMANDY
THE BREAKOUT
JULY 25 - AUG. 25, 1944

MILES 0 — 50
KM 0 — 50

N

ENGLISH CHANNEL

TWENTY-FIRST A.G.
MONTGOMERY

U.S. FIRST ARMY | BR. SECOND ARMY

Dieppe

Rouen

Le Havre
8/25

SEINE R.

PARIS LIBERATED
8/25

Paris

Chartres

Orléans
8/25

LOIRE R.

Blois

Tours
8/25

CAN. FIRST ARMY

Évreux

KLUGE
xxxx

Falaise

Argentan

Le Mans

Cherbourg

COTENTIN PEN.

St. Lô
7/25

Caen

Périers
Coutances

La Haye du Puits

Avranches

U.S. THIRD ARMY

Mortain

TWELFTH A.G.
BRADLEY

Angers

St. Malo

Vannes

Nantes

St. Nazaire

BRITTANY PENINSULA

L'Orient

Brest

BAY OF BISCAY

palacios

called it COBRA. The jump-off line was to be the Saint-Lô–Periers road. As the Americans saw it, the Germans were to be paralyzed by heavy bombing. Two infantry divisions would then attack. One was to hold the line open on the right. The second, with its flank on the Vire River south of Saint-Lô, would hold open the other shoulder. Once the gap had been opened and the flanks secured, Bradley intended to push two armored divisions and one motorized infantry division through the hole toward Coutances. If successful, the infantry would round up the German units drawn from seven divisions opposing Middleton's advance.

Although carpet bombing was not novel, no one had used it on the scale planned by Bradley and the air commanders. An important risk for the Americans was the possibility of inaccurate bombing that would hit the attacking troops. To increase the safety factor, the soldiers of General J. Lawton Collins's VII Corps, which was to deliver the attack, were to be withdrawn 1,500 yards behind the road marking the jump-off point. The Allied air command informed Bradley that 2,246 aircraft would be assigned to the mission—1,500 heavy bombers, 396 medium bombers, and 350 fighter-bombers. They were to be directed against five square miles of hedgerows and tiny fields beyond the road.

The air attack did not go according to plan. Bradley believed that the bombers would follow the Periers road. But the air force found this course time-consuming. The bombers flew in over the heads of the attacking Americans. When the bombs fell, both the Ninth and Thirtieth Infantry Divisions suffered heavy casualties and Lieutenant General Lesley J. McNair was killed.

The infantry began their advance across the bomb-pitted fields on the afternoon of July 25. The destruction that met the advancing Americans was on an unprecedented scale—burned-out tanks, dead Germans, fields and roads literally pulverized. By the evening of July 27, the First Division had fought its way into Coutances and the VIII Corps was moving delicately through the minefields that were strewn across its front.

On Aug. 1 the First Army had been split into the First Army and the Third Army, with the redoubtable General George S. Patton taking command of the latter. General Courtney H. Hodges assumed command of the First Army, and Bradley became commander of the Twelfth Army Group.

The whole line went forward. Two armored divisions rounded the bend at Avranches and led the VIII Corps toward the Brittany ports. The Germans, uncomfortably aware of the worsening of their position, had begun to move some of their armor from the British to the American front. But they were too late. The German left flank had been torn free with an ominous gap in the Avranches area.

Field Marshal Gunther von Kluge, who had replaced Von Rundstedt as commander in the west, had two options. He could withdraw his left flank and establish a new line behind which the Germans could begin a retreat to the Seine. Or he could attack toward Avranches, hoping to plug the hole and again pin his left flank on the sea. Either option was studded with difficulties. An orderly withdrawal was unlikely in view of the Allies' air superiority. Movement would be possible only by night. In retrospect this seems the wiser course. Air power operating effectively by day can disrupt a movement and inflict heavy losses. But it cannot halt it. On the other hand the alternative, the attack toward Avranches, held out prospects of restoring the German line close to its original positions and cutting off the American divisions that had sped toward Brittany.

Von Kluge chose the second option. He and his staff planners saw it as the more rewarding operation. They clearly underestimated the strength of the Americans in numbers of men, tanks, trucks, and the power of the Allied air forces. Nor did they understand the mobility of the American armies. They decided to strike. This decision cost them France.

About 1 A.M. on the morning of Aug. 7, five panzer and SS divisions attacked toward Mortain twenty miles east of the Bay of Mont Saint-Michel. The armor had come from the British front. Some of the infantry had been taken from the idle forces still awaiting an Allied attack in the Pas-de-Calais.

The German attack hit the Thirtieth Infantry Division, and within a few hours had penetrated its forward lines and cut off one of the battalions of the 120th Regiment. Much was at stake. If the Germans broke through to Avranches, they would cut the supply lines of the twelve American divisions that had passed through the gap.

The decision was up to Bradley. Should he play it safe and call back four divisions to strengthen the First Army's defenses at Mortain? Or should he hurl the divisions against the German flank in the hope of destroying the Seventh Army? Bradley, in his own words, decided to "shoot the works" and attack with his four divisions.

It was a very near thing. The German attack had opened a hole in the American line. The Thirty-fifth Division was taken from Patton and used to plug the gap. Oddly the Germans, without adequate air reconnaissance, failed to discover the gap. Had they diverted their tanks a few thousand yards to the south, they might have pushed through to Avranches.

The Thirtieth Division, under constant attack, held its ground. The German panzer units continued their attacks with their usual tenacity. On the second day they advanced with infantry clinging to the armor while the fifty-six-millimeter shells of the American antitank guns bounded off the tanks like peas from a blow gun.

Now the Allied air forces intervened. A mixed force of rocket-firing Typhoons of the RAF and American P-47's dealt the panzers a critical blow. Rockets were new on the Western European front, and the Typhoons swooped in to deposit their missiles under the bellies of the panzers. The P-47's then followed with their bombs. The infantry of the Thirtieth held on. The battle was won.

The consequences were enormous. At the time there was a furor over whether or not the famous Falaise Gap could have been closed by more energetic British and Canadian action and the whole of the German forces surrounded and destroyed. The argument over this point has engaged historians for nearly forty years.

Bradley, whose clear insight into the battle never faltered, knew that the Germans were beaten. Montgomery, no less the professional, held the same opinion. And on the other side, Ruge wrote somberly that the Allied advance could not be stopped, only delayed.

From the American breakout in Normandy, followed by the British push through Caen, a cornucopia of successes fell on the Allies. Patton pushed eastward. General Sir Miles Dempsey and the Second British Army drove north to Brussels. Paris and the Belgian capital were liberated by the Americans. The Germans withdrew toward their frontier, fighting stubbornly but taking heavy punishment from the Allied air forces.

In the wake of the Normandy campaign, one serious strategic question arose. It has not been settled satisfactorily to this day. Could the Allies, either in the south or in the north, have driven on into Germany and total victory in the late summer of 1944?

The arguments, pro and con, have been set out by the surviving generals and military experts. The question remains open. No matter. It was a famous victory.

XII

MacArthur and the Chinese Puzzle

CHONGCHON

The battalion headed for the Yalu River expected to meet nothing more serious on its front than the remnants of North Korean formations broken in the fighting of the last six weeks. The unit was from the Second Regiment of the Sixth Republic of Korea (ROK) Division. It moved confidently northward on Oct. 25, 1950. The cold was increasing, but there was a general feeling among the soldiers of this and other United Nations units that the war was almost over. Certainly it would be finished before the cold of the Asian winter settled over the battlefields.

The troops came under heavy fire south of Pukchin. The battalion was destroyed, not by North Koreans but by soldiers of the People's Republic of China.

That half-forgotten action in the desolation of North Korea was the first in a chain of events that would culminate in the defeat of the United Nations forces, largely American, on the Chongchon River. The immediate tactical consequence was the retirement of the American and other UN forces to the south and the transformation of the UN effort from a triumphant offensive to a dogged defense whose only solution, it became depressingly apparent, lay in a negotiated peace.

The battle on the Chongchon had other reverberations. The Chinese emerged from it as a primary Asian power, relatively weak in modern weapons but flexible, resourceful, and courageous in battle. Peking could no longer be considered a military appendage of Moscow. In the next twenty years, recognition of China as the major military power among Asian states influenced continually and at times decisively the policies of Washington, Moscow, Tokyo, New Delhi, and half a dozen other capitals.

The fighting in the last three months of 1950 also eroded to a considerable extent the towering military reputation of General Douglas MacArthur, the UN commander in chief, who on Oct. 21, proclaimed, "The war is very definitely coming to an end shortly." The results of that fighting and what now appears to be MacArthur's inability or unwillingness to understand its implications led circuitously but clearly to his removal in 1951 by President Harry S Truman after the most serious trial of strength in American history between the political and the military powers.

The *hubris* of MacArthur after he confounded his critics and landed successfully at Inchon, the failure of United States intelligence to estimate accurately the capabilities of the Chinese forces, the differences of opinion among government departments in Washington over Chinese intentions, and the skill shown by the Chinese in hiding the movements of very large forces into jump-off positions all contributed in varying measures to the UN defeat.

The Inchon landing was one of MacArthur's familiar military masterpieces. It had its genesis as early as June, when he visited Korea and found that the South Korean forces were in full retreat and that significant American reinforcements had not yet arrived. He realized that the advancing North Korean forces would find themselves at the end of long and vulnerable lines of supply and that a landing in their rear in the Inchon-Seoul region would disrupt those lines, many of which fed through that area. As the concept hardened in his mind, the general also recognized the considerable psychological advantage of retaking the South Korean capital of Seoul.

From the outset, the Inchon landing plan inspired strong opposition from the U. S. Navy and the Marine Corps. The marine division was to make the main attack on the city, with its right flank covered by the Seventh Army division. The navy was given the task of landing the ground forces in conditions which its officers outlined with gloomy relish. The sea approach to the harbor was through a narrow channel with a five-knot current, a channel dotted with rocks and shoals. The tidal range was enormous and, at the ebb, the harbor was transformed into a giant mud flat. The port facilities were inadequate. There were other tactical difficulties, not the least of which was the withdrawal of the marine division from the forces in the south.

All these arguments were well ventilated at a meeting at MacArthur's Tokyo headquarters on Aug. 23. This meeting was attended by General Lawton Collins, the Army Chief of Staff, and by Admiral Forrest Sherman, the Chief of Naval Operations, as well as by MacArthur and his principal subordinates. Collins was worried over the division of available ground forces in the face of a superior enemy. Rear Admiral James H. Doyle, a staff officer, rehearsed the navy's misgivings, including the navigational dangers of a landing.

MacArthur, puffing on the inevitable corncob pipe, heard them out and then defended his plan.

"The very arguments you have made to me as to the impracticabilities involved," he said, "will tend to insure for me the element of surprise. For the enemy commander will reason that no one would be so brash as to make such an attempt." With characteristic hyperbole, he ended, "I can almost hear the ticking of the second-hand of destiny. We must act now or we will die . . ."

They acted and they won. Inchon was taken with relatively light casualties. Seoul was retaken. But in that victory, one can conjecture, lay the germs of MacArthur's overweening confidence that led to disaster on the Chongchon.

At any rate, when the general met President Truman on Wake Island on Oct. 15, MacArthur was all confidence.

"The general assured me that the victory was won in Korea," Truman wrote later. "He also informed me that the Chinese Communists would not attack . . ."

Later MacArthur said that although there was very little chance the Chinese would enter the war, they might be able to get fifty or sixty thousand men into Korea, but since they had no air force, "there would be the greatest slaughter."

If MacArthur was confident, so was Truman. He returned to Washington, believing that the general was loyal to the President, to the Administration, and to United States foreign policy. But even as the President flew eastward in the *Independence,* MacArthur's forces were taking the first steps northward to the Yalu and defeat.

Pyongyang, the North Korean capital, fell to UN forces on Oct. 19. The enemy fled northward toward the Yalu. MacArthur, anticipating permission to cross the thirty-eighth parallel which divided the country, began to prepare for the conquest of North Korea. Very little attention was paid to the possibility of Chinese intervention.

There were ample reasons to consider that possibility, even without the warnings that began to emanate from Peking. American forces on the Yalu River would be on the border of Manchuria, China's most important industrial area. Its cities, industries, and mines would be within easy range of American bombers in Korea. But there were even more tangible reasons for apprehension.

After the success of the Inchon landing, Chinese statements about the progress of UN forces toward North Korea became more strident. It was clear that an advance into the region south of the Yalu would be intolerable to the Chinese. After South Korean forces had crossed the parallel, Chou En-lai, the Prime Minister, told K. M. Panikkar, the Indian Ambassador to China, that if American troops followed them, China would fight. When Pyongyang fell, the Chinese government broadcast a warning that the Chinese people could not tolerate an American invasion of the north because it would present a direct challenge to China's security.

Today these warnings seem reasonably clear and sufficient to give a prudent government pause for thought. But the China of 1950 was not the China of the 1980s. There was concern in Washington, but also a good deal of doubt. Ambassador Panikkar's message was transmitted to MacArthur, but Truman noted that the ambassador in the past had "played the game of the Chinese Communists fairly regularly, so that his statement could not be taken as that of an impartial observer. It might very well be no more than a relay of Communist propaganda."

The two governments had no diplomatic relations, no meeting ground. The Chinese believed they had to go to war to protect Manchuria. The Americans believed that to uphold the principle of collective security, UN forces must occupy North Korea and unite the country. When two governments hold such different positions and when each is inflamed with suspicion of the motives of the other, there is little room for brokerage.

Another element was the inadequacy of military intelligence. The withdrawal from Japan in 1948 of experienced intelligence officers had stripped the Far East Command, which supplied the Department of Defense with the bulk of its information, of many of its best men. Among other weaknesses was an alarming lack of trained photo-interpreters to evaluate reconnaissance photographs. In view of the Chinese ability to move by night and hide by day, such photographs might not have provided much. But they could have provided something.

MacArthur, as we have noted, had divided his forces for the Inchon landing. He tried it again for the drive to the Yalu. Not only were they divided, but the division was a particularly awkward one. The X Corps was to be carried by sea hundreds of miles around the Korean Peninsula to Wonsan on the east coast and to occupy northeastern Korea. The Eighth Army was to remain on the west coast for the drive into northwest Korea. The two commands would be separated by a gap of between twenty and fifty miles. MacArthur assumed, wrongly, that the terrain in the gap was too rough to permit large-scale operations. Both the Eighth Army and X Corps had to divert strong formations to safeguard these open flanks.

Whatever the strength and importance of the guerrilla activity, the separation of the two forces violated the doctrine of unity of command sacred not only to the United States Army but to all armies. MacArthur's intransigence in taking this risk survived opposition from three staff major generals and from General Walton H. Walker, the commander of the Eighth Army. His reasoning was that the separation of the two commands was dictated by geography. The Taebaek range, the spine of southern and central Korea, ran north and south and made an advance on two axes the only means of overcoming the geographical difficulty.

The X Corps was withdrawn from the Eighth Army on Oct. 7 and embarked. There followed a journey of 800 miles by sea to Wonsan, where the main body arrived on Oct. 19. The corps had to wait a week aboard ship until the navy cleared the minefields laid by the North Koreans.

The operational plan for a two-pronged advance to the north exacerbated MacArthur's feud with Washington. A directive from the Joint Chiefs of Staff of Sept. 27 had forbidden the use of non-Korean forces in the provinces contiguous to China and the Soviet Union. MacArthur flouted the directive on Oct. 24, when he ordered his commanders to "drive forward with all speed and full utilization of their forces." That day the Joint Chiefs complained that MacArthur's orders were "not in consonance" with their directive of the previous month. MacArthur replied that Secretary of Defense George C. Marshall had said that he was to be "unhampered" in his operations and that, in any case, the weakness of the ROK forces under his command justified his orders to push the American units forward.

Once again MacArthur had defied a clear order from the Joint Chiefs. Once again, he got away with it.

Now the taste of victory was in every mouth. Walker's motorized columns crossed the Chongchon at Sinanju and the Twenty-fourth Division of the I Corps struck westward along the coast road to the Yalu. By Nov. 1, the Twenty-first Regiment of the division was only eighteen miles from Sinuiju on the Yalu. Two British battalions followed and a third, the Middlesex Battalion, spilled into the Kuryong River valley about forty miles south of the frontier. The South Korean Sixth Division of the ROK II Corps drove west toward Chosan, its objective on the Yalu. On the morning of Oct. 26, a reconnaissance platoon of the division's Seventh Regiment was on the Yalu at Chosan. No other UN unit reached the river.

The first sign of trouble was the Chinese attack on the Koreans south of Pukchin. This was followed by the defeat of the Sixth Division by the Chinese in the Huichon-Onjong area and the dispersal of the Seventh Regiment after it had been surrounded by the enemy.

General Walker divined that this was no minor counterattack. The collapse of the Korean II Corps left his flank open. A regiment of the U. S. First Cavalry Division and another from the First ROK Division were sent to help. The American regiment was overwhelmed at Unsan in fierce fighting between Nov. 1 and Nov. 3.

The UN commander was now anxious to withdraw his forces behind the Chongchon and to hold bridgeheads in the Sinanju-Anju area in the event he was able to resume the offensive. Gradually the positions were stabilized and the Chinese offensive slackened. They had, however, begun to feed Mig-15's into the battle. The first jet air battle of history was fought on Nov. 8 when an F-80 of the American Fifth Air Force shot down a Mig-15 over Sinanju.

To the east, the Chinese had also been active and successful. The ROK Third Division ran into a Chinese force and fought a heavy action in the Sudong area. The Seventh Marine Regiment moved to the Koreans' assistance and fought a five-day battle with Chinese troops in the Sudong–Chinhung-ni area. But, as they had in the

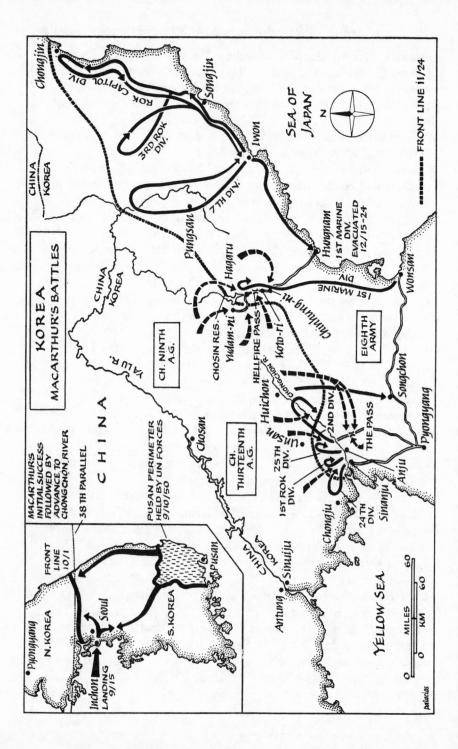

KOREA
MACARTHUR'S BATTLES

SEA OF JAPAN

N

FRONT LINE 11/24

CHINA
KOREA

Chongjin

ROK CAPITOL DIV.

Songjin

3RD ROK DIV.

IWON

7TH DIV.

Pungsan

Hungnam
1ST MARINE DIV.
EVACUATED
12/15-24

Wonsan

1ST MARINE DIV.

CH. NINTH A.G.

Hagaru

CHOSIN RES.

Yudam-ni

HELLFIRE PASS

Koto-ri

Chinhung-ni

EIGHTH ARMY

Songchon

VALU R.

CHINA
KOREA

Huichon

CHONGCHON R.

2ND DIV.

THE PASS

Pyongyang

CH. THIRTEENTH A.G.

Unsan

1ST ROK 25TH DIV.

Chosan

24TH DIV.

Sinanju

Anju

MACARTHUR'S
INITIAL SUCCESS
FOLLOWED BY
ADVANCE TO
CHONGCHON RIVER

38TH PARALLEL

PUSAN PERIMETER
HELD BY UN FORCES
9/10/50

Chongju

Sinuiju

Antung

YELLOW SEA

FRONT LINE
10/1

Pyongyang

N. KOREA

Seoul

PUSAN

S. KOREA

Inchon
LANDING
9/15

MILES
0   60

0   60
KM

palacios

west, the Chinese suddenly halted operations and withdrew to the shelter of the hills.

The initial Chinese intervention in the war, which lasted from Oct. 25 until Nov. 7, raised questions that neither MacArthur and his commanders nor Truman and his advisors were able to answer. How many Chinese were there in North Korea? Was this intervention, as MacArthur believed, only an attempt to save the shattered North Korean forces and hold part of the country? Or was it the beginning of a massive Chinese offensive?

Blinded by his own overweening optimism and relying on insufficient and inaccurate intelligence, MacArthur was slow to grasp the size of the Chinese forces opposing the UN troops. The intelligence estimate on Nov. 1 was that there were about 60,000 Chinese in North Korea. Actually, at that point in the Chinese deployment, there were about 180,000.

During the last half of Oct. 18, Chinese divisions had moved across the Yalu and into positions in North Korea. They were undiscovered by intelligence and unnoted by the few reconnaissance flights able to penetrate the heavy weather in the north. By the end of October, the Thirteenth Army Group of General Lin Piao's Fourth Field Army had concentrated in areas just north of the Chongchon, waiting for the Eighth Army attack. The Thirty-eighth, Thirty-ninth, Fortieth, Forty-second, Fiftieth, and Sixty-sixth Chinese Armies, each with three divisions or about 30,000 men, were concealed over a front of about 120 miles from Chongju in the west to the Choshin Reservoir in the east. In the first half of November, reinforcements came in the form of the Ninth Army Group of General Chen Yi's Third Field Army, composed of the Twentieth, Twenty-sixth, and Twenty-seventh Armies, each with four divisions. This force concentrated to attack the flank of the X Corps near the Choshin and Fusen Reservoirs. Altogether about 300,000 Chinese troops had been assembled in North Korea waiting for the resumption of the UN offensive.

The size of the Chinese forces was not known to the National Security Council when it met in Washington on Nov. 9 to discuss the situation arising from the first Chinese successes. But there were signs that someone at UN headquarters was rattled.

MacArthur claimed in his customary orotund phrases that the Chinese attack across the Yalu from "the privileged sanctuary of Manchuria" constituted "one of the most offensive acts of international lawlessness of historic record . . ." General G. E. Stratemeyer, the air force commander, was ordered to destroy the twin bridges which linked Sinuiju and Antung across the Yalu and over which, MacArthur believed, supplies were flowing to the Chinese in North Korea.

The order precipitated another contest of will between the commander in the field and his superiors in Washington. When the Administration heard of the order to Stratemeyer, the order was canceled and all bombing attacks within five miles of the frontier were banned. This elicited a furious protest from MacArthur. The traffic over the bridges, he raged, threatened "the ultimate destruction of the forces under my command."

Washington gave way. The bridges and the town on each side of the Yalu were attacked on Nov. 8 by seventy-nine B-29's and 300 fighter-bombers. The effect on the campaign, but not on the towns, was minimal. The Chinese by then were secure in their positions miles south of the Yalu.

The National Security Council's discussion of the next step dwelt on future strategy. Bradley, the Chairman of the Joint Chiefs, believed that MacArthur would be able to hold his positions against the Chinese threat. There was to be no question of operations against the Chinese bases in Manchuria; the Administration had promised the British that. Bradley conceded that a UN line farther to the south would be more defensible, but he pointed out that this retirement might well sap South Korean support for the UN effort.

Walter Bedell Smith, the Director of the Central Intelligence Agency, pointed out that the Yalu would be frozen in a few days in any case. That shrewd intelligence also reassured the Council on another point—the Russians, Smith said, were unlikely to go to war as long as the West was tied down in Korea.

Secretary of State Dean Acheson was more irritated by MacArthur's changes of mind than were any of the other participants. He wrote later that the five days of Nov. 4 to 9 gave "an excellent example of General MacArthur's mercurial temperament. In this period, he went from calm confidence, warning against hasty judgment until all the facts were in, to ringing the tocsin on the sixth to proclaim that hordes of men were pouring into Korea and threatening to overwhelm his command, to confidence again on the ninth that he would deny the enemy reinforcement and destroy him."

Such were the difficulties of dealing with the American Caesar from afar.

Acheson's contribution was a proposal that a buffer zone be established in North Korea under the UN. He reasoned that the Chinese were attempting to protect their frontier and especially the Suiho hydroelectric plant on the Yalu, upstream from Antung.

The upshot of all this argument left MacArthur free. He was not to bomb Manchuria, but he was at liberty to take other military steps that he found advisable. This clearly included a renewed advance by the UN forces to the north. The Administration was at once ignorant of the strength of the Chinese in North Korea and highly sensitive to the criticism it would get at home if it seemed to be holding back the Republicans' hero. The fact that the Republicans had made substantial gains in the November 1950 Congressional elections did not smooth the Administration's path.

Characteristically, MacArthur wanted to drive to the Yalu in a new offensive almost at once. Walker had a different opinion.

He wanted his army along the Chongchon with its supply lines open and secure. He moved the American IX Corps in the center with I Corps on the left and the South Korean II Corps on the right. MacArthur prodded Walker for an attack on Nov. 15. The army commander resisted with what, in retrospect, seems good reason. Not until Nov. 20 were the supply elements able to deliver the 4,000 tons daily that were required for a minimum of offensive operations. Finally, Walker agreed to attack on Nov. 24. A battalion commander in the Eighth Army recalled that even when the date had been set, "there was a certain uneasiness about the people at Army headquarters, rather like people who had agreed to step out of a brightly lit house into the dark."

The X Corps was in little better shape at the eastern end of the UN line. The dispositions of the corps seem foolhardy, even if full information on the extent of the Chinese intervention was lacking. They knew some Chinese were there; no one could say how many scores of thousands more would enter the war.

The American Third Division had landed at Wonsan on Nov. 5. About 200 miles to the northeast on the coast, the Capitol Division of the Korean I Corps was pushing steadily toward the Soviet frontier, with the Korean Third Division on its left, or inland, flank. The American Seventh Division was moving through Pungsan toward the

Yalu. Two regiments of the marine division in the center were driving north toward the Choshin Reservoir, sixty miles from the frontier.

On the maps at GHQ in Tokyo, all seemed to be going well. But not only had MacArthur, in his final determination, underestimated the Chinese, he had discounted the problems of winter. When the Seventh Marine Division occupied Hagaru at the southern end of the reservoir, the temperature was four degrees below zero. In addition to the cold, there was the gap of fifty miles between the Eighth Army and the X Corps. Guerrilla activity there appeared to be developing rapidly.

MacArthur tinkered with his plan. Major General Edward M. Almond of X Corps was instructed that the marines, instead of driving north to the Yalu as originally planned, were to advance to the west and link up with the Eighth Army, advancing in a northeasterly direction.

The directive stirred misgivings in Major General O. P. Smith, who commanded the marine division involved. He wrote to his superior, the Commandant of the Marine Corps, to question the wisdom of launching a campaign in the bitter cold of the Korean winter with his division scattered along one road from Hungnam to the Yalu. Smith also was worried by the gap between his division and the Eighth Army on his left.

For a marine general in the field to counsel caution in carrying out the orders of a Supreme Commander—and that commander a proven soldier of enormous popularity in Congress and the country —took courage. Whether or not Smith was encouraged, we do not know. But, as Rees points out, the marines' advance proceeded with a caution worthy of Fabius. The rate of progress was about a mile a day while Smith hurried the establishment of a base at Hagaru. As Rees saw it, "this caution in all probability saved the division from annihilation in the next few weeks."

So both Walker on the left and Smith on the right had strong reservations about the wisdom of the offensive. They were experienced military men, each the veteran of a dozen campaigns. As we have seen, there also were strong reservations in Washington. Did any of this matter to MacArthur, who had now recovered his poise, admittedly having been shaken by the first Chinese attacks? The second drive to the Yalu did not appear to him the stupendous risk that others saw it to be. Rather—and this is very hard to believe—

MacArthur envisioned the advance as an occupation rather than an offensive. He was still impatient of Washington's restraint, believing in his wildest moments that it was the result of a malign British influence.

MacArthur's dispatches at the time and his later testimony before various Congressional committees provide us with an insight, rare in military history, of the thought processes that led him to plan and implement the second offensive. As he saw it, he had three options: the UN forces could advance to the Yalu, they could remain where they were, or they could pull back to the waist of Korea.

A retreat to the waist, MacArthur reckoned, would result in a political disaster, for it would leave most of North Korea in Communist hands. To remain where he was offered no advantages, military or political. But an advance to the Yalu would fulfill the UN's purpose in Korea. The presence of UN forces along the Yalu would prevent any major Chinese incursion—a conclusion that indicates how far MacArthur and his intelligence service were out of touch with reality—but if there was a major Chinese offensive, then the UN forces would retreat rapidly and the Chinese would be exposed to withering artillery fire and almost unopposed heavy bombing attacks.

MacArthur was wrong in his estimates of the Chinese. He was foolish to discount the problems arising from the fierce cold of North Korea. He was, first, last, and always, culpable for dividing his forces in the face of an enemy that was clearly equal and probably superior in numbers if not in weapons. The reckoning was about to be paid.

Walker's offensive on the left kicked off without encountering any serious opposition on the first day. That was the last day of progress, easy or otherwise.

The Ninth Regiment of the Second Division, advancing northeast along the Chongchon valley, ran into a strong Chinese force. The advance was halted. On the night of Nov. 25–26, the Chinese attacked the Americans in their hilltop positions. The attack was accompanied by the sound effects that were to become dismally familiar during the remainder of the war: horns, whistles, and gongs. The Americans held on, but it was clear that their advance was effectively blocked. Worse was to come. The officers and men of the Ninth did not know it, but on Nov. 26 the ROK II Corps had disintegrated under Chinese attack, leaving the right flank of the Eighth

Army open and vulnerable. Three Korean divisions had vanished from the order of battle. The Chinese, attacking from their concentration area around Huichon, drove from the east across the Chongchon behind the American Second Division.

The Chinese ran over a Turkish brigade which had been sent up to reinforce the ROK II Corps before the army command realized that the corps had been destroyed. The American Twenty-fifth Division on the Second Division's left met some Chinese, fought hard, and planned to resume the offensive on Nov. 26.

It was at this point that the Chinese made their decisive move in the battle. Into the gap left by the Koreans, they poured eighteen divisions, six armies, to smash into Walker's open flank and his communications. The situation of the UN forces was grave. The right flank of the Eighth Army was nonexistent. The Second Division was falling back. The Twenty-fifth Division was withdrawing in the center under heavy pressure, and the two divisions on the Army's left flank, the American Twenty-fourth and the First ROK, were in danger of being cut off north of the Chongchon. All the ingredients for a disaster had been assembled.

The credit for averting that disaster belongs to the Second Division commanded by Major General L. B. Keiser. The division took defensive positions around Kunu-ri supported by reserves, the First Cavalry Division and the Twenty-seventh Commonwealth Brigade. Their task was to check the Chinese advance and buy time for the Twenty-fourth and Twenty-fifth US and First ROK Divisions to struggle past the crossing points of the Chongchon, already filled with all the debris of a retreating army, and to reach comparative safety south of the river.

About this time, MacArthur, in a message to the Security Council of the UN, a body to which he had paid scant deference in the past, announced that he was being attacked by more than 200,000 Chinese and that the world organization faced "an entirely new war."

Fortune favors the brave, and the Second Division was very brave and very effective in the next forty-eight hours. The divisional artillery, supported by stray batteries from other units inflicted heavy casualties on the advancing Chinese who, until that moment, had never encountered modern artillery served by experienced gunners. They remembered it. In 1976 I talked to a Chinese divisional commander in Manchuria, asking what he remembered best about Korea. Since he was a professional soldier and not a party propagandist, he said simply, "Your guns, so many, so well used. We lost many, many."

The stand at Kunu-ri could not last forever. More and more Chinese were marching to the attack. Major General John B. Coulter, the corps commander, on Nov. 29 gave Keiser permission to withdraw to Sunchon twenty miles to the south. The Commonwealth Brigade had marched to Sunchon to keep the road open but came under heavy attack. Under intense fire, the brigade was unable to progress beyond the pass in the road. The Chinese reinforced their troops along the road until by Nov. 30 an entire Chinese division was entrenched along the road.

There were two escape routes available. Keiser and the Second were committed to the Sunchon route. There was a route through Anju in the Twenty-fifth Division area, but Keiser did not know whether the division had cleared the Anju crossing. He felt that most of his people were still ahead of the advancing enemy. They were desperate men seeking desperate remedies.

Their situation makes the soothing "syrup" emanating from Eighth Army headquarters all the more difficult to comprehend. The UN attack, as that headquarters saw it, "probably saved our forces from a trap which might well have destroyed them. . . . the timing of our attack to develop the situation was indeed most fortunate."

The last act of the withdrawal from the Chongchon began on the morning of Nov. 30. It proved much more difficult than had been foreseen. One theory was that the Chinese had established only a roadblock which the Americans could smash through without undue casualties. Instead they faced a Chinese division well dug-in along six miles of the road to the pass. The task for breaking through was given to troops who had been fighting for five days in temperatures hovering around zero.

Chinese fire took out the leading vehicles of the division. The road was swept by the fire of thirty machine guns and, probably, a dozen mortars. The infantry inched forward, shaken, tired, and in some cases demoralized. The air force pounded the Chinese positions with conventional bombs and napalm, but there was no slackening in the enemy fire. It was a monsoon of bullets and mortar bombs.

At about 1:15 P.M. Keiser and his staff picked their way around American, Turkish, and Korean dead lying among burning trucks and jeeps. The last of the divisional artillery got through early on

Dec. 1, and small groups broke away from the road and escaped across the countryside to the lines of the Commonwealth Brigade and the First Cavalry. What remained of the rearguard escaped through Anju. The Second Division suffered more than 3,000 casualties and lost almost all its equipment in a day. If there was anything memorable in the battle, it was the behavior of the soldiers who failed to panic, kept discipline, and made their way through against insuperable odds.

The immediate consequence was that the Eighth Army was in full retreat. The rearguard was under heavy pressure from the Chinese. MacArthur, at this point, believed that to save the army a major withdrawal must take place. He ordered a retirement 120 miles south to the thirty-eighth parallel, north of Seoul.

Oddly enough, this precipitate withdrawal was not necessary. The Chinese, after six days of unremitting attack, had exhausted their supplies of ammunition and were unable to maintain the pressure they had first applied.

Washington, although it approved the order for the Eighth Army's retirement, was equally worried by the fate of X Corps. With the situation worsening, both in the west and the east, MacArthur finally was ordered to pull the corps out of northeastern Korea in a manner that would preclude their being flanked by the advancing enemy. Clearly Washington wanted to end the system of divided command.

The optimists were active at GHQ in Tokyo. Some suggested that Pyongyang could be held and used as a sally point for an attack on the rear of the advancing Chinese. This optimism foundered when the Chinese took Songchon on the Pyongyang–Wonsan road and it became clear that only disengagement could save X Corps.

If he had been beaten on the military battlefield, MacArthur remained resilient and formidable on the political one.

First the commanding general told the Joint Chiefs that he would be unable to hold the Korean waist because of the difficulties of terrain, logistics, and inadequate forces. He also announced that unless "some positive step and immediate action is taken . . . steady attrition leading to final destruction can reasonably be contemplated."

The reversal in North Korea had surprised the Administration almost as much as it had surprised MacArthur. The latter, however, had begun to publicize his views, views which inevitably led to the final break with Truman. MacArthur, in messages to friendly recipients in the United States, talked about "extraordinary inhibitions" on his command and emphasized that no blame should be attached to him and his staff for the defeat on the Chongchon. In official Washington, they were beginning to discuss in guarded whispers the evacuation of all of Korea.

Early on Dec. 5 a British rearguard evacuated Pyongyang, the only Communist capital ever to be held by the West. Surrounded by hordes of refugees, the troops drove south to the thirty-eighth parallel. Their campaign was over. For the First Marine Division, however, the campaign was continuing in zero weather and against huge odds.

The marine division was trapped. Their main elements were seventy-eight miles north of Hungnam at the Choshin Reservoir. Of these, two regiments at Yudam-ni were in the greatest immediate danger. On the night of Nov. 27–28, the marines were heavily attacked with the Chinese assailing their main positions and others farther south at the Toktong Pass.

Worse was to come. The Chinese fed twelve divisions, three armies of their IX Army Group, into the battle. By the morning of Nov. 28, the First Marine Division had been forced into three positions at Yudam-ni, Hagaru, and Koto-ri on the Changjin River. Three Chinese divisions were identified in the attacks at Yudam-ni and five more in an action against the supply route to Chinhung-ni.

The marines retreating from Yudam-ni headed for Hagaru, which was held by a regiment of the corps and some stray army detachments. The perimeter at Hagaru contained an airstrip and a supply base and, consequently, was of vital importance to the withdrawal. The regiments approaching from Yudam-ni would have to move through this thinly held perimeter.

Disengagement from the ubiquitous Chinese was the first problem for the approximately 10,000 marines moving to Hagaru from Yudam-ni. The Chinese had pressed so close to the single road to Hagaru that the marines had to launch repeated attacks to drive the enemy back and clear the road. The operation began on Dec. 1, and by Dec. 3 the first stage of what must be considered one of the most masterly withdrawal operations in the history of war, one fought at great odds, had been concluded when the first marines reached Hagaru. The remainder of the force entered the now-reinforced perimeter by the following afternoon.

The importance of holding Hagaru was emphasized by a relieving operation mounted by a force of about 1,000 men which struck north from Koto-ri. The force included marines, army, and British marine commandos. The Chinese ambushed the column at a point along the Changjin named "Hellfire Pass" by the embattled troops. Major General O. P. Smith, the marine commander, judged the relief of Hagaru so important that he ordered the force to break through at all costs. It did, but when the force reached Hagaru, it had lost sixty percent of its original strength.

The army suffered too. Three battalions of the Seventh Division, two of infantry, and one of artillery, were in the Shung-ni perimeter roughly eight miles north of Hagaru. For three days beginning on Nov. 27, the force was heavily engaged by the Chinese. After heavy fighting the remains of the force of 2,500 reached Hagaru—approximately 1,000 men, of whom only 385 were unwounded or incapacitated by frostbite.

During these actions, the Americans dominated the air. Chinese formations were strafed as they attacked in "human wave" formations. Under the fighters' escort, more than 4,500 wounded were evacuated from Hagaru airstrip.

The next phase in the withdrawal was a march to Koto-ri where about 4,000 men were surrounded by the attacking Chinese. The drive to Koto-ri began on Dec. 6 after the American forces had regrouped. They took thirty-eight hours to cover the eleven miles through the snow under incessant Chinese attack.

Smith again regrouped his forces and started southward for Chinhung-ni, ten miles to the south. The last ten miles from Koto-ri presented an additional problem. The bridge over the gorge in Funchilin Pass had been destroyed. The problem was solved when special prefabricated bridge-building equipment was dropped by parachute into Koto-ri. Engineers installed the new bridge across the gorge, and on Dec. 8 the first troops of a force of 14,000 men began to fight their way southward toward the sea and safety. On Dec. 9 the troops moved across the bridge. Early on Dec. 10, the forward elements of the column entered Chinhung-ni. The last elements were still in Koto-ri.

By Dec. 11 what remained of the command assembled in the Hamhung-Hungnam area and began preparations for evacuation. The Chinese failed to mount any heavy attacks on the Americans. The reason was that their IX Army Group had lost so heavily from the firepower of the marines and the continuing air attacks that it was incapable of renewing its assaults. Marines remember the withdrawal with pride, the Chinese with the rueful admission that in this campaign, too, they came to understand what modern automatic weapons, artillery, and fighter-bombers could do.

The marines' casualties were heavy. During the First Marine Division's campaign, beginning with the fighting around the Choshin Reservoir, it suffered nearly 4,400 battle casualties, including 718 dead. In addition there were more than 7,000 other casualties, the majority from frostbite.

MacArthur had ordered Almond to re-deploy his forces to the Pusan area in the far south and report to the Eighth Army. The evacuation, which was covered by seven navy aircraft carriers, had already begun when the weary marines reached the Hungnam staging area. On Dec. 10 Wonsan was evacuated. Four days later the last of the marines were embarked from Hungnam for Pusan. A total of 105,000 officers and men were evacuated, plus about 91,000 Korean refugees who had fled with the marines from Choshin. The operation involved over one hundred ships. When the last stages of the evacuation were completed on Christmas Eve, the port's waterfront was destroyed by hundreds of explosive charges. North Korea, half empty and devastated, was left to the Communists.

Strategically the UN defeat forced a drastic rethinking of plans and operations upon the Americans and their allies. MacArthur's reputation diminished appreciably, as much because of his unwonted optimism after the first rebuff of his forces as by his tactical error of dividing his forces in the face of the enemy. Officers who served in the campaign recall a loss of confidence in the high command which was exacerbated by the death in a jeep accident of General Walker on Dec. 22. Not until General Matthew Ridgway arrived to replace Walker did the command situation improve.

President Truman's political position was weakened by the defeat. His policy of limiting the war to the Orient in order to maintain NATO's strength in Europe was now under heavy attack by the Republicans, who once again demanded a more vigorous prosecution of the war in Korea.

Realistically the Administration's sights were lowered. It now appeared sensible to seek only the preservation of South Korea rather than the conquest of the entire country. This strategy, of course, was not acceptable to the hawks in Washington, but on balance it was the only practical one. There were to be other battles in Korea, but they were on a reduced scale. Even so, casualties became increasingly unacceptable to the United States and other Western countries that were furnishing troops for Korea.

MacArthur's loss of military reputation contributed considerably to his replacement by President Truman in 1951. The most notable American leader of World War II and of the opening campaigns in Korea was dismissed. Some claim that had MacArthur remained in command, the tide would have been turned. Nothing in the subsequent operations in Korea nor in national attitudes toward the war confirms this view. The drive to the Yalu was the last flare of MacArthur's genius and, perhaps, of the American willingness to take great risks.

The Chinese were the victors, militarily and politically. The People's Liberation Army achieved tactical surprise and used that surprise with skill and boldness. Even the deficiencies in MacArthur's intelligence, which he, an experienced general, should have suspected, cannot diminish the skill with which hundreds of thousands of troops were moved virtually undetected into their jump-off positions. The Chinese fought bravely in their first encounter with modern weaponry, and their casualties were very heavy. By the end of the serious fighting in Korea, the commanders of the PLA had begun to change their tactics and alter the organization of combat units to provide more firepower.

Politically the victory established China as the major military power on the Asian mainland and, consequently, increased Peking's political influence throughout the region. The assessment of Chinese military and political strength accepted by Washington after 1950 undoubtedly exaggerated that strength. But without diplomatic relations and relying for intelligence mainly upon the highly suspect reports of the Chinese Nationalists on Taiwan, the original exaggeration was woven into the fabric of American doctrine. A decade later, when the United States was involved in Vietnam, this overestimate of Chinese strength, both political and military, had a serious impact on policy making in Washington.

XIII

The Siege Without Hope

DIEN BIEN PHU

At about 6:30 on the evening of May 7, 1954, Jean Nicholas, a bone-weary, half-starved major of the French Moroccan infantry, saw a Viet Minh soldier approaching his position on Strongpoint Lily. A white flag was fixed to the barrel of the enemy's weapon.

The Viet Minh asked the Frenchman if he intended to continue firing. No, Nicholas said, he was not going to shoot anymore.

"C'est fini?" asked the Viet Minh.

"Oui, c'est fini," answered the major.

This quiet, almost polite exchange ended the Battle of Dien Bien Phu which had begun on March 13. Although a relatively small action as major battles go, it had consequences that shook the world. The long, bitter, bloody resistance of the French forces at Dien Bien Phu ended in a defeat that today is seen as a major turning point in the struggle by Asians against European colonialists.

Dien Bien Phu signaled the end of France as an Asian power. The North Vietnamese were established as the foremost military power of Southeast Asia. It was an inspirational factor in Algeria's successful revolt against French rule and, indeed, some of the most skillful Algerian revolutionary officers had fought with the French in Indochina.

Nor was the battle without impact on the course of French politics. Successive defeats in Vietnam and Algeria had a traumatic influence on French public opinion. The resulting national humiliation and frustration fused into a rampant French nationalism which carried General Charles de Gaulle to power in 1958, a nationalism still evident in France's sometimes abrasive relations with the United States.

Dien Bien Phu combined in the compass of one small valley the most primitive and sophisticated means of combat. The Vietnamese threw themselves in masses against French positions which, almost until the end of the battle, were sustained by airdrops of reinforcements and supplies. The Viet Minh, however, had abundant artillery, particularly antiaircraft guns, sighted and served with remarkable skill. The French, who enjoyed regular radio contact with commanders in Hanoi and Saigon and daily intelligence reports, were supported by fighters and bombers, while the Viet Minh had no airpower. But by the end, the siege became a struggle between little groups of French and Vietnamese fighting with grenades, rifles, and bayonets. The struggle was as brutal, as confused as any battle of the century, not excepting Stalingrad.

It is easiest to describe the defenders as French, but in fact they were a polyglot force that included the Foreign Legion composed of Frenchmen, Germans, various Eastern Europeans, and Spanish Anarchists. There were also Moroccans and Algerians from North Africa, Vietnamese largely recruited in the south, and T'ai irregulars from the surrounding countryside.

The survivors' record for stubborn valor is unmatched in the long history of France in Asia. They endured agonies of hunger and thirst. They lived for days in thick mud in which many of the wounded died. They were harassed almost incessantly by artillery, mortar fire, and sniping.

The same cannot be said for their commanders. The original French concept of the campaign and much of the direction of the battle from a distance was marred by a startling underestimate of the Viet Minh capabilities and an exaggerated opinion of French soldiers, weaponry, and skill in logistics. These two errors of judgment afflicted Western commanders in Asia from Korea to the later American experience in Vietnam as well.

The contest between France and the Viet Minh, a military and political organization, had been going on intermittently since 1945, when the defeated Japanese withdrew from Indochina. Ho Chi Minh was the leader of the Central Committee of the Communist Party of Indochina, which as early as 1941 had established as its main goal the elimination of the French power in the region. On Sept. 2, 1945, Ho proclaimed the establishment of the Democratic Republic of Vietnam and demanded the total withdrawal of the French.

The reaction by Paris was recognition of the DRV within the French Union. The French also proposed a national referendum to determine whether North Vietnam and South Vietnam, where French influence was strongest, were prepared to unite under Ho's government. A series of futile negotiations between the two governments followed, with no agreement on the key issue of total independence for Vietnam.

The contest quickly shifted from the political arena to military combat. Guerrilla activity spread throughout the northern region of the country. The Viet Minh registered a number of successes which emboldened Ho to decide on major campaigns to drive the French out of the north and central regions. General Vo Nguyen Giap was chosen as the field commander of the Viet Minh.

Giap, who was forty-four at the time of Dien Bien Phu, based his strategy and tactics on the experiences of the Communist Chinese in their wars against the Japanese and Chiang Kai-shek's Nationalists. Against the French and later against the Americans, Giap showed little concern for the very heavy losses incurred by his tactics or for the sufferings the war inflicted on local populations. The villagers, who made up most of the population, had only the vaguest comprehension of the aims of the new government; indeed, in some of the more remote areas they had little knowledge of the French presence which had been established in 1883.

By late 1953 the war had assumed a familiar pattern. The better-armed French held the majority of the cities and towns. The Viet Minh dominated the countryside. After 1949 the rebel leaders established contact with Mao Tse-tung's now-unchallenged People's Republic of China. The connection had two advantages for the Viet Minh. They began to receive modern arms from the Chinese, although the volume was never as great as the French assumed and many of the young Vietnamese leaders were trained in China by specialists in guerrilla warfare.

The establishment of what the French call a *Base Aéro-Terrestre,* or air-land base, at Dien Bien Phu was the first significant action taken by the new French commander in Indochina, General Henri

Eugène Navarre. He had succeeded Marshal Jean de Lattre de Tassigny, who had returned to France in ill health after months of hard but largely unsuccessful campaigning against Giap's guerrillas. At the time of Navarre's arrival as commander in chief of the French forces, Giap commanded more than 120,000 men and was capable of assembling at least three infantry divisions, well supported by artillery and mortars at any point where Navarre chose to strike.

Navarre believed that his best chance of inflicting severe losses on the Viet Minh was to provoke Giap into fighting conventional rather than guerrilla actions. In such battles, he was confident, the superior discipline, training, weaponry, and airpower of the French would prevail. He knew, and exaggerated, the amount of military aid the DRV was receiving from Mao's People's Republic, but he appears to have discounted this factor.

On Dec. 3, 1953, Navarre presented General René Cogny, the French commander in the north, with his directive for the battle to be fought in the far northwest. Navarre was then in Saigon, the French military and political capital; Cogny in Hanoi, the northern command headquarters.

Navarre's stark first paragraph said, "The defense of the Northwest shall be centered on an air-land base of Dien Bien Phu which must be held at all costs." The commander in chief then outlined the scenario for the battle as he saw it developing after the arrival of the French and the concentration of the Viet Minh against them. First there would be a period of approach and reconnaissance in which the enemy would assess and probe the French defenses. This would be followed by the attack stage, "lasting several days," which "must end with the failure of the Viet Minh offensive."

In retrospect the plan reeks of overconfidence. Navarre knew nothing at first hand about the problems of jungle warfare and very little about the courage and flexibility of his enemies. He did not believe the Viet Minh would be able to concentrate more than a division—about 10,000 men—against the French, and he believed that the French air force, unopposed by Vietnamese aircraft, would smash any Viet Minh attempts to concentrate larger forces against the French at Dien Bien Phu. Navarre was convinced that the Viet Minh strength was at its height and that Giap would be unable to mount a prolonged offensive, requiring continual reinforcement against the French forces. This underestimate of the Viet Minh, coupled with the overestimate of the French resources, was the primary error in the planning of the battle.

The plan was criticized from the first, although the criticism was rather muted—probably a tribute to the hierarchical principle of acceptance of the commander in chief's strategic and tactical policies, a principle which was still strong in the French officer corps. General Cogny, however, perhaps because of his higher rank, went further in his criticism. He told Navarre that one of the objectives of the operation would not be obtained. Navarre had reasoned that the occupation of Dien Bien Phu would close the road to Luang Prabang in Laos and cut off the Viet Minh's rice supplies from that area. Cogny answered: "In that kind of country, you can't interdict a road. This is a European-type notion without any value here. The Viets can get through anywhere. We can see this right here in the Red River Delta."

This abrupt dismissal of one of his chief's arguments for the operation was followed by Cogny's highly pessimistic forecast of the consequences of the battle: "I am persuaded that Dien Bien Phu shall become, whether we like it or not, a battalion meat grinder with no possibility of large-scale radiating out from it as soon as it will be blocked by a single Viet Minh regiment . . ."

Dien Bien Phu is in a valley less than twenty miles from the border of Laos and Vietnam and roughly one hundred miles west of Hanoi. The Chinese frontier runs seventy-five miles to the north. Hills covered with thick jungle vegetation surround the valley, which in summer collects more rain than any other region of Vietnam. The winter, from November to April, is relatively cool with precipitation in the form of a damp drizzle. Summer sees the temperature rise to the nineties, with heavy rains and occasional typhoons. These weather conditions affected the French operations. Obviously the establishment of a fortified position from which troops could meet the first enemy onslaught and, later, push out into the countryside against Viet Minh strongholds had to be carried out in winter.

The high command, with the exception of Cogny, put great store in these offensive operations which, it believed, would lure Giap to battle and defeat. Cogny, the commander in the north, was, as we have seen, not as sanguine.

The first step on the long trail that led to the French defeat was taken on Nov. 20, 1953, when the entire French air transport force of sixty-five elderly C-47's was deployed to drop parachute troops into the valley. The French planned for an initial drop of 1,500 troops into three zones to the northwest and south of the village of Dien Bien Phu, which was believed to house a small Viet Minh garrison.

The drop did not come up to expectations. Some of the paratroops landed well outside their zones and, in consequence, were ambushed by parties of Viet Minh as they moved to their rally points. On Nov. 20, 700 additional paratroops and additional equipment were dropped into the valley without opposition, and by night the village was in French hands.

Superficially, the French had done well. They had landed 1,827 paratroops in a defended position 220 miles behind enemy lines with relatively light losses—eleven dead and fifty-two wounded. After less than six hours of desultory fighting, the position was secured and the enemy attacks died.

They had not, however, encountered the main Viet Minh forces. The 148th Regiment of the Viet Minh Army was in the hills surrounding Dien Bien Phu, and scattered throughout the jungle, in the rear, unobserved by French aircraft, was the 116th Division: three regiments of infantry supported by 120-millimeter mortars and 75-millimeter recoilless rifles.

Cogny had supervised the drop. These were his troops, the best he had at his disposal. Now he was succeeded by a new commander, Colonel (later Brigadier General) Christian Marie Ferdinand de la Croix de Castries.

De Castries was the type of elegant adventurer in war that European armies, the British more than the French, attract. He had been an aviator, a horse-show star, and a racing driver, and was known throughout the army and Parisian society as an indefatigable womanizer. He was also an experienced and competent soldier. He had fought bravely in 1940. After capture by the Germans, he had escaped and joined the Free French forces and fought in Africa, Italy, and southern France. In 1951 he had commanded the forces in the critical Red River sector of Vietnam.

His friends noted an odd streak of detachment in De Castries. He could fight furiously, inspiring his troops by his personal bravery. But at times, sometimes critical ones, he would withdraw mentally from the battle. He appeared, at those moments, to be above the fight, watching it from a distance. This was the man designated to command Dien Bien Phu in France's last great battle in Asia.

The French buildup, which put 4,500 troops into the valley by the end of the first week, demonstrated a striking difference between the situations of the two forces. The French troops were entirely dependent on air supply, and for this they had to rely on less than one hundred transport aircraft. The Viet Minh on the other hand had neither air support nor air transport. They relied on a logistical system as old as war: human bearers. Tens of thousands of coolies carried staggering loads of shells, mortars, artillery tubes, food, and water through the jungles and over hills to maintain the fighting forces. Giap gave the coolies no less than their due when in his proclamation of victory he paid tribute to "the ardor and the enthusiasm of the People's Porters of the population of the Northwest and of the rear areas . . ."

Dien Bien Phu's central command post was based in the village whose original name was Muong Thanh. A series of strongpoints formed the French outer ring of defenses. These were known as Beatrice, Gabrielle, Anne-Marie, Dominique, Huguette, Françoise, Elaine, and Claudine. Well to the south lay Isabelle. This strongpoint guarded the only escape route to the south, and it was the last of the strongpoints to surrender on the final day of the siege. Numbered combat positions dotted each strongpoint.

Construction of the strongpoints and of fortifications for the main headquarters and the airfield at Dien Bien Phu disclosed a serious logistical weakness. The French were thinking in terms of a defensive system with a perimeter of approximately thirty miles. It soon became clear that the materiel required could not be airlifted from Hanoi in addition to food, ammunition, and other supplies without a drastic and unattainable reinforcement of the airlift command. In consequence the defensive positions, although imposing enough on a map, often were flimsy and makeshift, inadequate to withstand the pounding of Viet Minh guns and artillery.

By Dec. 3, however, the French were fully committed to Dien Bien Phu. Navarre's directive ordered that the village and the airfield must be held, even if this meant abandoning some of the strongpoints. Four battalions of infantry, five batteries of 105-millimeter guns and two batteries of 75-millimeter recoilless rifles were sent to reinforce the garrison. Again the reinforcements appeared impressive. But Navarre and his staff discounted two factors. First, the Viet Minh were concentrating far more powerful forces around Dien Bien Phu. Second, French air resources were inadequate to supply the garrison in the face of increasingly heavy and accurate antiaircraft fire and in deteriorating weather conditions.

By early January 1954, the French had completed their preparations. The polyglot force was established in field positions surrounded by barbed wire and protected by the strongpoints. Gun emplacements had been strengthened and a system of dugouts built. Every move was observed and charted by the Viet Minh who, however, forbore to attack until they had concentrated adequate forces. The Crickets, light spotter aircraft operating from the airstrip, while useful enough in action, were unable to detect the gradual consolidation of the enemy forces. The Viet Minh's apparent inactivity and the success of their reinforcement encouraged the French to begin aggressive patrolling.

The results were disappointing and ominous. One of the first patrols was destroyed only a few miles from Dien Bien Phu. The Viet Minh encountered were not unorganized and ill-armed guerrillas but a unit of the 176th Regiment. Lieutenant Colonel Victor Guth, De Castries's chief of staff, was killed by enemy fire on a patrol a few hundred yards north of the Anne-Marie strongpoint. A Foreign Legion force attempting to clear a road beyond the village of Ban Him Lam was badly mauled by the Viet Minh. After a month the French realized that aggressive patrolling into the jungles wasted men and provided little accurate information about the enemy.

Giap began to close the ring. The Viet Minh's 304th, 308th, and 316th Divisions were established in the hills north and northeast of the airstrip. One by one the French strongpoints came under fire from the Viet Minh's 105- and 75-millimeter guns. The airstrip was shelled, aircraft damaged, and incoming transport planes harassed by antiaircraft guns.

The French retaliated by turning their B-26 bombers and Bearcat fighters onto the gun positions. Attacks by napalm, rockets, and other bombs failed to silence the enemy batteries. Small groups of infantry, using commando tactics, sought without success to attack Viet Minh gun and mortar positions. The losses were heavy.

Ten tanks were flown in to reinforce the garrison. They were assembled and armed under fire, but they had little effect on the battle. By the middle of February, De Castries's losses amounted to a little under a thousand men killed, wounded, or missing—just over a battalion. Meanwhile the enemy continued to build up strength.

According to Bernard Fall, who wrote one of the best accounts of the battle, the Viet Minh had assembled 49,500 combatants supported by 31,500 support personnel, largely coolies. In addition Giap had 23,000 other troops along his main line of communication running north to the Chinese frontier. The French had about 13,200 men in the valley, of whom 7,000 were rated front-line combatants. Giap's forces thus enjoyed a superiority in manpower of five to one and immeasurably greater firepower.

Many authorities, Fall among them, believe that the battle was won by the coolies who kept the supplies moving toward the front over 500 miles of jungle road. More than 20,000 coolies and local tribesmen rebuilt Route 41 leading to Dien Bien Phu and widened the turns so that the road would take artillery pieces and the 800 Soviet-built Molotova trucks. These and the thousands of coolies were the core of the Viet Minh supply system.

The first major bombardment of the French fortress, at 5 P.M. on March 13, 1954, signaled the opening of the siege. Navarre and his staff, naturally, had envisioned a siege and, if things went badly, the evacuation of the French forces. But neither Saigon nor Hanoi were able to provide the garrison with the men, guns, ammunition, materiel, and air support that would enable the French to withstand the siege or, in the worst case, to break out to safety. It was another example of their persistent underestimation of the Viet Minh's capabilities.

Giap fed another 11,000 troops into the battle as it intensified and steadily increased the strength of his artillery. The Viet Minh deployed eighty 105-millimeter howitzers, twenty-five 75-millimeter howitzers, and twenty heavy 120-millimeter mortars. French aircraft drew fire from thirty-six 37-millimeter guns, Soviet-made; another fifteen 75-millimeter pack howitzers were added to the Viet Minh artillery. There were also thirty recoilless rifles and a number of Soviet-made rocket launchers.

The French reinforcement was puny by comparison. During the siege, 4,000 men were flown in or dropped into the battle area. The besieged had no artillery to compare with that assembled by the Viet Minh. At the height of the battle, the French deployed six batteries of 105-millimeter howitzers and four of 155-millimeter howitzers. Three companies of 120-millimeter mortars were assigned to Strongpoints Claudine, Anne-Marie, and Gabrielle. The total was twenty-four medium and four heavy guns, twenty-four heavy mortars plus four 50-caliber machine guns for use against enemy infantry. The machine guns were an afterthought. An American officer had told the French that such guns had inflicted heavy losses on the attacking Chinese in Korea.

Beatrice, the strongpoint northwest of the airstrip, was the first Viet Minh target. On the morning of March 13 its defenders reported that they were completely encircled by enemy approach trenches, some within 50 yards of the French positions. When the attack began the strongpoint was hit by a hail of artillery shells and mortar bombs. At the same time Viet Minh antiaircraft batteries opened up from hills 633, 674, and 701 on aircraft taking off from the airstrip. Until then, the guns had been undetected.

Around 6:30 P.M. the command bunker on Beatrice took a direct hit. The commander was killed along with his staff. Another shell hit a subsidiary command post. The Viet Minh infantry blew gaps in the barbed wire with explosive charges. The advance cost the attackers dearly, for the remaining French brought heavy automatic rifle and machine-gun fire to bear on the enemy. One by one the French positions were overrun. By 8:30 P.M. all the officers were dead or wounded. One company under a sergeant held out for another two hours assisted by the fire of the French howitzers. But the Viet Minh were too strong. Early on the morning of March 14, the remnants of the Third Battalion, Thirteenth Foreign Legion Half Brigade (a peculiarly French formation), slipped out of the strongpoint and into the jungle, where they hid until dawn. The first day of the Battle of Dien Bien Phu thus ended with the loss of a strongpoint.

Giap's tactics now settled into a monotonous pattern—a storm of artillery and mortar fire followed by wave upon wave of assault infantry. The next target was Strongpoint Gabrielle, lying north of the airstrip and important to its security. The French considered it the best built of all their positions. As it happened, it proved one of the more vulnerable.

Counterbattery fire failed to reduce the Viet Minh barrage or to affect its accuracy. All the officers at Gabrielle, which was manned by Algerian troops, were killed or wounded in the first phase of the battle. Hundreds of infantry threw themselves against the barbed wire covering the main position, the living clambering over the bod-

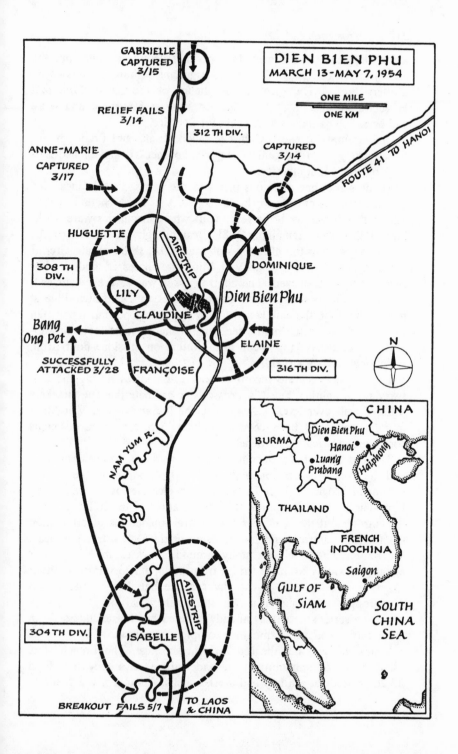

ies of the dead. The French fire was mercilessly accurate, but the enemy attack continued. Slowly the Algerians withdrew, harassed by artillery fire. A few reached the shelter of the Anne-Marie and Huguette strongpoints. They had lost at least 800 men, and there had been 700 casualties in the fight for Beatrice.

One attempt to relieve Gabrielle failed. Tanks and French infantry attacking from the central sector were checked and then driven back by Viet Minh infantry.

At the same time a serious threat to the garrison's sole means of contact with the outside world developed. Viet Minh shells began to fall on the airstrip, with the revetments where mechanics were working on the seven remaining F-8F Bearcat fighter-bombers as the prime targets. On the afternoon of March 14, three of the aircraft got away to Haiphong. The Viet Minh fire increased and the last Bearcats were destroyed. The control tower was severely damaged, and the radio beacon, which guided planes to Dien Bien Phu at night or through the clouds and fog, was smashed beyond repair. On the second day of the battle, the garrison had lost its local air support. It would have to depend in the future on missions flown from Haiphong's Cat-Bi airfield.

There is no accurate record of Viet Minh losses during the first two days of fighting, but it is a reasonable estimate that the attackers suffered well over 3,000 casualties in the initial assaults. Viet Minh morale, nourished by success, remained high, and reinforcements continued to reach the battlefield.

The outcome of the opening days of the siege, heavy casualties, and the loss of two strongpoints deepened pessimism in the French command. Cogny in Hanoi began to consider the loss of Dien Bien Phu. The reversal there and the deterioration of the military situation throughout the Red River Delta strengthened his determination not to throw more troops into a losing battle. De Castries's appeals for reinforcement fell on stony ground. Navarre in Saigon was equally unwilling to move troops from the south to reinforce either Cogny or De Castries. Eventually a single battalion of paratroops was dropped into Dien Bien Phu; the numbers did not suffice to replace the serious casualties already suffered by the defenders. With the paratroop infantry came three complete gun crews.

Manpower was not the only critical shortage. The French were running out of ammunition. In under three days they had fired 23,200 rounds of artillery and mortar shells. An appeal was made to

Cogny for a drop of shells, dismantled artillery pieces, and infantry ammunition.

Viet Minh saboteurs were active. They infiltrated the airfield and blew up most of the remaining supplies.

By March 16, the third day of the battle, the situation within Dien Bien Phu was deteriorating rapidly. Jean Peraud, a French photographer, left this graphic picture of the battlefield: "Air drop on March 16 . . . Viet Minh bombardment of DZ [Drop Zone] and headquarters . . . Cavalcade of soldiers under fire . . . Our artillery smashed up by Viet Minh . . . Attempts at embarkation of wounded under fire of Viet Minh 105's . . . Tragic . . . Many wounded . . . Gloomy atmosphere reminds of German concentration camps . . . Catastrophic."

De Castries sought to encourage his men with an order of the day which promised more reinforcement, a promise he could not be certain would be filled, and emphasized the importance of the battle: "We are undertaking at Dien Bien Phu a battle on which the whole fate of the Indochina War will be decided." In this he was correct.

On March 17 came the first desertions. Strongpoint Anne-Marie was held by the T'ai irregulars recruited from the surrounding countryside. The position itself was an easy target for the Viet Minh gunners. On the morning of March 17, the French artillery observer on Anne-Marie reported that the T'ai were deserting *en masse*. The irregulars who had held positions 1 and 2 in Anne-Marie's defense were slipping through the barbed wire and heading for their homes in the mountains on the skyline. The few French officers and non-commissioned officers could not stop them.

The Viet Minh now concentrated their attacks on Anne-Marie 4, held by a single company. Positions 1 and 2 were occupied by a handful of French and a few loyal T'ai. By night the Viet Minh had taken the high ground on the strongpoint and Anne-Marie was lost.

A lull followed. Giap had expended enormous amounts of ammunition. He had lost thousands of his best troops. The moment had come for the reorganization of his infantry. But artillery and mortar fire was maintained on the French positions and on the drop zones into which French aircraft were parachuting supplies. In effect Giap had closed the ring around the fortress, Isabelle in the south had been isolated, and air supply of the garrison was increasingly hazardous. The rains were coming, and Giap was content to wait and reorganize. He wasted no men in mass assaults but set his coolies to work digging a communications trench system around the outer perimeter of the fortress. One trench system ran through the only direct route from Dien Bien Phu to Isabelle.

During this period, the Viet Minh redoubled their efforts to sap the morale of the garrison. Communist leaflets had had some effect on the desertion of the T'ai from Elaine. Other appeals were directed at the non-French elements in the garrison, chiefly the Algerians and the Germans, in the form of leaflets and loudspeaker broadcasts.

Cogny in Hanoi was increasingly worried over the morale, not of the troops but of the high command in Dien Bien Phu. On March 20 he sent a somewhat ambiguous message to De Castries. This enjoined the latter to "keep in view the success of the battle," promised that an airborne regimental group "is being speedily activated" and warned that the only "immediate possibility" of reinforcement would be one battalion, "but even the dropping of that battalion can only be permitted on the condition that the integrity of the fortified camp be guaranteed."

The fifth paragraph of the message offered even less hope. "In the unfortunate and infinitely improbable hypothesis which has been considered [De Castries' gloomy message of the previous day forecasting further reverses] an eventual operation for the rescue of the breakout forc*e has been studied.*" (Author's italics.)

The battle's tempo began to accelerate on March 22, when a French counterattack was launched against the Viet Minh forces, blocking the French approach to Isabelle around Ban Kho Lai. The paratroops of the Foreign Legion and a tank platoon were thrown into the firefight. Little progress was made until the French committed their last four tanks. The attackers made contact with a force striking from Isabelle at noon. It was the first French success since the battle opened. The losses were heavy—151 dead, seventy-two wounded, and one missing. Viet Minh casualties also were severe. Only nine members of one company of the Fifty-seventh Regiment survived.

The Viet Minh could sustain such losses. The French could not. It was clear that they could not continue to commit infantry and their few precious tanks to keeping open the road to Isabelle.

The continued extension of the Viet Minh trench system around Dien Bien Phu raised curious echoes of World War I. De Castries was ordered by Cogny to destroy the enemy trench system with counter-mines. But not until late March did De Castries issue an order that all strongpoints were to be connected with trenches and that the Viet Minh trenches should be mined and booby-trapped by raiding parties working at night.

The Viet Minh's next target was the high ground east and south of the airstrip and east of the Nam Yum River. De Castries and his staff regarded these hills as vital to the defense of the garrison's command post and the airstrip. Moroccan and Algerian troops and a few French paratroops held most of the area, with the French most numerous at Strongpoints Dominique and Elaine. The defenders' position worsened as the first heavy rains began to fall, reducing the reliability of airdrops to the garrison. C-47's were still landing on the airstrip to take off the wounded, but Viet Minh antiaircraft fire became increasingly heavy and accurate. Three of the transport planes were lost in a few hours on March 26. Late that evening, a C-47 flew through the flak to land. It took off in a hail of mortar shells carrying nineteen wounded who had been waiting in a drainage ditch next to the airfield. It was the last flight to take off safely from the fortress.

The attack on the hill positions followed a familiar pattern. Despite the loss of three 75-millimeter howitzers to French counter-battery fire, the Viet Minh plastered the positions with artillery and mortar fire. The infantry stormed across the bullet-swept terrain unshaken by heavy casualties. The Viet Minh infantry charged across minefields and over barbed-wire entanglements, apparently oblivious to bursting mines and the fire of French automatic weapons. Four of the five major positions were stormed. The French took more than 2,000 casualties, and some Algerians and Vietnamese irregulars broke and ran for the shelter of the jungle.

To the losses in personnel, the French had to add the destruction or capture of guns and mortars and the probability that antiaircraft guns installed on the hills would further reduce the effectiveness of airdrops.

De Castries now ordered Major Marcel Bigeard to launch a limited attack against the concentration of light antiaircraft guns near Bang Ong Pet, about 1½ miles west of Strongpoint Claudine. The operation, involving elements of five battalions, air support from bases 200 miles distant, and the fire of two artillery battalions, was a limited success. The French struck early in the morning of March

28, behind a heavy artillery barrage and strengthened by the presence of a tank platoon.

Viet Minh resistance around Bang Ong Pet temporarily checked the advance of one battalion of paratroops. But once again the half-forgotten garrison at Isabelle intervened. Led by a tank platoon, troops from Isabelle smashed into the Viet Minh flank. The parachutists resumed their attack and, suddenly, the enemy broke and fled leaving 350 dead, seventeen antiaircraft weapons, and hundreds of rifles and machine guns on the battlefield.

It was a notable raid. But like all other French offensive actions during the siege, it could not be exploited. French losses were heavy, and no major reinforcement was in sight. By midafternoon Bigeard ordered a retirement to the main lines of resistance. From that point onward, Isabelle played little part in the main battle for Dien Bien Phu.

By the first week in April, the French position had worsened generally. Counterattacks against the Viet Minh forces at the north and west of the airstrip, pushed with vigor and daring, temporarily halted Viet Minh attacks on Strongpoint Huguette. Again the Viet Minh lost heavily. Giap, whose total casualties since the start of the siege now had reached approximately 9,000 men, called for reinforcement from the divisions waiting in the jungles to the rear. The French reinforcement position was far more difficult. They too had lost heavily in the fighting, and the troops parachuted into the fortress as replacements failed to make up for the losses.

Nevertheless, De Castries persisted in his counterattacks. On April 10 a counterattack was launched against Elaine with the support of fighter-bombers and artillery. The Viet Minh reacted furiously. Thousands of infantry threw themselves against the advancing French, only to be slaughtered by automatic-weapons fire or blown to bits by grenades and bombs. For once, a Viet Minh attack was unsuccessful. The French recaptured and held positions at Elaine.

It is probable that the heavy Viet Minh losses suffered in these two actions forced Giap to alter his tactics. Instead of human-wave assaults by infantry, he intensified and extended his trench system in the hope that the attackers would be able to come to grips with the French without exposing themselves to heavy fire as they crossed no-man's-land. The digging operations provided the defenders with a brief respite from attack but none from the increasingly serious problem of supply. Rain and clouds made accurate drops of ammunition, food, and other necessities increasingly difficult. The French counted it a victory when on April 9 almost 180 tons of supplies were dropped in the valley with only a ten percent loss to the Viet Minh. But 180 tons does not sustain a garrison in action for very long, especially one in which the hopes of relief from outside were fading rapidly.

For a moment the scene shifted from the fog-shrouded valley shaking with the thunder of the guns to quiet offices in Paris, Washington, and London. Warned by Navarre, General Paul Ely, the French Chief of Staff, had informed Premier Joseph Laniel's French government of the increasing precariousness of the French situation at Dien Bien Phu. The French were also worried over the possibility that the Chinese air force would intervene to help the Viet Minh. As it happened, Chinese military intervention was limited to the deployment by the Viet Minh around Dien Bien Phu of modern antiaircraft guns supplied by Peking.

To the French government the situation now was one which demanded Allied support, particularly American. Laniel and his colleagues were encouraged by a speech made by Secretary of State John Foster Dulles on March 29. In it he warned that "the imposition on Southeast Asia of Communism should be met with united action" which might involve serious risks. These risks, he added, would be far less than those the West would face "if we dare not be resolute today." Dulles also reminded his audience that President Dwight D. Eisenhower had declared that Southeast Asia was of "transcendent importance" to the West.

Dulles's comments understandably encouraged the French government. It soon learned, however, as others had, that there always was a considerable gap between the Secretary of State's fiery utterances and American military action. The first barrier was congressional approval. Eisenhower and Dulles, supported by Admiral Arthur W. Radford, Chairman of the Joint Chiefs of Staff, wanted a joint Congressional resolution permitting the use of air and sea power in Indochina.

Radford told a bipartisan congressional group that the operation, code-named Vulture, would be carried out by the aircraft carriers *Essex* and *Boxer* reinforced by land-based bombers from Clark Field in the Philippines. As the planning progressed, the scale of American intervention escalated. To the original force, the Air Force added ninety-eight heavy B-29 Superfortresses. Two wings of these bombers, the most advanced then in service, were stationed on Okinawa, a third at Clark Field. Each carried fourteen tons of bombs. In addition there would be 450 American fighters available if the Chinese were to attack the bombing missions. Although at the time the French discussed the use of "atom bombs" (as they were then called) in the relief operation, there does not appear to have been any serious American military consideration of so extreme a step.

The senators and congressmen were not impressed. They recoiled from the idea of unilateral American intervention to save Dien Bien Phu. The Administration was told that such intervention would be possible on three conditions: (1.) Intervention would take place only in company with the British and other free nations of Southeast Asia such as the Philippines. (2.) The French must agree to accelerate their independence planning for the three Indochinese states so that the United States could not be accused of supporting colonialism. (3.) The French must guarantee that they would remain in the war.

These conditions effectively killed American military intervention. The British would not go along for political and military reasons. Dulles, as was his habit, attempted to place all the blame upon the British, but it is clear from other sources that, aside from Radford, the American military leaders were less than enthusiastic. The Chief of Naval Operations, Admiral Robert B. Carney, and the Chief of the Air Force Staff, General Nathan F. Twining, doubted in a meeting with Eisenhower the feasibility of the intervention as planned. But the most decisive intervention came from General Ridgway, the Army Chief of Staff and the former commander in Korea. Ridgway believed, as did Sir Anthony Eden, the British Foreign Secretary, that air strikes would be followed by the deployment of large American ground forces in Indochina and by their involvement in another inconclusive Asian war.

Eisenhower's feelings, as expressed in his memoirs, were that "if the United States were unilaterally to permit its forces to be drawn into conflict in Indochina and in a succession of Asian wars, the result would be to drain off our resources and to weaken our overall defensive position."

There were purely military arguments against the proposed air strike. The British experience against guerrillas in Malaysia was that weeks passed before there was any evidence that heavy, high-altitude bombing had been successful against troops covered by the jungle. Both American and British airmen pointed out that the French and Viet Minh forces at Dien Bien Phu were so intermingled that heavy bombing could well kill as many French as Viet Minh.

There was one final factor in the death of Operation Vulture. Eisenhower, Dulles, the American military leaders, and to a lesser extent the British all were more concerned over future military action by the People's Republic of China than they were over a relatively minor battle raging around an obscure valley in northern Vietnam.

The French were thrown back on their increasingly limited resources. Two operations were planned to relieve Dien Bien Phu. One, Condor, envisaged an infantry thrust out of Laos to link with airborne forces flying from Hanoi. Eight battalions would then drive toward Dien Bien Phu. To work, Condor would have to be supported by around 115 C-47's each day, plus a sizeable fighter-bomber force. This was beyond French air resources. Nevertheless the planning went forward until late in April, when Navarre held up the second or vital phase of the operation—the linkup between the infantry and the airborne—because, as he should have known, the operation was beyond the capacity of the air force. It could not drop supplies into Dien Bien Phu and at the same time supply the Operation Condor forces.

Albatross, the second operation, planned a breakout from Dien Bien Phu by the garrison. Fall writes that Navarre directed Cogny's staff to prepare plans for this operation only on May 3, 1954, by which time the fortress was all but lost. The breakout, as planned, was to be preceded by very heavy artillery and mortar fire. The severely wounded would be left behind, and the lightly wounded would provide covering fire for the breakout force. The dash for safety was to be made at the end of the day so that the force could reach the twin shelters of the jungle and darkness as rapidly as possible.

De Castries was not pleased with the plan transmitted from Hanoi. The breakout was to be toward the south, and he pointed out in a message to Cogny that the tracks in that direction would not support the movement of 6,000 men. The only feasible operation would be a simultaneous breakout in various directions, De Castries declared.

If De Castries was uncertain about Operation Albatross, so was the staff in Hanoi. One staff appreciation called the operation "both impossible and inconceivable" and urged De Castries and his men to continue to resist because they continued "to tie down Viet Minh troops."

De Castries, the flamboyant, dashing soldier, does not emerge from those last days as the decisive field leader many thought he was. After dithering over the operation, he apparently decided on May 7 to execute the Albatross breakout. By then it was too late.

The situation within the Dien Bien Phu perimeter worsened daily. There was the weather—torrential rain that transformed the positions into hillocks of mud, fierce heat, and high humidity. On April 24 the staff took stock of its position. There were 3,250 infantrymen in Dien Bien Phu who were in condition to fight. This figure was an elastic estimate, for many of these had lost an arm or an eye. Isabelle's garrison, isolated to the south, reported 1,400 men fit for combat. In addition there were 878 seriously wounded under care in the main hospital, in battalion aid stations, and in trenches dug alongside the communications trenches. The artillery and mortar support available to the infantry had been cut in half by Viet Minh shelling and the inevitable mechanical breakdowns. The French were, to be sure, receiving air support from the fighter-bombers and light bombers based in Hanoi. But as they had since the opening of the campaign, the commanders overestimated the effect of air strikes upon the Viet Minh.

Giap and his forces were in good shape for the final act. He had about 35,000 troops ready for action, plus another 20,000 reserves. The Viet Minh artillery, guns, howitzers, mortars, and antiaircraft pieces, were vastly stronger than those of the French, and there was no shortage of ammunition. Over the hills, through the mud and heat, long columns of coolies fed the Viet Minh guns.

The last act of Dien Bien Phu was fought out on an area less than a mile square south of the airstrip. The slow shrinkage of the garrison area naturally made it far more difficult for the aircraft dropping supplies and ammunition to the troops; food and other necessities fell with increasing frequency behind the Viet Minh lines. Airdrops also had become doubly dangerous because of the increasing accuracy of the Viet Minh antiaircraft guns. Finally the monsoon, now in full force, impeded the dropping of supplies; less than thirty tons of supplies were received on April 29. No reinforcements parachuted in to the garrison. The remaining defenders went on half rations.

The final Viet Minh attack may be said to have begun on April 29.

Heavy artillery and mortar fire fell on the garrison area. Enemy infantry were observed moving into assault positions. The next day the Foreign Legion's paratroopers who were holding Huguette 5 were fiercely attacked by an infantry battalion supported by artillery that fired *down* on Dien Bien Phu from gun positions newly established in the hills around the fortress. In one case the Viet Minh had dug tunnels through a hill so that their seventy-five-millimeter recoilless rifles could be fired and withdrawn before French counter-battery fire could take effect.

But there was still life in the Legion. The paratroopers counterattacked out of post 2 of Strongpoint Elaine on the night of May 3–4. A small group penetrated the Viet Minh lines and blew up a Communist position with explosives. But this minor success was balanced by the Viet Minh's own mining operations. The defenders at point 2 could hear the enemy digging and scraping beneath their position as part of a mining operation.

Efforts to supply and reinforce the garrison continued, despite the monsoon and Viet Minh antiaircraft fire. On the night of May 4, 125 men of a colonial infantry battalion and a small headquarters unit dropped into Dien Bien Phu. With them came fifty-seven tons of supplies, of which about forty percent dropped into the hands of the Viet Minh.

Giap chose Huguette 4 as his next point of attack. The size of the attacking force gives some idea of the disparity in strength. The Viet Minh deployed a full regiment from the 308th Division, three more battalions from other formations, and an additional battalion of the 312th Division. They were supported by the howitzers of the Thirty-fourth Artillery Regiment. The attack, which opened at just after midnight, was met by eighty-one Moroccans and Legionnaires. They had hoped for support from the guns at Isabelle. But these were silenced by a withering interdictory fire from Viet Minh artillery.

The tiny force on Huguette 4 held on despite heavy losses. The Viet Minh also were suffering, so much so that the original field commander was sacked and replaced by another. At 3:35 there still were ten Moroccans fighting. A young lieutenant told De Castries on the radio that the enemy had leaped into his trench. There was the sound of shots, a scream, and then silence.

Elsewhere on Huguette, a force of about one hundred Moroccans and paratroops attempted yet another counterattack. The group managed to fight its way almost to Huguette 4 when it was driven back by the concentrated fire of 2,000 Viet Minh infantrymen and heavy shelling.

Huguette 4 was lost. It had cost the French fourteen dead, fifty-eight wounded, and 150 missing. Isabelle had lost two dead and thirty wounded.

By May 4 the senior officers knew there was no hope for the garrison. Vulture, the American air operation, never left the ground. The Condor force was stuck in Laos. The trenches and dugouts were flooded. The wounded were piled in muddy holes and were being devoured by maggots. As the rain seeped through the fortifications, the roofs of dugouts began to collapse. The ammunition supply was shrinking. The gunners reported that on May 4 they had fired 2,600 rounds of 105-millimeter ammunition; forty tons of supplies fell within the perimeter of the position.

Reinforcements dribbled in out of the clouds, seventy-four paratroops on May 5. By now all the reserves were committed to battle and the ammunition level was at its lowest. That day more dugouts collapsed under the unrelenting rain.

Although the senior commanders in Dien Bien Phu and in Hanoi and Saigon were shrouded in pessimism, the troops and the junior officers displayed a marvelous resiliency which was all the more remarkable when it is realized that most of them were living in appalling weather conditions on half-rations. Morale rose whenever a supply drop was halfway successful, such as that on May 6 when 196 tons of supplies were dropped into the fortress. That night, another ninety-one soldiers parachuted into the doomed fortress. The men in the French outposts continued to check Viet Minh attacks and followed them with counterattacks. If the generals—De Castries had been promoted to brigadier general during the siege—were giving up, this motley force of French, Vietnamese, and North Africans was not.

The French dispositions for the final battle were a sad reflection on their losses since the start of the siege. The Sparrowhawk position and Dominique 4 were held by the remains of a parachute battalion. To the northwest, 160 paratroopers of the Legion clung to what was left of Huguette 3 and 4. Lily 1 and 2, on the west, were held by Moroccans and Legionnaires. Claudine, to the southwest, was intact—as was Juno, the site of the hospital which was held by an Air Force detachment employed as infantry, some T'ai tribesmen, and some colonial infantry. Juno's dugouts and trenches held over 600 wounded.

The strongest French position was Elaine. Vietnamese, colonial infantry, French paratroops and combat engineers, and Moroccan riflemen were distributed through the strongpoints. About 750 paratroops held the main line along the tops of the hills that formed Strongpoint Elaine. They could expect no reinforcement from the main garrison and little artillery support.

At a little after noon on May 6, the Viet Minh began their final attack with the introduction of a new weapon, Soviet six-tube Katyusha field rockets fired from mobile launchers. The rockets fell on all the French positions. At the same time, mines laid under the French bunkers exploded. Dugouts collapsed. Electricity failed. The wounded died, suffocated in the mud. The first two salvos from the Katyushas broke the back of Dien Bien Phu's fortifications. Ammunition dumps exploded. Three fourths of the bunkers on Strongpoint Claudine collapsed. The first two salvos of the Katyushas and the exploding mines literally broke the back of Dien Bien Phu's fortifications.

Late in the afternoon, Giap switched to the firing of artillery, to which the French could offer only a feeble reply. The dazed defenders on Strongpoint Elaine and elsewhere burrowed into the earth to escape the shelling.

The first Viet Minh infantry attack developed in the early evening, when about 1,000 men sprang from their approach trenches and moved up the eastern slope of Elaine 2. Opposing them was a small force of French paratroops, backed by such artillery as the defenders could muster. The last remaining howitzers and mortars hammered the assaulting Viet Minh. The paratroops added fire from automatic weapons. The waves of attackers receded, leaving at least 200 dead behind.

The reverse had little lasting effect on the Viet Minh. They retaliated with heavy artillery fire against the French atop Elaine 2. Other batteries opened on Isabelle, and just before midnight eight of the nine 105-millimeter howitzers there had been knocked out of action.

The attackers' tactical pattern developed as the night deepened: heavy artillery attacks, exploding mines beneath French defensive posts, and mass attacks by waves of fanatical infantry. The French fought well; no troops could have fought better. Little knots of men withstood the pounding of the enemy guns, fought off with rifle and grenade the charging infantry, and then somehow drew on a last reserve of courage to launch counterattacks.

This happened on Claudine's post 5. But there were not enough defenders. The position fell at two in the morning.

Meanwhile heavy attacks had been launched on posts 4 and 10 of Strongpoint Elaine. The weight of the infantry assault struck a unit of Vietnamese paratroops, possibly because the Viet Minh commanders believed that these colonial soldiers would break. They did not. They fought the first attacking wave to a standstill. But there, as everywhere in the battle, they were too few to hold for long. By three in the morning, Elaine 4 was gone and Elaine 10 was held by about twenty men, many of them wounded.

Elaine 2 was destroyed just before midnight by the explosion of a huge Viet Minh mine built out of captured French 1,000-pound aerial bombs. Miraculously six men of the garrison survived. When these soldiers recovered from the shock of the explosion, they rallied and opened heavy fire on the masses of Viet Minh infantry advancing across the muddy slopes below them. Reinforcements were promised. Some of the soldiers were destroyed in the open; others ran into fierce firefights around other positions. Some thirty eventually reached the position, and by four in the morning they represented the entire garrison of the post.

Ammunition stocks were now desperately low—100 rounds of 120-millimeter bombs, 300 shells for the seven remaining 105's, and eleven shells for the sole remaining 155. Despite this serious shortage, the heavy losses and incessant fighting of the night, when dawn broke on May 7, the French still held Dien Bien Phu. Positions which had been lost had been regained—Elaine 4, for example. Clerical staff at the headquarters were hastily armed and fed into the fight. De Castries transmitted a somber estimate of the situation to Cogny at Saigon.

Just after eight in the morning, the enemy guns opened on Elaine 4. As usual, the artillery preceded a charge by hundreds of infantry, many of them wearing French uniforms and American helmets taken from airdrops that had fallen into Viet Minh hands. Despite the intensity of the attack, a few paratroops held on without reserves and short of ammunition.

About this time Dr. Paul Grauwin, the head of the medical services in the fortress, reported to De Castries that men were suddenly dying at their posts with no visible signs of wounds. They were dying, the doctor deduced, from fifty-five days of insufficient food and rest and the stress of constant combat.

The Viet Minh, scrambling over the mud and into the French positions, drove the defenders out of their trenches and into the open. The remnants from Elaine 4 attempted to escape to Elaine 10. Across the shattered fortress, little groups of French held out, taking a heavy toll of the attackers. But the Viet Minh came on. Elaine 11 and 12 were submerged under the tide of infantry after some of the Moroccan and T'ai tribal levies had hoisted the white flag. De Castries methodically reported the fall of successive strongpoints to Cogny by radio. At this late hour, Dien Bien Phu's commander suddenly revived the idea of a breakout, an operation that by now had become all but impossible. Cogny assented. The conversation, recorded at the time, has an air of fantasy. While it was being held, the entire French position was falling apart.

The last heavy firepower left to the French were the .50-caliber machine guns still blasting into the Viet Minh ranks with abundant ammunition. Elsewhere the positions on Claudine were eroding; the force at Sparrowhawk was pulled back to a new position close to the main headquarters.

In the midst of chaos, there was hope. The remaining French began to prepare for a breakout effort. Only those in good physical condition who had fought well during the siege would make the effort. Each man would carry a double load of ammunition. The remaining officers knew that the attempt was a very long shot. Some troops, those that broke westward toward the shelter of the hills, might make it. Others were sure to be met by overwhelming numbers of Viet Minh infantry and destroyed.

Two columns were assembled, and the commanders decided to draw straws to determine the routes. Those who attempted a breakout toward the hills had a marginally better chance than those who attacked elsewhere in the hope of breaking out to another position.

French planning for the breakout was interrupted by an aerial photograph dropped into the fortress. This showed that three new Viet Minh trenches had been dug over the last stretch of open terrain. De Castries and his subordinates realized that any attack by troops in poor condition could not hope to succeed and would result in heavy casualties.

Meanwhile Giap had called on his apparently inexhaustible reserves to mount another attack across the Nam Yum River. In twos and threes and, in one case, a lone man wounded but firing his automatic rifle with serene bravery, the French opened fire on the new attack. But others, the Moroccans among them, either surrendered to the enemy or collapsed from fatigue and hunger.

De Castries held a last meeting with his senior commanders. All knew now that Dien Bien Phu could not be held until nightfall. This grim estimate led inevitably to the realization that if the wounded were to be saved from massacre, French resistance should cease at a given time. The troops still fighting on Isabelle to the south were given the option of surrendering or attempting a breakout. The soldiers on Isabelle decided on a breakout.

De Castries selected 5:30 P.M. as the time for the cease-fire. Points 11 and 12 on Elaine fell around 4 P.M. and the last bridgeheads east of Nam Yum with them. The mortars were running out of ammunition. Infantrymen were down to their last few cartridges. Huge columns of black smoke rose from shattered positions as the surviving French destroyed everything that could be useful to the enemy.

The commanding general now put the cease-fire time forward by half an hour, and the message was transmitted by radio to the few remaining centers of resistance. De Castries, meanwhile, plunged into his last dialogue with Cogny. The latter realized that the end had come. His only command contribution was to order De Castries not to raise the white flag; there must be no capitulation.

At 5:50 P.M. came the last recorded message from Dien Bien Phu, "We're blowing up everything, *adieu.*"

The force on Isabelle fought on. By nine o'clock the preparations for the breakout had been completed and a series of explosions marked the destruction of the heavy equipment.

T'ai irregulars, Legionnaires, and tank crews fighting as infantry made up the force. They never had a chance. The first group followed the Nam Yum southward for about six miles where it ran into a strong Viet Minh force. Only three French and ten T'ai got away. The second force was ambushed half a mile south of Isabelle. In the darkness and confusion discipline broke. Only the tank crews managed to escape. Early on the morning of May 8, a French scout plane over the battlefield picked up the last message from Dien Bien Phu. It said simply, "Sortie failed—STOP—Can no longer communicate with you—STOP AND END."

Across the world in Paris, Laniel, dressed entirely in black, mounted the tribune of the National Assembly and spoke:

"The government has been informed that the central position of Dien Bien Phu has fallen after twenty hours of uninterrupted violent conflict."

The siege of Dien Bien Phu had lasted fifty-six days. The French casualties during the fighting, in the long march to the Vietnamese prison camps, and in the camps themselves were heavy. Most experts on the battle agree that about 2,200 men were killed, 6,000 wounded, and 6,000 taken prisoner. More than half of the latter died either on the trek to the camps or in the camps. Without any air force of their own, the Viet Minh antiaircraft gunners shot down forty-eight French planes over the valley, and sixteen others were destroyed on the ground. At the end of the battle there were slightly more than 9,000 troops left in the garrison. These included about 2,000 deserters, mostly North Africans, Vietnamese, and T'ai, who had hidden from the battle and hoped to slip away when the end came. The great majority failed.

During the siege the French dropped or flew in 4,000 reinforcements to replace casualties, and 6,500 tons of supplies were flown or parachuted into the valley. Less than five-sixths of the supplies reached the defenders.

The Viet Minh, who fought with fanatic bravery, paid heavily for their victory. Casualties were never announced, but the consensus is that there were at least 8,000 killed and 10,000 wounded.

The fall of Dien Bien Phu naturally provoked extensive analysis by the French and by their allies, particularly the Americans. Hundreds of staff studies, memoranda, and personal memoirs of the battle have appeared. The losers and their allies naturally were seeking the causes of the defeat.

The great majority of the troops at Dien Bien Phu, that polyglot army of different religions, customs, and training, cannot be faulted. They fought as brilliantly as any troops in history. The young French officers and the noncommissioned officers of all nationalities offer a shining example of personal leadership under desperate conditions.

A study of the various accounts leads to the conclusion that there were two main causes for the defeat.

The first was the insufficiency of French air force resources. Stewart Menaul draws a striking comparison between what the French were able to do at Dien Bien Phu and the American and South Vietnamese performance in the siege of Khe Sanh in 1968. In this action two North Vietnamese divisions numbering over 20,000 men besieged a garrison of 6,000. The siege lasted for seventy-eight days. In that time American air force and navy pilots flew 24,000 sorties in which more than 95,000 tons of bombs were dropped on the enemy. The defenders received over 12,000 tons of supplies from 1,200 supply sorties. In Menaul's view, "the garrison held out entirely due to the right application of air power in the right strength at the right time." Such an effort was well beyond French capabilities.

There is general agreement that the second major contribution to the French defeat was the persistent underestimate of Viet Minh capabilities and an overestimate of their own. They could not believe that the Viet Minh could supply so large a force in such forbidding terrain; at the same time they considered that the terrain would not prove any serious impediment to their own sorties. The generals in Hanoi and Saigon were surprised by the weight of firepower the besiegers were able to bring on the fortress and by the virtual collapse of their own supply system in the last days of the battle.

Consequently the greatest measure of blame must be assigned to the staff officers who planned the operation and then, when the situation began to deteriorate, failed to call a halt and to direct De Castries to cut his way out when he still had sufficient men and ammunition.

Did the Americans and other allies learn anything from the siege? The American performance at Khe Sanh is part of the answer, but only part. For the same underestimation of enemy capabilities and overestimation of our own contributed to the early American reverses in the Vietnam War.

One of war's grim axioms is that no power ever learns from another's defeat.

XIV

Military Victory and Political Defeat

TET

The Tet Offensive of 1968 in Vietnam is the outstanding example in this century of a military defeat that led to a political victory. The North Vietnamese and the Viet Cong were defeated everywhere, often with crippling losses. Yet almost before the echo of the guns had died, the psychological process had begun that drove a President of the United States from office and prodded his successor onto the long, wearying, but eventually successful road to peace. In the process the self-image of a great and powerful nation, the United States, was altered from one of confidence and resolution to one of uncertainty and whining self-doubt.

The political impact rather than the military operation gives the Tet Offensive its distinctive position among the battles of this century. Indeed there are few parallels. One must go back in our own history to Bunker Hill to find another battle in which the military losers accumulated so much political profit.

In any recounting of battles, men—especially those nurtured in the groves of academe—are prone to take the position that battles proceed according to plan and their outcome may be credited to the theories of Marshal X or General Y or Admiral Z. The end result may represent a facsimile of the words of the sainted Clausewitz. But except when a master is in command—a Wellington, a Lee, a

Rommel, an Alexander—the winner, when the odds are anywhere near even, usually just muddles through.

Because the battle and its consequences aroused such fierce controversy in the United States and, indeed, throughout the world, many of its salient points, such as the degree of surprise enjoyed by the Vietnamese, remain shrouded in a fog of words.

For example, in the immediate aftermath of Tet many Americans, not all of them opponents of the war and the Johnson Administration, believed that the offensive had been a complete surprise to the United States and South Vietnamese forces. No one bothered to ask why a force that had achieved complete surprise was completely defeated. Surprises there were. But they involved the enemy's targets and tactics, not the offensive itself.

The prescient reader will contend that this was true of the great German offensive in Flanders in the spring of 1918. Certainly the British and French knew that they were about to be attacked on a massive scale. What they did not know was that the Germans would use new tactics to achieve success. There the parallel ends. The Germans were largely successful and came within a hand's breadth of winning the war. The North Vietnamese regulars and Viet Cong guerrillas were defeated utterly on the battlefield.

The military and political origins of the Tet Offensive lie in the position of North Vietnam and its Viet Cong puppets in late 1967. The year had not been a good one. Faced with increasing numbers of American troops provided with overwhelming firepower, the North Vietnamese suffered heavy losses. The support of the peasantry, on which the Viet Cong counted, wavered. Supplies of war materials from the Soviet Union continued, but the People's Republic of China, the reluctant, uncertain, and resented ally, was in the throes of the Great Cultural Revolution which was to reduce Chinese political and military influence for a decade.

Sometime during the winter of 1967–68, the Vietnamese high command decided to take the offensive in the form of a co-ordinated and general offensive throughout South Vietnam. Whether, as General William C. Westmoreland believed, the objective was a popular uprising by the South Vietnamese against the Saigon government and its American supporters, we do not know. The Vietnamese accounts of the battle are either so wrapped in Communist ideological folderol or so self-serving that we have no clear evidence.

Whatever the objectives and the rationale for them, General Vo

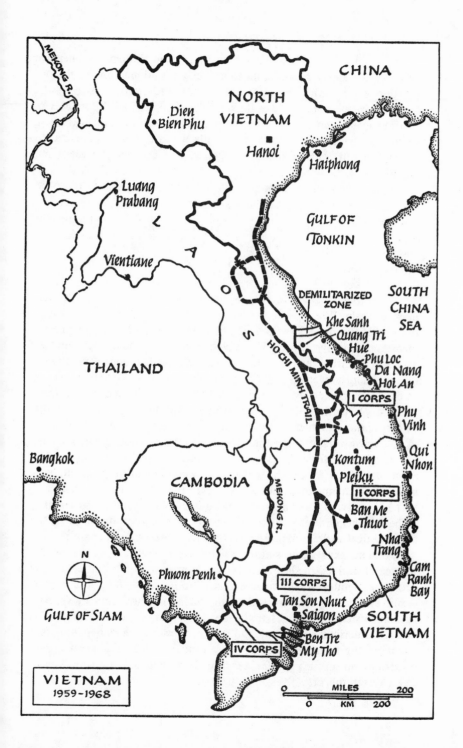

Nguyen Giap, Hanoi's Defense Minister, began to plan the offensive that winter. In his planning he consciously abandoned one of the operational tactics which, since the Vietnamese uprising against the French, had served them well. With the exception of the great victory at Dien Bien Phu, the Vietnamese, North and South, had clung to the doctrine and practice of guerrilla warfare. Giap's plans called for attacks in conventional style against positions held, in the main, by well-armed, well-trained troops.

It was, militarily and politically, a tremendous gamble. In spirit, at least, Giap was one with the Marquis of Montrose, who wrote:

> He either fears his fate too much
> Or his deserts are small,
> Who dares not put it to the touch
> To win or lose it all.

Or in the language of a less literate age, Giap was to "go for broke."

The Vietnamese intention, if not the detailed plan of operations, was known to the United States high command. Intelligence detected a methodical buildup of supplies and the concentration of manpower in the vicinity of cities and towns in South Vietnam. These measures were accompanied by feints intended to draw American units toward the border with Cambodia and to lure them away from the areas in which they would defeat individual operations of the Tet Offensive.

To these preparations the Hanoi government added an offensive in psychological warfare. In a thousand villages Viet Cong agents spread the word that the Americans were preparing to get out of Vietnam. Before they did so, the misinformation pattern said, the Americans would form a coalition government with the Viet Cong. There was nothing to these stories of American collusion with the enemy, but they probably served the purpose of weakening the resolve of some supporters of the Saigon government.

More than a decade later, Hanoi's approach to the battle remains unclear. Some students believe that Giap hoped to force the Americans and South Vietnamese into one or more Dien Bien Phu's, battles in which his enemies would be slowly destroyed. To believe this pays little tribute to Giap's military prescience. He understood that American manpower, firepower, and mobility were far greater than those of the French. There were no Dien Bien Phu's in the American Vietnam War.

If he did not aspire to a series of smashing military victories in the field, Giap did envision, I think, a series of attacks throughout Vietnam against targets of political and propagandistic importance. The attacks, successful or not, would have an impact on the course of American politics—it was an election year—and on the growing antiwar sentiment within the United States.

The North Vietnamese already were demonstrating their awareness of the strength and gullibility of the antiwar forces. Every antiwar speech by every obscure academic in an equally obscure college was seized upon, often edited, and circulated around the world as proof that America's heart was not in the war. Professor Knowitall from Whatzis Agricultural College became a weapon.

The celebration of Tet, the Lunar New Year, is a major event throughout Vietnam, a time of holiday and relaxation when the national guard is down. Giap chose well when he decided to launch the offensive at Tet. But Hanoi was reluctant to launch the offensive without giving its people a holiday.

Consequently the North Vietnamese government announced that the start of the Lunar New Year would be on Monday, Jan. 29. This meant that celebration in the North would begin on Sunday, Jan. 28. The North, then, would have three days of holiday before their troops in the south began the offensive after the true start of the Lunar New Year before daylight on Jan. 31.

Saigon made its own arrangements. After consultation with the Americans, President Nguyen Van Thieu announced that a cease-fire would be in effect from the evening of Jan. 29 to the early hours of Jan. 31. Hanoi, having ensured that its people would have a brief holiday, ordered the Viet Cong to announce a seven-day Tet truce beginning at sundown on Jan. 27.

The Communists' move was not particularly successful. All through the autumn, American and South Vietnamese intelligence had been picking up hints that a major operation was in the offing. The number of small but aggressive attacks around the country was increasing. Prisoners under interrogation talked about the approaching "final victory." The strength of the North Vietnamese and the Viet Cong in the Demilitarized Zone rose, and truck sightings along the Ho Chi Minh Trail rose by about 200 percent.

As the stream of intelligence reports swelled to a flood, interpretations of what they meant multiplied. For a brief period Westmoreland believed they indicated a major attack in the I Corps

Zone, the northernmost of the four corps zones into which South Vietnam was divided by the Army. But no one could be sure. In the autumn of 1968 Giap published an article in an official publication in which he urged the conservation of forces for a long war of attrition. If he were to be taken at his word by the Americans, then there was no sense in preparing for a general offensive by the enemy.

The American command was not duped. The signs of a major attack were too many. Moreover Giap's sudden conversion to the doctrine of attrition was not easy to reconcile with the tactics he had used at Dien Bien Phu. There, with the help of French stupidity, he had directed brilliantly a siege that culminated in the greatest victory scored by the Vietnamese in the long years of war. Would Giap, now, with his resources growing, be content to return to a war of ambush, sniping, and demolition?

If some Americans had any doubts about what the Vietnamese had in store, their doubts were dissipated when on Nov. 19 the 101st Airborne Division captured a document that appeared to be an outline for a major offensive—the "final phase" of the war, it was called. "Central Headquarters," the document said, "concludes that the time has come for a direct revolution and that the opportunity for a general offensive and a general uprising is within reach."

The South Vietnamese were becoming uneasy. In such circumstances racial identity among sworn enemies often speaks louder than volumes of intelligence intercepts. General Tran Ngo Tam told Westmoreland that he sensed that the enemy was planning a decisive blow.

The American general had reached the same conclusion. On Dec. 20 he had cabled General Earle G. Wheeler, Chairman of the Joint Chiefs of Staff, that the enemy had decided "that prolongation of his past policies for conducting the war would lead to his defeat and that he would have to make a major effort to reverse the downward trend."

The popular misconception of the American forces before and during the offensive is one of a huge, unwieldy force in static positions unprepared for surprise. In fact the Americans in the III Corps area opened a new series of offensive operations in Phuoc Long province to the northeast of Saigon, while other forces began a sweep to the Laotian frontier through the four northern provinces that would re-establish control of the A Shau Valley.

Sloppy Vietnamese reconnaissance and prisoners' reports slowly built up a picture of Giap's tactical intentions. A North Vietnamese scouting party at Khe Sanh was eliminated by a Marine patrol, but the dead included a North Vietnamese regimental commander and his operations and communications officers. Khe Sanh, evidently, was to be one of the foci of Giap's offensive. The two Marine battalions there were reinforced. The depth of reconnaissance patrols was increased. Plans were made for the co-ordination of artillery and air strikes around the post.

The document captured by the 101st Airborne Division was now released. It did not divulge the timing of the offensive, but it did give a clear picture of the tactics that would be used:

"Use very strong military attacks in co-ordination with the uprising of the local populations to take over towns and cities. Troops should flood the lowlands. They should move toward liberating the capital city (Saigon), take power, and try to rally enemy brigades and regiments to our side one by one. Propaganda should be broadly disseminated among the population in general, and leaflets should be used to reach enemy officers and enlisted personnel."

The events leading to the Tet Offensive began to take on the color of a Victorian melodrama in which each step leads inevitably to the startling *denouement*. A North Vietnamese defector at Khe Sanh provided a fairly complete description of the plans to capture Khe Sanh. To the south, soldiers of the Fourth Infantry Division picked up "Urgent Combat Order Number One," which gave a detailed plan for attacks in Pleiku province to begin "before the Tet holidays." Major General Charles F. Stone, the divisional commander, put his troops on alert and deployed a tank company as a reserve in Pleiku city. The South Vietnamese commander, Vinh Loc, was less energetic. But, he told the Americans, something was coming.

He did not cancel his plans for spending the Tet holiday in Saigon. The Americans, including Westmoreland, had a low estimate of Vinh Loc's capacities as a soldier. But he was there, and there was nothing they could do to get rid of him.

By the middle of January, North Vietnamese moves in preparation for the offensive became more obvious. Patrols of the Fourth Division reported movement behind the Cambodian frontier of two regiments of a North Vietnamese division that had fought skillfully at Dak To in November. Bombers and artillery attacked the regiments so successfully that, when the Tet Offensive began, only one battalion was able to carry out its assignment.

In the III Corps Zone there were signs that the Vietnamese were moving from positions along the Cambodian frontier to concentrations around cities and towns, including Saigon. Offensive operations were suspended, and the First Cavalry Division was ordered to move north into Thua Thien province.

By now the debate at American headquarters was not over whether there would be an enemy offensive but when it would come. Westmoreland thought that the attacks would be launched before Tet. His chief of intelligence, Brigadier General Phillip B. Davison, believed that the Vietnamese would use the cease-fire period to concentrate and then strike after Tet.

Few in the high command believed that the offensive would be launched on the day of Tet. They could not conceive, and their South Vietnamese allies were even less ready to think, that the enemy would open an offensive on the great national holiday. The reasoning was good, if wrong. The start of an attack on the holiday would turn against the attackers the very people whose help they sought for a national uprising. Westmoreland had some second thoughts. In a message to General Wheeler on Jan. 20, he mentioned the possibility that the offensive might start "during Tet."

Neither Westmoreland nor his deputies and staff envisaged the scope and fury of the Vietnamese attacks. Indeed, Westmoreland in his official report said, "It did not occur to us that the enemy would undertake suicidal attacks in the face of our power. But he did just that."

By the last week of January, the American high command was convinced that a prolonged celebration of Tet would be dangerous. Westmoreland went to President Nguyen Van Thieu and General Cao Van Vien, the South Vietnamese commander in chief, to propose that the cease-fire over Tet be canceled entirely or be cut from forty-eight to twenty-four hours. The Vietnamese refused. Cancelation was out of the question. The blow to national morale would be too severe. Under a drumfire of argument from Westmoreland, Thieu finally agreed to reduce the cease-fire to thirty-six hours, to limit leaves for the South Vietnamese forces and to keep at least fifty percent of all troops on duty at full-alert status.

What then was the American position on the eve of the battle?

Westmoreland and his chief of intelligence, General Phillip B. Davidson, knew that an enemy offensive was in the offing. Identification and location of the hostile units involved was correct. They knew that attacks were planned on cities and towns, although they did not guess the extent and weight of those attacks.

It was this failure to estimate accurately the scope of the attacks which prompted the shoot-from-the-hip criticism that the Americans had been taken by surprise.

"Even had I known exactly what was to take place," Davidson said later, "it was so preposterous that I probably would have been unable to sell it to anybody. Why should the enemy give away his major advantage, which was his ability to be elusive and avoid heavy casualties?"

Neither the high command of Americans and Vietnamese in Saigon nor the Administration in Washington was prepared for the political consequences of Tet. Westmoreland is not alone in blaming these consequences upon the media.

"No one to my knowledge," he wrote later, "foresaw that in terms of public opinion, press and television would transform what was undeniably a catastrophic military defeat for the enemy into a presumed debacle for the Americans and South Vietnamese, an attitude that still lingers in the minds of many."

The factor that was overlooked at the time of Tet and for some weeks after the offensive was that it was launched at a point in the war when President Lyndon B. Johnson and his chief aides, including the then-Secretary of Defense Robert S. McNamara, had been exulting publicly in American military success and predicting regularly that the end was in sight. The climate thus was prepared for a humbling of the mighty.

The North Vietnamese planning for the offensive was excellent. Not so their timing. Just after midnight on the morning of Tuesday, Jan. 30, the start of the Year of the Monkey, six mortar rounds burst in the Vietnamese Naval Training Center in Nha Trang. An hour later the streets of Ban Me Thuot in the Central Highlands were hit by rockets and mortars. This was followed by a two-battalion attack. Tan Canh, a tiny town that was a district capital, was attacked by a battalion. A half-hour later three battalions assailed the city of Kontum, the capital of the provincial highlands. Other enemy attacks were launched on Nha Trang, Hoi An (another district capital), Da Nang (where the headquarters of the South Vietnamese I Corps were located), Qui Nhon, and Pleiku.

Even today no one knows the reason for these premature attacks. The assumption is that because they all occurred in the same enemy area, Military Region V, someone in the regional headquarters either misinterpreted his orders or decided to launch the attack on his own.

The allies moved rapidly. President Thieu canceled the cease-fire, and Westmoreland told all American units that "troops will be placed on maximum alert with particular attention to the defense of headquarters complexes, logistical installations, airfields, population centers, and billets."

The offensive went into high gear late on Jan. 30. The most spectacular and reportable attacks were those on Saigon. But in addition to those, assaults were directed at thirty-six of the forty provincial capitals, five of the six autonomous cities, sixty-four of the 242 district capitals, and about fifty hamlets which were considered to have military importance. After Saigon, the most important objective was the old imperial capital of Hue, to the north in I Corps Zone.

The numbers conceal the sweep and fury of the attack. Read the words of Tom Hayden, now a major in the Marine Corps, then a civilian commanding a group of South Vietnamese irregulars. Late in the night of Jan. 30, Hayden walked the streets of Phu Vinh, capital of Vinh Binh province in the south. He recalls that an eerie feeling came over him.

"The streets were abandoned. No police patrols, no military sentries—nothing. I walked up one block and found nothing. Down a second block and still nothing."

Just after 3 A.M. on the morning of Jan. 31, the storm burst.

"I don't know which awoke me first—the gunfire or Lieutenant Colonel Girdner pounding on my door. I awoke in a fright. 'Something's going on. Get your weapon.' I heard a lot of people moving outside my window across the street. There is a small yard just before the street. I pushed open the shutters on my window and there they were. A whole platoon of armed men—twenty to thirty. It was 0310 hours.

"At first I thought they could be friendlies. But then I saw them shooting into the Provincial Government Compound.

"I quickly dressed, put on web gear with grenades and extra ammo, flak jacket, helmet, and grabbed my boots. Lieutenant Colonel Girdner and I maneuvered out of the front door and into the darkness. I could see that the VC were *inside* the Provincial Compound shooting at the Province Chief's House. I had seen a VC squad starting into the back of the yard just as we were going out the front of the house."

Hayden and Girdner took position on the porch of an adjacent house while the Viet Cong in green jackets and shorts slipped up to the wall of the compound.

"We watched the activity in the courtyard. The VC were running around, laughing, yelling, and calling each other by name. There were at least fifty VC in the courtyard. They were shooting at the Province Chief's houses and up and down the road in front of the house. Two heavy machine guns were inside the Compound shooting in all directions. A heavy firefight was going on behind us."

By 4:30 the VC appeared to have engulfed the area. Hayden and Girdner were in the midst of the attack, isolated on the porch of their landlord's house. The counterattack developed.

"By 0600 hours, armored personnel carriers had arrived from Cang Long and were linking up with elements of the Fourteenth Regiment. By 0615 the Fourteenth Regiment and the APC's [Armored Personnel Carriers] were moving. They moved into the center of the town and began fighting their way toward the Provincial Compound."

The APC's arrived in front of the house that held Hayden and Girdner at about 6:30 A.M.

"They immediately came under heavy fire from the Provincial Compound and the houses off to the right of our area. I realized that they didn't know where the VC were and neither did Sector TOC. I moved up to the front wall of my compound and started directing the APC's and the TOC by PRC-25 radio . . . This was the first time that I was really scared.

"The APC's didn't know I was there, and they were shooting the hell out of everything. Rounds were ricocheting all around me. One APC was shooting down the street past the front wall and, as he moved his machine gun, rounds would hit the wall in front of me, ricocheting inside, and [would] tear holes in the corner wall that I was leaning against. It reminded me of a knife thrower who would outline a figure against a target."

Hayden continued his radio instructions to the South Vietnamese who had arrived to counterattack the Viet Cong. The personnel carriers were now moving down a street into heavy concentrations of the enemy.

"The VC's opened up with B-40 rockets and machine-gun fire. As the APC's were trying to move back, two took heavy hits and had to be pulled out."

Communications between Hayden and the relieving force were difficult.

"There were at least five stations talking on the radio. And with the deafening explosion of .50-caliber machine guns, M-79 grenade launchers, and VC weapons, especially B-40 rockets, I could hardly hear. I pressed against the wall expecting the wall to explode."

The APC's continued to hammer at the Viet Cong with their heavy weapons aiming at the buildings in the Provincial Compound occupied by the Viet Cong.

"The sun had come up, and I finally realized that the VC had stopped firing and all the shooting was being done by our side."

Hayden walked over to talk to some of his Vietnamese irregulars.

"The explosion knocked me into the open bunker. I felt burned and dazed. The right side of my body was shaking uncontrollably . . . left arm covered with blood, left side of my face and neck dripping blood . . ."

Hayden survived this near-miss by a rocket to finish the war. His story tells us, in the cant phrase of the day, "like it was" to be caught in the Tet Offensive. Because of Hayden and his Vietnamese and American comrades, the point of the offensive was broken—but not before it had done the maximum psychological and political damage.

The most spectacular attack, that which won the most attention in the American media, was launched against the United States Embassy in Saigon. The Viet Cong sent an engineer unit against this objective, and for a time the fighting was heavy.

The Viet Cong blew a hole in the wall of the embassy compound. They exchanged fire with two military police and lost the first two men into the compound as a result. An American jeep patrol entered the fight and lost two men. At dawn the tide turned. A military police patrol entered the compound, picking off the Viet Cong one by one. Then a platoon of the airborne troops landed on the helicopter pad on the roof of the Embassy Chancery and entered the fight. Fifteen Viet Cong were dead when the scrap ended, and five Americans and four South Vietnamese embassy employees. One of the latter, Westmoreland reports, may have been a Viet Cong collaborator.

At the same time the Viet Cong also were attacking the Presidential Palace, the Vietnamese Joint General Staff Compound, and the Tan Son Nhut Airbase complex. They also overran the Phu Tho racetrack, which became their base for the remainder of the operation.

By the second day of the offensive, the elements of seven American battalions were operating in Saigon. Westmoreland has been criticized, mostly by writers whose military experience is extremely limited, for concentrating so many men around the capital. None of these writers offers an alternative strategy. Whether or not the commander's tactics were an example of overkill, they worked. Most of the attacking force was killed. Some became prisoners. Aside from the attack on the embassy, a dash into the rear area of the Vietnamese General Staff Compound, and two isolated raids on the perimeter of Tan Son Nhut Airfield, the American military position in Saigon survived almost undamaged.

But if the military position was unchanged, the attacks in Saigon had radically altered the viewpoint of the American media representatives covering the battle and, as a consequence, the attitude of their readers and viewers in the United States. Before we discuss the major Vietnamese operations elsewhere in the course of the Tet Offensive, the impact of the Saigon attacks must be assessed.

The Embassy of the United States, the armorer and paymaster of South Vietnam, had been boldly and bloodily attacked by enemy troops in the center of the capital. Editorial writers consulted their files to find when another such outrage had been perpetrated. It did not seem to matter to editorialists and commentators that the attackers had been killed or made prisoner. The assumption was that the American military had proved powerless to prevent an assault on the very heart of the United States position in Vietnam.

The rage, shock, and disillusion that arose from the attack on the embassy is more explicable when the comments of government leaders are examined. In the Vietnam War there was no one in high position in the Administration with any close and continuing experience with warfare, be it conventional or guerrilla. There was, in fact, no one in the White House able on the basis of personal experience to question the conclusions of the CIA briefing officers who daily presented *their* views on the military situation.

According to an informant who must be nameless because of his present position, President Johnson invariably took the most favorable view on the basis of the intelligence summaries provided by the military. When, as often happened, a general, an admiral, or a State Department official spoke up to suggest that the situation was not quite as favorable as the President appeared to think, he was told to "shut up." American military policy before, during, and after the Tet Offensive operated on the quicksands of wishful thinking.

Repulse of the attacks on Saigon led to a dangerous overoptimism about the attacks on Hue. The North Vietnamese and the Viet Cong made a far larger investment in the attack on the old imperial city than they did in Saigon. The reason, as with the majority of Communist operations, was based on political rather than military reasoning.

To Vietnamese, both North and South, the city of Hue was the symbol of Vietnamese nationalism. Take Hue, and a symbol for victory would be established for all Vietnamese. Whatever the reason, Hue was the focus of the largest offensive of the Tet battle. Most accounts agree that eight North Vietnamese and Viet Cong battalions launched the initial attack under the cover of heavy fog, and that these were later reinforced by another Viet Cong battalion and elements of two North Vietnamese divisions. By the end of the battle, about twenty North Vietnamese and Viet Cong battalions had been identified in and around Hue.

In view of the intelligence reports circulated by headquarters in Saigon, there should have been no surprise. But by daylight on Jan. 31, most of Hue was in enemy hands, including parts of the Citadel. The American compound housing the United States advisors was under siege. The blue-and-red Viet Cong flag with its yellow star flew from the flagpole of the Citadel. Its presence emphasized the extent and success of the enemy's offensive. But that offensive provoked a massive and highly effective counterstroke by the Americans and the South Vietnamese. This involved at the outset the First South Vietnamese Division and the only available American reinforcement, a company from the First Marine Division. The other companies in that company's battalion were fed into the battle as it developed.

Westmoreland reports that the South Vietnamese and the Marines in their initial counterattacks did not call in artillery, armored, or fighter-bomber support. They hoped, he wrote later, to spare "the venerable city." Perhaps. Commanders in desperate situations, as this one was, seldom fail to call for all the firepower available. Was it available at this juncture in the battle?

President Thieu, possibly under goading by the Americans, finally authorized the use of whatever means were necessary to retake Hue. The destruction was what might have been expected in war. Curiously, many Americans who were familiar with far worse destruction in Manila, Saint-Lô, and Aachen were shocked by what had happened in Hue in the twenty-five days of combat required to destroy the Viet Cong and the North Vietnamese presence.

Most of the Citadel and the residential sector of Hue south of the Perfume River was in ruins. Other areas in the city had been severely damaged in street fighting that, as Westmoreland said, was the closest approximation in Vietnam of the street fighting in Europe in World War II.

One aspect of the battle for Hue which should have had but did not have an enlightening effect on Americans was the disinterment by the Americans and South Vietnamese of those who had been killed and buried by the Communists during their occupation of the center of the city. All told about 2,800 people had been killed by shots in the back of the head, by formal firing parties, or by burial while alive. They included school teachers, civil servants, government officials, South Vietnamese soldiers and militia, priests, policemen, and hundreds of young men of military age with no connection with the South Vietnamese forces. A number of Americans, entitled to the usual favors given a prisoner of war, also were executed. No thought was given to them, nor tears shed in the groves of American academe.

American troops were committed in a number of other areas where the local situation proved beyond the capacities of the South Vietnamese. The Americans went "in" at Kontum city, Phu Loc, My Tho, and Ben Tre. In most of these areas and particularly at Quang Tri city, it was a close-run thing. At Quang Tri city a battalion of the First Cavalry Division arrived in time to break an attack and kill more than 400 of the attackers.

Westmoreland and other reporters on the defeat of the Tet Offensive are generous in their praise of the South Vietnamese forces, or the ARVN (Army of the Republic of Vietnam), as they were known to the Americans. The American involvement was important. Isolated units, military policemen, individuals like Hayden—all were drawn into the firefights that sparkled across the countryside. But as Westmoreland records, the "major share of credit for turning back the offensive" must go to the South Vietnamese.

They fought effectively. And despite the preliminary propaganda from Hanoi and the Viet Cong, no South Vietnamese unit broke in battle or defected under stress. In this, the climactic battle of the allied side of the war, they bore themselves as soldiers and patriots. By 1975 and the fall of South Vietnam, there were many in the United States prepared to disparage the South Vietnamese army. But the effort of that army's soldiers in the Tet Offensive should not be forgotten.

The enemy losses were severe. The official American estimate—and nothing in the interval has altered it—was that between Jan. 29 and Feb. 11, when the offensive had been stifled, the Communists lost 32,000 killed and 5,800 captured. This is close to half of the force committed to the offensive. The Americans lost 1,001 killed; the Vietnamese and allies, 2,082. After the North Vietnamese and the Viet Cong had been driven out of the major cities, the American estimate of enemy losses was fixed at 37,000 killed.

Was the figure exaggerated? On the one hand there are those who believe that body counts during the Vietnam War were so exaggerated by the American command that all estimates are suspect *per se.*

Bernard Brodie wrote that "the entire discredited system of 'body counts' for determining enemy dead has such a scandalous history in the Vietnam War that there would have to be an extraordinary and inexplicable shift to virtue during the Tet Offensive for one to accept as even nearly correct the figures for dead claimed by the allies."

An interesting comparison may be made with the French losses at Dien Bien Phu, which Brigadier General Peter Young puts at 2,293 killed and about 10,000 prisoners between March 13 and May 8, 1954.

The numbers game can go on into eternity. The effect of the battle on the Viet Cong and the North Vietnamese is more important. On Feb. 1 the Viet Cong headquarters called for a continuation of the offensive, a call that fell on deaf or dead ears, and conceded failures in the Tet operation:

"We failed to seize a number of primary objectives and to completely destroy mobile and defensive units of the enemy. We also failed to hold the occupied areas. *In the political field we failed to motivate the people to stage uprisings and break the enemy's oppressive control."* (Author's italics.)

This minatory message has attracted little attention among critics of the war, although its meaning is clear and highly significant. The North Vietnamese and Viet Cong are saying that not only had they failed to achieve their military objectives, but that the main political air, the uprising of the people against Saigon and Thieu and the Americans, never got off the ground.

The military victory of the allies was offset to some extent by Tet's disruption of the countryside and the cities. Westmoreland estimates that it created 600,000 new refugees and that the pacification program suffered because the teams operating in rural areas were driven into cities and towns where they stayed, fearful of a renewal of the enemy attack.

Under American pressure, the field pacification teams filtered back into the rural areas, and damage to the program proved less extensive than originally estimated. In the end, the refugee problem proved more serious. Intensive politicking by the Americans, and a recognition by Thieu of the dangers inherent in more than a half million rootless refugees that led to a welfare program certainly had some basis in fact. But no government program in Southeast Asia under any government—democratic, fascist, or communist—goes forward without corruption.

This is deplorable. But it is the way things happen to be.

One important effect of Tet on the Vietnamese was the enactment of a mobilization decree by the South Vietnamese National Assembly. The decree had been promulgated in the preceding autumn, but Thieu's government had feared it would be incapable of implementing it. After the citizens of cities and towns, until then largely apart from the struggle, had seen the consequences of the North Vietnamese and Viet Cong attacks, they were ready to contribute to what they now saw as a common struggle. The bill providing for the drafting of youths of eighteen and nineteen was passed, with only minor amendments by the assembly.

So making due allowance for exaggeration in the American estimates of enemy losses, for the social and economic consequences of an addition of 600,000 refugees, and for the continuation of corruption within the Saigon establishment, the reckoning must show that the Tet Offensive was a military defeat for the North Vietnamese and the Viet Cong.

This in sum is the military result of Tet. An enemy had used many of his best, and some of his least, battleworthy formations, in an offensive that had been destroyed by the South Vietnamese and the Americans. But the seeds of political victory were contained in the dimensions of the military defeat.

The Viet Cong had penetrated into the American Embassy compound in Saigon. The penetration had no military effect beyond the expenditure of the lives of a good many Vietnamese and some Americans. But the political effect in the United States was extensive and damaging. "Wow," as they said on the campuses where the anti-war legions were mobilizing for battle in their jeans and T-shirts.

Lyndon B. Johnson charged in *The Vantage Point* that there was "a great deal of emotional and exaggerated reporting of the Tet Offensive in our press and on television." Certainly there was. But in a simpler day American reporters, nurtured on a tradition of victory extending back to 1942, were not prepared to see American embassies attacked. They might have been "emotional" in their reporting, but their subject matter was of a kind that was bound to excite emotions even in the most objective reporter. The reporting appears to have been exaggerated in the first eight hours but, looking over the reports of those days, the exaggeration may have been more the work of headline writers than of correspondents in the field.

President Johnson argued that the performance of the South Vietnamese after the passage of the mobilization decree "was never made clear in most day-to-day reporting." A counterargument could be made that it *was* made clear, but that any reporter believing in balance would have a mandate from his editor to describe the other side of the war story as well.

What the Administration could not obscure was the impact the reports, accurate or exaggerated, of the Tet Offensive had had on the peace movement in the United States. It may well have been that the media reports had only a marginal effect on this movement. Like all mass movements of its kind, it was intolerant of fact, except when fact served to confirm its own emotions, and quick to take to heart the most outrageous fabrications put out by the North Vietnamese and circulated around the world by what are called "freedom-loving" or "progressive" associations.

There were those in the Administration and in the field who realized that the Communists were attaining their political objective of weakening the United States's will to war. General Earle G. Wheeler, the Chairman of the Joint Chiefs of Staff, said that although he could see no reason for "all the doom and gloom we see in the U.S. press, most of the setback was here in the United States, which was one of their objectives."

Similarly President Johnson, after a discussion with Vice President Hubert Humphrey, was convinced that "we were defeating ourselves."

It is perhaps too early to say whether this judgment was accurate. But it is a matter of record that the clamor against the war on the campuses, among liberal politicians, in academic circles and, most important, among patriotic middle-class families was rising. The last were the most important, because their support in that or any war is essential. Once even a fraction of them became convinced that their sons were being sent to fight in a war that could not be visibly won, they opted out.

The Viet Cong and the North Vietnamese had won.

No single motive is responsible for a human being's decisions. But it is possible to discern in Lyndon B. Johnson's decision on March 31, 1968, not to run for re-election, the impact of Tet. The war had continued despite the enemy losses in that offensive. New requirements for more men and more arms were encountering increasingly effective opposition in Congress and the media. European and Antipodean allies, while mouthing lip service to American policy, were evading moral, not to say material, support of the war effort. The popular appeals for a bombing halt, for negotiation, for American withdrawal, increased in volume and in fervor. Mass demonstrations against the war in Washington and a hundred other cities, led by respected members of the clergy, academics, and politicians, were proliferating. Kent State was just around the corner.

Lyndon Johnson decided not to try again for the Presidency. The enemy had lost the Tet Offensive. But they had forced the United States government into a "no-win" position.

Could the war have been won militarily? A majority of army, navy, and air force officers who were there believe that it could have been won if two conditions had been established at the start by their masters in Washington. The first was that the Administration should have jettisoned the, on the face of it absurd, fiction that American troops were in Vietnam solely to protect the government of South Vietnam and announce that North Vietnam was the enemy. The second was that from this announcement American military efforts would have been directed at Hanoi, Haiphong, and the other centers of North Vietnamese military power. Granted the American superiority at that time in the air, on the ground, and at sea, there is at least the probability that North Vietnamese power would have been destroyed.

Would this have ended the war? The likelihood is that the Vietnamese, North and South, would have continued the guerrilla war although without the support of Hanoi.

But from the standpoint of the United States position in the Far East, would that situation have been worse than that in which the Republic now finds itself? Vietnam triumphant from the South China Sea to the borders of Thailand? The great bases at Cam Ranh Bay and Da Nang now open to Soviet fleets?

In the Tet Offensive, the Viet Cong and the North Vietnamese won, and won more than they could have envisaged at the time.

XV

"If You Can See It, You Can Hit It. If You Can Hit It, You Can Destroy It."

THE BATTLE OF THE BRIDGES, HANOI

In the second week of May 1972, small forces of aircraft drawn from the Eighth Tactical Fighter Wing based on Ubon in Thailand destroyed two Vietnamese bridges and irrevocably changed the nature of war. The American aircraft launched precision-guided bombs—or as they were then called, "smart bombs"—and the Vietnamese employed surface-to-air (SAM) guided antiaircraft missiles against them, with little success. The consequences of this air-ground battle have had an enormous and continuing influence on defense ministries, arms industries, and general staffs around the world. Tactical warfare concepts long held and revered are being reviewed and revised. Strategists are re-examining the potential military strength of those smaller countries that have access to the new weapons. The revolution in war may not be as great as that which followed the introduction of gunpowder, as some assert, but it certainly is comparable to the introduction of the tank onto the battlefields of World War I.

The background of the battle against the bridges provides clues to understanding the significance of their destruction. The bridges were targets of the highest priority. The Paul Doumer Bridge on the outskirts of Hanoi, named for a former Governor General of French Indochina, was built between 1896 and 1902. The bridge carried railway traffic into the North Vietnamese capital from the port of Haiphong to the east and from Lao Cai in the west. As traffic expanded under the stress of war, the bridge also carried trains from Kep, Thai Nguyen, and Dong Dang to the north. As the war grew, so did the volume of truck traffic across the bridge over the Red River.

The bridge was 5,532 feet long and thirty-eight feet wide, supporting a one-meter railroad track in its center and a ten-foot highway on each side. Its nineteen spans rested on eighteen massive concrete piers with ten through-truss spans, eight of 350 feet and two of 250 feet, and nine cantilever spans, each of 246 feet. Including the approaches, the total length of the structure was 8,467 feet. In extent and solidity of structure, the Paul Doumer could be compared to the great railroad bridge across the Rhine at Cologne which for so long resisted Allied air attacks in World War II.

The Thanh Hoa bridge, which spans the Ma River three miles north of Thanh Hoa, the capital of Annam province, was relatively new. The Viet Minh had destroyed the original bridge in 1945. The new bridge had been completed in 1964 with the help of Chinese technicians. The North Vietnamese called it Ham Rung, or Dragon's Jaw.

The Dragon's Jaw was smaller than the Paul Doumer, being 540 feet long and fifty-six feet wide. A one-meter-gauge railway track ran down the center with twenty-two-foot-wide highways cantilevered on each side. Although crude in finish, the bridge was strong. The two steel through-truss spans rested in the center on a massive reinforced concrete pier sixteen feet in diameter and on concrete abutments at the ends. The Vietnamese, fearful of bombing, had added eight more concrete piers close to the approaches to provide added resistance.

As early as 1965, President Lyndon B. Johnson and the Joint Chiefs of Staff, casting about for a means of forcing the North Vietnamese to reduce their support of the Viet Cong, recognized the two bridges as vital links in the North's communications system. The Battle of the Bridges was about to begin, with the air force and navy pitted against North Vietnamese armed with Russian Mig fighters and an increasing supply of SAM's.

The first American raid on the Dragon's Jaw was executed on

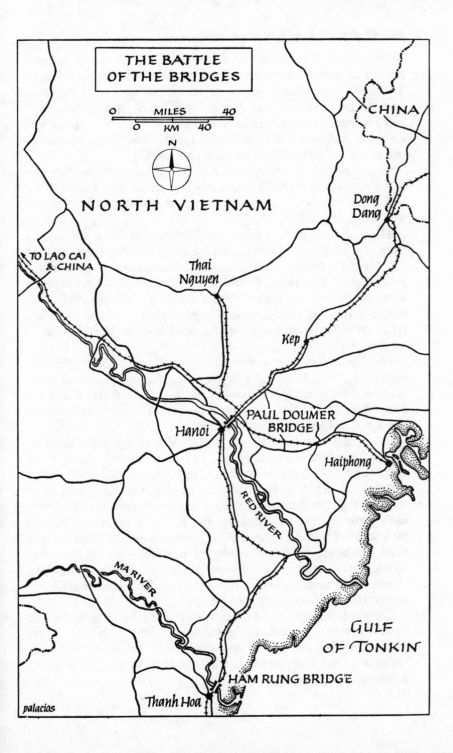

THE BATTLE
OF THE BRIDGES

0   MILES   40

0   KM   40

N

CHINA

NORTH VIETNAM

Dong
Dang

TO LAO CAI
& CHINA

Thai
Nguyen

Kep

PAUL DOUMER
BRIDGE

Hanoi

Haiphong

RED RIVER

MA RIVER

GULF
OF TONKIN

HAM RUNG BRIDGE

Thanh Hoa

palacios

April 3, 1965. The attack was a heavy one, but the bridge suffered far less damage from the conventional bombs than was anticipated. Two aircraft were lost. The pattern thus set endured until the President ordered the cessation of bombing; heavy attacks, invariably pressed home, caused considerable damage—twice the bridge was closed to traffic—but with no lasting results. Two planes shot down one day, three on another, two more on a third.

At this point in the war, the air force and the navy had been ordered not to attack the Paul Doumer Bridge. Some critics have described this denial as a salient example of the folly of waging war with only one hand.

The American efforts against the Dragon's Jaw were not entirely without reward. Aerial reconnaissance in late March 1968 reported that the main structure was a mass of charred, dented, and twisted steel girders. The railroad tracks were twisted and bent. Craters along the approaches made vehicular traffic almost impossible. The bridge still stood, but it would require prolonged and extensive repairs if it was to resume its old importance in the North Vietnamese economy.

The North Vietnamese were granted time to make repairs. On March 31, 1968, President Johnson ordered a halt to air and naval bombardment north of Latitude 20 North and asked Hanoi to enter peace talks to end the war. The President also announced that he would not seek or accept another term.

During the bombing halt, the Thanh Hoa bridge and dozens of others throughout the country that had been seriously damaged or destroyed by air attack were repaired or rebuilt. As American troop withdrawals began, the Vietnamese ground and air forces were strengthened. On March 30, 1972, almost four years after Mr. Johnson's order to halt the bombing, the North Vietnamese launched their major invasion of the war, smashing across the Demilitarized Zone into South Vietnam's Quang Tri province. The air force was called upon to check the offensive and to attack communications targets in the north. The air strategy included a co-ordinated interdiction campaign against the two bridges.

The air crews and ground crews were doing business at the old stand but with a difference. Their armament now included the first precision-guided munitions. These were electro-optical–guided bombs (EOGB's) and laser-guided bombs (LGB's) weighing 2,000 and 3,000 pounds respectively.

The EOGB's had a small TV camera attached to the nose, which transmitted a picture of what it was viewing to a scope in the attack aircraft. The pilot then pointed the aircraft and weapon at the target area, allowing the weapons systems operator in the rear cockpit of the F-4 Phantom to find the target on the scope, refine the contrast-aiming point, and designate the target to the weapon. Once this was done, the pilot released the bomb and flew out of the target area, leaving the EOGB to guide itself.

Bad weather or smoke that obscured the target robbed the EOGB's of much of their effectiveness. But if the weapon could see the target when it left the aircraft, it would usually hit it.

In the LGB's, a laser sensor was mated to the nose of a 2,000- or 3,000-pound bomb, which enabled it to guide itself toward a target illuminated with low-power laser energy. The problem that confronted the bomb's builders was illuminating the target. This was solved by attaching a pod beneath the fighter. The pod held a laser-emitting device and an optical viewing system operated by the weapons systems operator.

The pilot flew the aircraft toward the target. The operator located the target-aim point and illuminated it with his laser equipment. The pilot released his bombs, and the attacking plane left the target area. An obvious advantage of this "smart" bomb was that more than one aircraft at a time could drop LGB's on the same target, with all the weapons using the same illumination point as a guide. The disadvantage was that the target had to be continuously illuminated. If clouds obstructed the view, the LGB became an unguided bomb. Both EOGB's and LGB's meant less aircrew exposure and greater accuracy.

The advances in sophisticated weaponry were not all on the American side. As early as July 24, 1965, an air force F-4C had been shot down by a North Vietnamese surface-to-air missile. Thereafter the number of SAM sites multiplied, although the air force estimated that about sixty-nine percent of its losses were due to antiaircraft fire. In all of 1965 the Vietnamese fired 180 SAM's, destroying eleven planes. During the 1972 air offensive, more than 1,000 SAM missiles were launched, knocking down fifteen B-52's and three other aircraft.

The first Russian SAM's were guided by either radar or optical sighting. Then the SA-7 was added; its guidance was either optical aiming or infrared homing.

Initially the SAM's were deployed in a circle around Hanoi. Later the network was extended to cover the railroads to the northeast and northwest and the major airfield at Yen Bai. According to General William W. Momyer, the SAM's at all sites were operated almost entirely by Russians and North Vietnamese, with the Russians gradually turning over operational control of the sites to their allies.

By the time the air force opened the 1972 offensive, there were about 200 or more SAM launchers in North Vietnam with 300 battalions of rocket troops maintaining about 100 missiles on launchers at any given time. The total inventory of missiles in the country was estimated at between 400 and 500, with about 200 at launch sites and the remainder in the supply system. During the 1972 American offensive, pilots reported sharp decreases in the launching rate after two or three days of operations. The Vietnamese supply system, it was assumed, was not efficient.

Whatever their strength, the SAM's presented a new threat to the American aircraft, one unprecedented in aerial war. At the start, most pilots believed their aircraft had sufficient maneuverability to escape damage from the new antiaircraft weapon. Pilotlike, they did not wish to trade this maneuverability for the installation of electronic countermeasures (ECM) equipment that would divert and mislead the missiles. In the end the pilots gave way, and ECM became standard throughout the air force. Since 1972, it has become more complex with the introduction of electronic counter-counter-measures (ECCM) and other instruments of electronic wizardry. But it was in Vietnam, in that final air offensive, that ECM's, like the SAM's and the smart bombs, took center stage in the long, tragic drama of war.

The effectiveness of the smart bombs—the precision-guided munitions or PGM's, as we shall call them henceforth—naturally was the most significant test of the new weaponry.

May 13, 1972, brought an attack by fourteen strike aircraft on the Thanh Hoa bridge. The planes were armed with nine 3,000-pound LGB's, fifteen 2,000-pound LGB's, and forty-eight 500-pound conventional bombs. The attack was launched in perfect weather. The postattack reconnaissance photographs showed that the western span of the bridge had been knocked off its concrete abutment and that the bridge's superstructure had been grotesquely twisted by the bombs. Traffic over the bridge was halted for several months.

The PGM's that knocked out the Dragon's Jaw had a similar

effect on the attacks on the Paul Doumer Bridge. On May 10, sixteen F-4's were loaded with PGM's, three flights with LGB's, and
one with EOGB's. The attackers met a very intensive defense. The
estimate is that 160 SAM's were fired at the strike force that day
and that forty-one Mig's intervened in the battle. Not a single American aircraft was lost.

The strike aircraft dropped twenty-two LGB's and seven EOGB's
on the target. One span of the Paul Doumer Bridge was destroyed.
Several others were severely damaged. Rail traffic from the north to
Hanoi was halted. But to make assurances doubly sure, the air force
ordered another mission for May 11. Only four F-4's were sent, but
their results were phenomenal by the standards of those days.

Eight 2,000-pound LGB's were dropped. Three of the bridge's additional spans were knocked into the Red River and three more
wrecked. On Sept. 10 the air force had one more crack at it. Two
more spans were destroyed. The Paul Doumer Bridge was out of action for the rest of the war.

An unofficial air force history of the operations against the two
bridges comments, "A significant factor in this success story was
[the] phenomenal accuracy achieved with guided bombs. With
fewer strike aircraft required to assure target destruction, more targets could be attacked and a larger number of aircraft assigned to
defending the strike force. The higher bomb-release altitudes helped
keep the fighters out of the deadly AAA range, thereby lowering loss
rates significantly."

Phenomenal accuracy, economy of force, lower losses—these
were the lessons that the first use of PGM's taught the military
world. In World War I, the significance of the birth of the tank went
largely unrecognized by rigidly conservative generals; in the high-
technology era of the second half of the twentieth century, this professional blindness did not recur. Military and civilian authorities
grasped the significance of the new weapons. They recognized that
the weapons were operationally and economically feasible. Naturally
there was an almost universal surge in military circles to apply the
principles of the PGM's to other fields, particularly to antitank
weapons.

The axiom was that what the new missiles could see, they could
hit—and that what they hit, they could destroy. By the end of the
decade, the pace of development was so great that a dozen or more
new PGM types reached the testing stage around the world each

year, and they proliferated beyond the superpowers and their alliances into Third World countries.

The advent of any new weapon raises questions about its effect on warfare. But the RPM (Remotely Piloted Munitions), unlike other twentieth-century weapons such as the tank or the submarine, is not confined to one element. The RPM's are applicable to war on the ground, at sea, and in the air. They can be launched by troops on the ground against aircraft, by aircraft against other aircraft or ground forces, by submarines against surface ships or shore targets, by surface ships against hostile vessels or enemy aircraft, by ground forces against enemy tanks or artillery or depots or headquarters. Their variety is almost infinite.

So is the number of tactical questions their use provokes. What is the future of the main battle tank, now costing in the United States more than $1 million each, when confronted with scores of antitank RPM's costing about $23,000 for the missile and its guidance unit. An SAM such as the Soviet SA-7 is capable of knocking down a multipurpose, advanced fighter aircraft. The SAM may cost about $10,000; the fighter costs well over $10 million.

Quite aside from economic considerations, will there be a place in future battles for the main battle tank, the advanced fighter-bomber, or even the aircraft carrier? Remember that in addition to the relative cheapness of manufacture, many of the weapons can be operated by the average soldier, sailor, or airman. The weapons themselves and their maintenance are becoming more complex. But the task of sighting and launching them is not.

The RPM's will have impact both on the tactics of tomorrow's battles and on the overall balance of power between the United States with its NATO allies and the Soviet Union with its satellites of the Warsaw Pact.

Let us examine the first impact as it is seen by military and civilian specialists.

Does the introduction of RPM's restore the importance in battle of small units armed with these weapons or even with the devices required to sight them? It may be that in a future war the key will be a large number of small squads of men, afoot or in light vehicles, roving a battlefield.

James Digby of the Rand Corporation, in an excellent early paper on the effect of RPM's, pointed out that as concentrations of vehicles and men become "less practical," concealment will become more important and smallness and mobility will make concealment easier. From this it can be argued that RPM's will make it unwise to concentrate military value in a single vehicle—an aircraft, a tank, an aircraft carrier. The alternative, on land at least, may be a multiplicity of lightly armored, fast, and agile vehicles. Even as the United States Army was unveiling its new Abrams main battle tank, some skeptics were arguing that the RPM's made the tank a risk and that the more sensible course was lighter, less heavily armed vehicles.

Since the German invasion of France and the Low Countries in 1940, the ideal offensive has consisted of masses of tanks, highly mobile artillery, and a cover of fighters and light bombers, today combined into the strike aircraft. How applicable is that ideal to the new era heralded by the RPM?

The argument among military planners goes both ways. One school contends that swarms of RPM's will halt the tank masses and destroy their air support, thus restoring primacy on the battlefield to the defense. Others argue that self-propelled guns and long-range RPM's will eliminate the defenders' fire and that mobile SAM's will provide the necessary protection against enemy aircraft, which, of course, will be armed with air-to-surface RPM's.

The argument will go on. If there is anything clear about this picture of the future, it is that the recognized and accepted modes of battlefield alignment and support will give way to less-ordered situations in which forces will be intermingled and in which the destruction of enemy resources, from tanks to command centers, will be more important than securing territory.

What does this mean to the balance of conventional power between the United States and NATO and the Soviet Union and the Warsaw Pact?

The RPM's in their present form, and in the next three or four generations, clearly favor the defender. No one, except Russian propagandists, has ever conceived of a NATO offensive against the Communist powers. Indeed, almost all the planning for NATO in Western Europe has concentrated on defending the region in the face of Russian attack.

The conclusion, today, must be that the RPM's have given NATO at least a chance to stabilize a front in Germany. This does not mean that the alliance's lines would be impervious to a massive Russian offensive at a chosen point where the Russians would have the advantage in tanks of at least three and possibly four to one and in aircraft of about two and one half to one. It does mean, however, that the defensive capacity of NATO forces armed with RPM's would suffice to check the Soviet offensive after perhaps thirty-six hours of progress.

It will be argued that Russian artillery and bombers would suppress the NATO RPM's. If these weapons were lined up truck to truck with the launchers in a neat row, Soviet suppression would be a probability. But the mobility of RPM's makes the difference. The Russians cannot expect to find their targets exposed and vulnerable. Instead they must reckon that every copse, every farmhouse, every hamlet houses its RPM's, whose mission is to destroy armored vehicles and shoot down the accompanying aircraft.

But what of the Russian masses behind the front prepared to enter the battle, what of the depots and headquarters? The answer there may lie in the perfection of another sophisticated weapon, the cruise missile, a self-guided missile of great precision. This weapon, fired from mobile launchers in the air, on or under the sea, or on the ground, may prove to be more effective against distant battlefield targets than the manned bomber. Again it is relatively economical. Compare the cost of fifty advanced manned bombers and fifty cruise missiles.

Two final considerations.

As has been proven, Third World countries, once equipped, can use RPM's with deadly effect. As the weapons grow simpler, their effectiveness in the hands of soldiers, sailors, and airmen with relatively low technological background will increase. The production and maintenance of RPM's, of course, will demand a high level of technological skill and heavy expenditure, either by the user nation or by the country that has provided the weapons. From this it can be suggested that we have seen the end of superpower intervention with minor losses against trained troops in a Third World situation. It is impossible to think of the United States Marines making a low-cost landing on a coast whose defenders are armed with RPM's. It is equally difficult to envisage the Russian naval infantry storming ashore against forces similarly armed.

A second consideration is that through strengthening the defensive capability of the NATO allies and friendly states the world over— Australia, Chile, the Philippines, to name three—the advent of RPM's may result in lowering the nuclear threshold. It is difficult to believe that the Soviet Union, once launched on a massive invasion and halted by an equally massive use of RPM's, would not resort very soon to tactical nuclear weapons. This would be the first step in the escalation of any conflict to an intercontinental exchange.

We are, therefore, living through the first phase of a revolutionary change in the nature of war which will be of enormous significance to future conflicts. We cannot today accurately chart the changes in formations, weaponry, and tactics that will ensue. But we can safely assume that with the coming of RPM's, war will change and change rapidly.

XVI

Victory on the Knife Edge of Defeat

THE YOM KIPPUR WAR

Early on the morning of Oct. 27, 1973, Major General Adly el-Sherif marched from the Egyptian lines around the city of Suez toward a huge tent marked with the Star of David. The tent was pitched at Wadi al-Jandali, not far from a milestone on the Suez–Cairo highway sixty-three miles from the capital of Egypt.

Standing in the starlight was Major General Ahron Yariv, the former head of Israeli intelligence and now designated the chief negotiator for Israel in the preliminary Egyptian-Israeli peace negotiations. "Two valiant armies have fought for three weeks," Yariv said. "Now let's try to work out an honorable peace."

The meeting ended one of the most important conflicts of the century. Although it is usually called the 1973 War, or the Ramadan War by the Arabs, or the Yom Kippur War by the Israelis, it was in fact a single campaign fought on two fronts. From a historical perspective the time spent fighting was brief; the campaign was concluded in fewer days than it took the Normandy invasion to develop its second phase; in the great encounter at Stalingrad, the Russians and the Germans had only begun after twenty-one days to feel out each other's strengths and weaknesses.

But neither the duration of battles nor the numbers engaged is the true criterion of their importance.

In this case the war may be said to have been planned as far back as the summer of 1967, when the Egyptian and Syrian forces, badly beaten by the Israelis, returned to ponder the lessons of defeat. Whether or not the Arab losers in 1967 completely assimilated those lessons we cannot tell. We do know that on Aug. 22, 1973, eight Egyptian and six Syrian senior officers met in the headquarters of the Egyptian navy, the old royal palace of Ras el-Tin in Alexandria. General Ahmed Ismail Ali, the Egyptian Minister of War, with a nod to General Mustafa Tias, Syrian Minister of Defense, called the meeting to order.

The business of the meeting was both complex and simple. It was to add the last delicate touches to the plan for a simultaneous offensive on Israel in the Sinai and in the Golan Heights, some time in the autumn. The plan represented not only military thought but emotional, nationalistic commitment. Like the French high command between 1900 and 1914, whose views seldom wandered far from Alsace and Lorraine, the Arab officers concentrated on the recovery of their lost territories.

This had been the goal of warring states since the beginning of time. In that sphere of reference the 1973 conflict was unexceptional. However, it is exceptional on two other counts. Politically and psychologically it restored to the two Arab combatants a confidence and pride they had lost in the humiliating defeats of 1967. Or, as a rough-tongued British officer said in Cairo just after the war, "the Arabs got their balls back." Militarily the campaign opened a new era in warfare, faintly foreshadowed by the American air force's use of guided bombs in the final phase of the Vietnam War.

In the Sinai and on the Golan, the entire arsenal of American and Russian precision-guided munitions were used with, as we shall see, drastic effects on the tactics of both sides. Like the advent of the tank in World War I or the employment of the railroads and telegraph by the North in the Civil War, the massive use of RPM's in a two-dimensional campaign changed the nature of war.

Aside from the impact on military doctrine arising from the use of these new weapons, the campaign had other lasting physical and psychological results. For the first time since the War of Independence, Israel suffered relatively heavy casualties—an estimated 4,100 killed and wounded. But it was not simply the quantity but the quality that told that Israel's losses in junior officers, both in the army and in the air force, were high. In view of the character of Israel's citizen-forces, this meant that the country had lost not only skilled and experienced officers but skilled and experienced farmers, mechanics, civil engineers, and administrators as well.

The Arab casualties also were high—7,500 Egyptians killed or wounded and 7,300 Syrians. But these losses were from populations far larger than that of Israel. They could be, and were, made up within a year.

Between the two Arab allies, the effect of the first few days of success was probably greater among the Egyptians than among the Syrians. The successful Egyptian assault against the Israeli forces in the Bar Lev Line on the east bank of the Suez Canal was a brilliant feat of arms, proving to the Egyptians and to watchers in the Western and Eastern world that not only were the Egyptians brave, but that they were resourceful and technologically advanced as well. In addition, the Arab strategists, Syrian as well as Egyptian, had surprised Israeli forces commonly accounted then and now as the best in the Middle East.

The campaign can be divided into three acts. The first saw the initial Arab offensive into the Golan and across the Suez Canal. The second, and in retrospect the most important, was a period of attack and counterattack in which, on both sides, errors of perception and mistakes in judgment played an important part. The third was an orchestrated Israeli climax with forces crossing the canal westward, "into Africa," as the triumphant troops proclaimed, and driving out of the Golan toward the Syrian capital of Damascus.

The overture to Act One, as we have seen, was written years earlier and practiced since then. Its first practical step may have been taken in May 1972, when Magirus Deutz Fire Protection Techniques, a company based in Ulm, Bavaria, received an order from the Egyptian government for two TST 40/7 pumps for testing. These are portable but powerful turbine-driven machines. Magirus is a major manufacturer of fire-fighting equipment. The explanation that must have come to mind was that Egypt intended to equip its fire fighters with new machines. The TST would be what was required; it could pump a thousand gallons a minute.

But it was the Egyptian army's engineer corps, not the Cairo fire department, that tested the pumps. After the first two pumps had been tested, Egypt ordered another one hundred. A windfall for Magirus—so much so that the Egyptians were quoted a special low price. The pumps, as we shall see, played an important role in Egypt's first major success of the campaign.

With the exception of the Japanese against Russia early in the century and against the United States in 1941, few powers have achieved surprise comparable to that won by the Egyptians and the Syrians when the war opened on Oct. 6, 1973. The impact of this surprise dominated the first days of the campaign, and to understand the fighting we must understand why the Israelis, the military masters of the Middle East, were surprised.

One factor was a complacent overconfidence. The writer, visiting the Bar Lev Line on the east bank of the Suez Canal in 1972, was told that only two infantry battalions with a third in reserve held more than twelve miles of the line. The Israeli colonel rejected the idea that his forces were very thin on the ground. If he faced an attack by American, British, or German troops, he said, they of course would be much stronger. But Egyptians? His boys could handle them.

Beyond this there was an overall failure to foresee the Arab offensive. This was a failure of Israeli intelligence which, at that time, was considered the best in the Middle East—not only in the collection of information, but in the assessment of that information in the Tel Aviv headquarters.

All the branches of Israeli intelligence, particularly Mossad, the secret intelligence service, had suffered from the placidity of five years of comparative peace. There was no lack of information. From what I have learned, every item of Egyptian or Syrian equipment was located and catalogued by intelligence. Military intelligence did suffer from the retirement of Major General Yariv, a skillful practitioner of his trade, but at the time this did not seem to matter very much.

Another aspect of the intelligence problem was Israel's preoccupation, natural enough in the circumstances, with the Palestine Liberation Organization. The PLO, which had expanded after the 1967 War, largely as a means of saving Arab pride, had given Israel a diet of isolated bombings and shootings which caused Israel to concentrate its intelligence services on PLO leaders and tactics. The Israeli defense forces coped easily with the PLO's raids into Israel. But the PLO was there, a tiny pebble in the boot of a military giant. Inordinate expenditures of men and materiel were devoted to it. There is some evidence that the Israeli intelligence apparatus in Egypt, by far the most powerful potential enemy, was thinned out to provide operatives for use against the PLO.

Ultimately the Israeli intelligence problem in 1973 came down to one familiar to all intelligence agencies; Mossad, military intelligence, internal security, and Shabak, the Foreign Ministry's research department, fully understood the capabilities of the potential Syrian and Egyptian enemies. What they did not know were the intentions of the high commands in Damascus and Cairo. This ignorance, reinforced by military complacency, led both the government and the military to ignore or at best discount Arab preparations for war. These, at the outset, were political.

Anwar el-Sadat, the President of Egypt, like all officers and functionaries of his regime, could not stomach the Israeli occupation of the Sinai Peninsula, a result of the 1967 War. He also could not live with the assumption, then widely held, that the Egyptians were bad soldiers, ineffective both in battle and in the maintenance of their equipment. He had furthered the programs of his predecessor, Gamal Abdel Nasser, aimed at modernizing the Egyptian army, with Soviet help. This meant not only the introduction of new weapons and training soldiers and airmen with them, but the elimination of what a British officer called "the pot-bellied, bemedalled no-accounts you see in the Cairo night spots."

Military reforms were accompanied by political moves. In March of 1973, Sadat sounded the Syrian government on the establishment of a common policy toward Israel. What was another war to be about? The Syrians wanted to eliminate the state of Israel. The Egyptians were chiefly concerned, in the first instance, with recovering their lost territory. Did not Syria wish to recover the Golan Heights?—Sadat asked. So the political maneuverings went on. It should be remembered that at the time Egypt represented the most powerful Arab military entity. The Syrians were willing to drop their nationalist pride and talk about strategy with the Egyptians.

The first serious meeting was held in Cairo on April 21, 22, and 23 of 1973. The object was to review Israel's military position. The input from the Egyptian Minister of War, General Ahmed Ismail Ali may have been decisive in those talks.

His appraisal was that the Israelis had four primary advantages: air superiority, technological skill, intensive and almost universal military training, and a "reliance on quick aid from the United States that would ensure . . . a continuous flow of supplies." But the

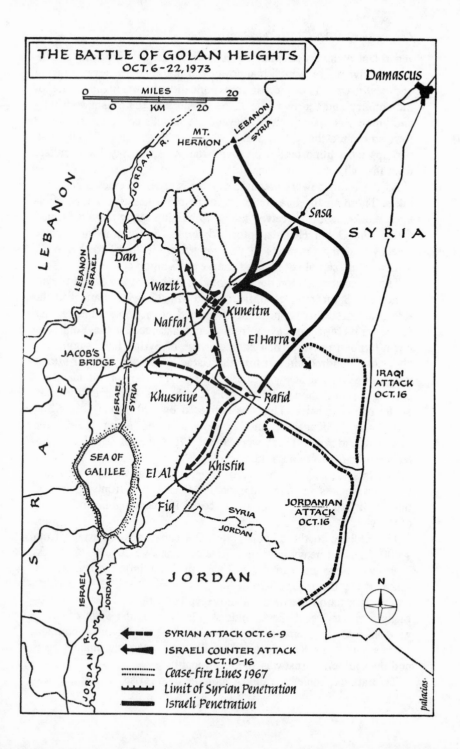

THE BATTLE OF GOLAN HEIGHTS
OCT. 6-22, 1973

MILES
0 — 20
0 — 20
KM

Damascus

LEBANON

MT. HERMON

LEBANON
SYRIA

Sasa

SYRIA

Dan

Wazit

Naffal

Kuneitra

El Harra

JACOB'S BRIDGE

LEBANON
ISRAEL

ISRAEL
SYRIA

Khusniye

Rafid

IRAQI ATTACK
OCT.16

SEA OF GALILEE

El Al

Khisfin

Fiq

SYRIA
JORDAN

JORDANIAN ATTACK
OCT.16

ISRAEL

ISRAEL
JORDAN

JORDAN

N

JORDAN R.

⬅ ⋯ SYRIAN ATTACK OCT. 6-9
⬅ ISRAELI COUNTER ATTACK OCT. 10-16
⋯⋯⋯ Cease-fire Lines 1967
Limit of Syrian Penetration
Israeli Penetration

palacios

general also discerned what he considered Israel's immediate military disadvantages. Israeli manpower did not encourage a protracted and costly war. The lines of communication between the center of the country and the two fronts, the Golan and the Sinai, were long and vulnerable. Ismail also believed that Israel's economic resources were so limited that a long war was out of the question. Finally, and perhaps most importantly, he saw Israel as an enemy "who suffers from the evils of wanton conceit."

As the Arab powers prepared for the war, both sides made mistakes. Those on the Israeli side were the more harmful. Israeli intelligence, although it perceived the Arab buildup along the Suez Canal and in the Golan Heights, informed the U. S. Central Intelligence Agency that the prospects of war ranged from "low" to "remote." This was an example of Ismail's charge of "wanton conceit."

That conceit was soon demonstrated. Just before 2 P.M. on the afternoon of Saturday, Oct. 6, five Syrian Mig-17 fighters attacked the Israeli armored forces on the northern end of the Golan lines. Many of the tank crews were away from their tanks reciting the Yom Kippur afternoon prayer. Then another wave of Syrian fighter-bombers, about one hundred aircraft hit other Israeli positions. The air attack was followed by a heavy artillery barrage. The Israeli commanders, peering through the smoke of shells and bombs, perceived the start of the main offensive. This was delivered by 700 Syrian tanks; 300 drove toward Kuneitra; another 400 attacked along the Sheikh Miskin–Rafid road. There were about 175 tanks of two Israeli armored brigades to oppose them.

The Israeli forces on the Golan Heights were in a desperate situation, but no less so than those on the Suez Canal front. It was on that front that the Egyptian army scored its most significant victory of the war.

The prelude to the assault across the canal was a barrage from 4,000 guns and heavy mortars. Three sectors were chosen for attack. These were: around Kantara in the north, Ismailia in the center, and south of the Bitter Lakes from Shaluga to El Kubri. Dispute exists among Israelis on the focus of the Egyptian attacks. Most of the Israelis who survived believe, understandably, that the main offensive was directed on their particular position. Their Egyptian counterparts say that the Kantara and Ismailia areas were the main targets and the southern thrust was an afterthought.

The attack achieved almost complete surprise, something extremely rare in war. One reason was Israel's refusal, on the highest political level, to recognize the high probability of an Arab attack. Another was the failure of Israeli intelligence to assess accurately the concentration of Arab forces in the sector facing the canal and, indeed, in the tank-assembly areas close to the Golan.

On the Sinai front, one example should suffice. The thirty-one strongpoints and twenty rear posts of the Bar Lev Line along the canal should have been manned by at least 4,000 men. An American commander would have considered this number the bare minimum for a successful defense. When the Egyptians attacked, there were about 600 men on the line, many of them reservists. They were the Fifty-second Battalion of the Sixteenth Brigade. This battalion had an activated strength of 800 men, but 200 had been given leave for Yom Kippur.

Even this small force might have sufficed to hold the canal had the Egyptians' enterprise not eliminated the Israeli's secret weapon.

Beneath the redoubts of the Bar Lev Line, the Israelis had installed a series of oil tanks. The pipes from these led to nozzles on the edge of the canal. The objective was to spread a film of oil over the canal which could be ignited by a grenade.

Here, again, the Israelis underestimated Egyptian enterprise and courage. The tanks were embedded deep to be secure from Egyptian artillery fire from across the canal. The Egyptian high command decided, on the basis of scouts who had crossed the canal at night and who were undetected by the complacent Israelis, that the system could be immobilized by sealing the sprays. On the Friday night before hostilities began, selected teams crossed the canal and stopped the sprays with cement or wooden bungs.

Since the war, Israeli military sources have contended that the "river-of-fire" device had been recognized as impractical by the high command. This may have been so. The fact is that the Egyptians made it useless as a weapon against their forces crossing the canal.

This action was one of the many that facilitated Egypt's successful assault on the Bar Lev Line, which, it must be remembered, was considered all but impregnable by the authorities in Tel Aviv. It took just about six hours to penetrate the line using modern weapons and Egyptian ingenuity.

The sand ramparts raised on the Israeli side of the canal were scaled by Egyptian infantrymen. But these were the infantry of the new warfare. Some carried canvas-covered suitcases, or so they appeared to the besieged Israelis, and some had tubes slung across their backs. The Israelis opened what fire they had upon these troops, expecting an assault upon their bunkers. But the Egyptian infantry pushed beyond the Israeli fortifications to seek out the Israeli armored formations that provided the principal counterattacking force. The assault on the Bar Lev Line was left to the second wave.

The Israeli defense concept of that line was based on the positioning of tanks behind each of the line's main bunkers. These tanks, dug in hull down, were expected to deliver a devastating fire on any force attempting to cross the canal. On Oct. 6, 1973, the tanks were not there.

The Fourteenth Armored Brigade had about one hundred tanks, almost half of those available in the Sinai. When the attack began, about half the tanks were available for action at the front. The remainder were about five miles to the east from the canal. Two skeleton brigades were even farther to the east, guarding the mountain passes. Most of the tanks were elderly American M-48 Pattons.

The armored formations supporting the Bar Lev Line were the first in history to experience the lethality of precision-guided antitank missiles. The "suitcases" carried by the Egyptian infantry contained the Soviet antitank guided missile code-named "Sagger" by NATO. This missile is directed to its target by the soldier firing it, guiding wires unreeling behind the missile in flight.

The Israeli armor already was under fire from the Egyptian artillery and tanks on the west bank of the canal. One by one the tanks were silenced under a rain of missiles and shells. Egyptian flags began to appear where crossings had been successful.

The Israelis held out in their bunkers, and automatic rifle and machine-gun fire took a heavy toll of the second wave of Egyptian attackers. But meanwhile the first wave spilled out into the desert beyond the Bar Lev Line to prepare for further counterattacks by the Israelis. There they brought into action the third new weapon, the Soviet SAM-7 antiaircraft weapon that had its baptism of fire in Vietnam.

Within a few hours, a new technology of ground warfare had been introduced. An attacking force had used guided antitank missiles in conjunction with artillery to stall an armored counterattack and had carried with it the antiaircraft weapons that might do the same for fighter-bombers on the same mission.

The Egyptian infantry's role was to establish positions beyond—that is, east of—the Bar Lev Line, to prevent Israeli interference with the movement by bridge across the canal of the main body of the attackers. At this point the Egyptians encountered the formidable sand barriers raised by the Israelis on the east bank of the canal.

"Sand" is a misnomer. These barriers were actually part sand, part gravel. The Egyptians knew from tests that neither explosive charges nor artillery fire over open sights would open the holes required for the movement of tanks and other vehicles through the Bar Lev Line into the open desert beyond. The fire pumps ordered from Magirus Deutz seventeen months previously provided the answer. Mounted on pontoons in the middle of the canal, the fusillades of water from the pumps rapidly tore holes in the sand ramparts. An Israeli artillery officer after the war remarked that it had been "a brilliant concept, brilliantly implemented," and added plaintively, "Why didn't we anticipate it?"

The canal was crossed by infantry in rubber boats. The next Egyptian problem was to establish bridges. The Egyptian bank of the waterway was under intermittent fire from the Israelis holding out in their bunkers. Any attempt to follow the then-conventional bridging procedures involving pontoons floated into a line across the canal, put into place by river craft and covered by a roadway, would expose the bridge builders and any follow-up force to severe casualties.

Here again the Egyptians used another innovation, also of Soviet inspiration and design. As a result of their planning for a campaign in Western Europe with its large number of rivers, the Russians had developed what they called the PMP bridge. This is a series of box-shaped pontoons, each of which is carried on a single truck. The trucks form a line along the edge of the water obstacle. The pontoons slide into the water and are extended to their maximum width. Then they are clipped together. The bridge is then swung across the waterway. The Russians estimate that such a bridge can be laid at a rate of twenty-one feet a minute. The Egyptians, under heavy fire, took somewhat longer, but the canal was bridged at the points where the fire hoses had torn down the sand castles of the Israelis.

Despite the Egyptian success, the Israelis still possessed one inestimable advantage: room. Hard-pressed as they were, they could retreat to their own bases in the Sinai Peninsula, relying on the air force to cover their retirement and inflict the maximum penalties on their pursuers. But these tactics did not work out quite as the Israeli commanders on the ground and their superiors in Tel Aviv anticipated.

The situation on the Golan front was much different. Seventeen miles separates the bluffs looking down on Israel from the Syrian starting line onto the plain that is called the Golan Heights. There was room for maneuver, but none for an Israeli retreat into Israel itself. The Israeli forces on the Heights had to stop the Syrians or the Arabs' armor would spill down into northern Israel. After visiting the battlefields on both fronts shortly after the end of the war, I concluded that the stand of the Israeli armor on the Golan Heights was the principal factor in saving the Jewish state from defeat. The Egyptian breakthrough of the Bar Lev Line, the subsequent tank battles at the Chinese Farm and elsewhere, and General Ariel Sharon's crossing of the Suez Canal "into Africa" were more spectacular, but the most critical battle of the campaign was fought in the north.

In their tank attack, the Syrians followed tactics similar to those of the Germans in their last great offensive in March 1918. The tanks did not stop to assail Israeli strongpoints but flowed around them in a seemingly irresistible flood.

One axis of advance was along the Kuneitra road; the other followed a course to the northwest from Rafid to Khusniye. In both cases Naffal was the objective. The headquarters for the two Israeli brigades were there, and it stood on the main highway into Israel from Golan, a path followed for centuries by camel caravans moving from Damascus to Cairo.

In October 1973 the Golan was empty. The Arabs had fled. Kuneitra was empty, half in ruins. A few villages of Druze remained on the slopes of Mount Hermon, and the boys went out as they have since the beginning of recorded time to tend the goats and, now, to watch the roaring, creaking, steel monsters move westward toward Israel.

There were four possible crossings into Israel, and to make good their offensive the Syrians had to take at least two of them. In the north a road snakes from the foothills of Mount Hermon across the frontier to the kibbutz of Dan at the top of the valley of the Jordan River. Another road in the southwest of Golan winds through the cliffs to Lake Tiberias, the Sea of Galilee. There are only two other practicable entries into Israel. The more important of these is the steel bridge over the Jordan called the Bridge of the Daughters of Jacob, which carries traffic from Kuneitra and Naffal. The other is the Bailey Bridge below Wazit to the north.

The first casualty to the Syrian advance was the fortified settlements that Israel had built on the Golan Heights. They had been built and fortified as a passive defense line against incursions by Palestinian guerrillas. Each settlement had its watch towers and barbed wire, its patrols of hardy, resolute settlers; but these were unable to cope with the flow of Syrian armor.

After the war, an Israeli report concluded that "the line of settlements contributed nothing to half [of] the Syrian attack. In fact, the ones which fell to the Syrians served them for solid bases for continuing their attack." In the light of this battlefield experience, the Israeli government's decision to fortify areas of the West Bank with similar settlements is almost incomprehensible.

Two Israeli tank brigades, both understrength, were given the unenviable task of halting a Syrian thrust into northern Israel.

Both the officers and the men knew that they could not expect early reinforcement. Israeli mobilization was just underway, and even under the best of conditions it would be thirty-six hours before tank reinforcements could reach the Israeli formations on the Golan. For these troops there followed some of the most intense and precarious fighting of the campaign. They had 176 tanks, and they could have lost the war in three hours of fighting.

One of the two brigades, at a strength of about seventy-five tanks, covered the southern and central sectors of the road which led from Kuneitra to the Bridge of the Daughters of Jacob. The Syrians had an overall superiority in tanks of five to one, and at important tactical points they could muster twelve to one.

The initial Israeli response was to bite into the Syrian vanguard. By twos and threes the attacking tanks went up in flames. The battle called upon the best tactical abilities of the Israeli tank corps—maneuvering under heavy fire in conditions of smoke and dust, sparing but effective use of the guns, and above all leadership by young tank commanders, a leadership that says not "go" but "come."

In the first stage of the battle, the rigid armored tactical doctrine inculcated into Syrian tank commanders by their Soviet instructors proved little short of disastrous. Attacking on a single axis of advance, tank after tank came "in line ahead," as sailors would say, and was destroyed by the Israeli tank gunners.

But the side that has the numbers in any battle can compensate for such mistakes. In this case the Syrians finally adjusted and sent forces around the Israeli tanks and, meeting no opposition from artillery or infantry, spread into an open formation and swept around the knots of Israeli armor. The Israeli tanks by now were short of ammunition. Their only recourse was a fighting withdrawal, in the prayerful hope that the Israeli artillery now slowly entering the battle would check the enemy attacks.

The rigidity of Soviet doctrine served the Syrians badly. The battle plan set out that the Syrian tanks, who unwittingly had won the day, called for a halt at El Al, their objective for the first day's fighting, on the road to Lake Tiberias. At El Al they would stop, and they did. An Israeli commander with the game in his hands would have gone on through the night. This was not the last time that Soviet tutelage cost the Arabs dearly. The Israeli tanks drew back, perilously close to the edge of the Golan, counting their losses.

The first day of battle on the Golan had turned out to have been not too disastrous to the Israeli defenders. In part this was due to the terrain. When I went over the battlefield three weeks later, a young Israeli tank major pointed out that the small hills, ruined villages, and groves of trees would impede any armored advance "and of course provided us, the defenders, with some difficulties."

By the second day the Israelis were receiving the combined arms support that had been absent in the first battles. More and more Israeli fighter-bombers swept over the battlefield. The artillery began to take its toll of the advancing Syrians. The tank force pushing north of Kuneitra was halted. The regiment driving south of the town was chewed up and forced to halt by Israeli fire.

Credit is due the Israeli air force. The A-4 Skyhawks descended like a plague of locusts on the Syrian tank spearheads. They attacked unmolested by the Syrians' Migs because Israel's air-to-air fighters, F-4 Phantoms and Mirages, flew sentry watch in the sky above the battle.

The air attack, although successful, was costly. The Syrians had moved up two of the most notable antiaircraft weapons of the war: SAM-6 missiles and ZSU-23 antiaircraft batteries that were radar controlled. One foreign observer of the battle estimated that Israel lost three of every five aircraft involved. These were grievous losses. The Syrians were halted, but for how long?

The situation on the Golan was fairly uncomplicated as battle situations go: tanks and aircraft and artillery defending against tanks and abundant antiaircraft resources. On the other end of the Israeli front, the situation was more complex. Brigadier General Rafael Eytan, who took over the defense of the Golan, had to weigh what he could deploy against the demands of the mounting battle in the Sinai.

The Egyptians, by crossing the Suez Canal, had won a great offensive victory. The question was: what would they do with it? The answer was that the infantry who had stormed the canal went on the defensive. Some critics have seized on this as the major Egyptian mistake of the war. But in retrospect it does not appear that this was true.

The Egyptian high command counted on the aggressive spirit of the Israelis to present the Egyptian forces, now entrenched across the canal, with the opportunity for a successful defensive battle. The Egyptian infantry were known for their tenacity. That quality was now enhanced by new defensive weapons, the Soviet surface-to-air and antitank guided missiles. The Egyptian generals were reasonably sure that the Israelis would throw their tanks against the Egyptian lines and suffer ruinous casualties.

A spirited, coherent, and well-armed defense can break any offensive, as the Allies demonstrated in the Battle of the Bulge. But it cannot be considered a means of winning a battle or a campaign and surely not a war. If the Egyptians were to get into the important Israeli rear areas, they would have to seize and exploit one of the three passes that run through the mountains which form the spine of the Sinai Peninsula—the Mitla Pass in the south, the Gidi Pass in the center, and the Khatmia Pass in the north.

There is another inviting and dangerous entry into Israel along the coast road that runs between the sea and the sand. But no commander is likely to choose that route, open as it is to air and naval bombardment with the sea on one flank and the shifting sands of the Eastern Desert on the other.

The Egyptian forces' task then was to seize one of the passes through the mountains. To do this, the attackers had to establish a bridgehead over the canal sufficiently deep into the Sinai to allow for a sizeable buildup of tanks, artillery, infantry, and supplies. General Ismail estimated that his forces could bite into the Sinai for twenty miles until they occupied a series of sand hills which would serve as defensive positions against Israeli counterattacks.

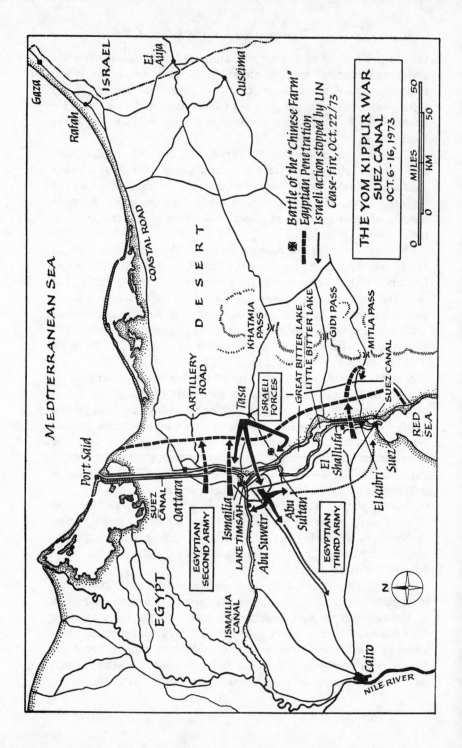

"Those were the orders," an Egyptian brigadier general said not long after the war. "We accepted them, but we didn't believe them. We were all schooled in the campaigns of Rommel, Patton, and Guderian. We didn't think we should stop until we got to the passes. What's that poem the British quote, 'Ours not to reason why . . .'?"

The battle that developed took place in a barren triangle of land about sixty-five miles from north to south and opposite the Mitla Pass, only twenty miles deep. This area is a wasteland. Quicksand, isolated groups of stringy trees, and ridges of sand or rock give it the appearance of the surface of the moon. It was not much to hold, but the Israelis held it. But before they were asked to do so, they benefited from that rigidity in tactical doctrine that influenced both Arab military establishments. After the crossing of the canal, the Egyptians had the initiative and, more important, the ammunition and the gas to drive on. But they halted.

"I was half an hour from the Mitla Pass," the Egyptian tank brigadier general told me two weeks after the battle, "just half an hour." I asked him why he had not advanced. "Ask Cairo," he said, shrugging his shoulders.

What was happening on "the other side of the hill"? General Abraham "Bren" Adan recalls that just after noon on Oct. 7 he and other local commanders received orders from General Shmuel Gonen, chief of the southern command, to form a new defensive line along the lateral road twenty miles east of the canal. Small mobile forces were to be sent into the area of the Artillery Road, eight miles east of the canal. The lateral road, however, was to be Israel's main defensive line, and Gonen ordered that the strongpoints still occupied by Israeli infantry be evacuated wherever this was possible. At the same time he asked for, and got, the promise that all available Israeli bombers and fighters would go into action on his front.

The period from Oct. 7 to Oct. 10 must be considered the critical phase of the campaign for both sides. Many elements made it critical: the fumbling of the Israeli high command, indecision on the part of the Egyptians, the introduction of precision-guided munitions which were widely known but had been little experienced previously.

The Israeli fighters and fighter-bombers, Phantoms and Skyhawks, had been equipped with American electronic countermeasures against surface-to-air missiles. This equipment had proved adequate in Vietnam. Now the Egyptians and Syrians deployed SAM's that the Israeli aircraft could not counter; the SAM-7 and the SAM-6, which home on heat-seeking infrared sensors that aim the missile to the aircraft's exhaust.

For the aircrews there was no warning, unless the pilot or the copilot glimpsed the wisp of white smoke that marked the launching of a SAM-6. If they were lucky, their electronic countermeasure apparatus might be tuned to the frequency on which the missile was operating. If not, and this happened very often, the crew had to evade a missile moving toward their aircraft at a speed of Mach 2.7. The preferred maneuver by pilots was to turn into the missile's path in an attempt to break its lock on the aircraft.

The prodigal employment of these missiles by the Syrians and Egyptians reduced but did not eliminate the impact of the Israeli air force on the battle. After the campaign was over, it was learned that Egypt had forty-six SAM-6 batteries and Syria, thirty-two. Each battery had four launchers and each launcher, three missiles. In these circumstances Israel's attainment of the air superiority it had enjoyed in 1967 would be costly, if not impossible.

Israel's ground forces also were encountering difficulties. The Egyptian infantry, liberally equipped with antitank missiles, checked tentative Israeli counterattacks. These were not delivered as an "all-arms" operation because the bulk of the Israeli air force on the Sinai front had been directed to the destruction of the Egyptian bridges across the Suez Canal. The bridges, like every other important target on the campaign's two fronts, were protected by SAM's and the ubiquitous ZSU's, the quadruple-mount, radar-guided antiaircraft guns.

The Egyptians, showing more enterprise than the Israelis could believe, also moved some of their twelve bridges from point to point along the canal. Moreover, when a pontoon was hit, it could be unlinked and another put into place. The Israeli air and artillery attacks—the 155's and 175's from the Artillery Road now had the range—disturbed, at times dislocated, but did not halt the stream of Egyptians crossing the canal. By now, it was evident that the expansion of the Egyptian bridgehead had to be halted, but halted not by the establishment of a defensive line but by an armored counterattack.

There is a streak of emotionalism in the decision to launch this attack. Even Adan, an experienced and logical soldier, records that the "problem of concern to us all was the situation of the men in the strongpoints, all of which were under siege; most had many wounded and dead, and all were crying for help." Emotion in war is as poor a guide to success as it is in other fields of human endeavor. In this case the emotional approach, wholly understandable then and now, had to, but did not, take into account the poverty of Israeli resources on the spot.

Adan at his conference with Gonen pointed out that he expected to have 200 tanks by the evening of Oct. 8, but that he had only ten guns in his sector and could not expect artillery reinforcement until Oct. 9. He was also short of infantry.

The attack was launched on Monday afternoon, Oct. 8. One Israeli division, Adan's, fell on the Egyptian Second Army bridgehead in the north. Ariel Sharon's division was assigned the task of cutting through the Third Army in the south. Sharon, who like George Patton was a brilliant tank commander with a talent for self-advertisement, claimed later that his mission was to "strike at the canal with a crossing on the other side, in order to destroy the self-confidence of the Egyptians."

The first Israeli counteroffensive was a failure. Not a disaster, as the Egyptians trumpeted to the world, but a failure nevertheless.

Adan, like all Israeli armored officers, had studied the tactics that would be most profitable in an attack against an enemy well equipped with antitank guided missiles. His solution, which he shared unknowingly with many American, British, West German, and Russian officers, was to assault missile-armed infantry with widely separated tanks, moving at maximum speed and throwing out smoke shells. The tanks were to lead infantry in armored personnel carriers who, once dismounted, would take care of the enemy infantry after they had been savaged by the tanks' secondary armament.

It did not work that way. Adan, by the time the attack developed, had about one hundred tanks. These did not suffice to break through the stubborn Egyptian infantry. The Egyptians stood, fired their antitank missiles, and were rewarded by a succession of "kills." When the attack petered out, the desert sand was dotted with burning tanks.

Sharon's share in the offensive never started. His story is that his force was held in reserve and "I watched and saw his [Adan's] force slaughtered." Another version is that Sharon had started south with his force when the impact of Adan's losses convinced Gonen that the battle plan was unworkable. Gonen's people say that Sharon was ordered to return, if possible to extricate Adan's forces. He was too late for that. The counteroffensive had collapsed. For the time being, the Egyptians were masters of the field. Along the canal a few isolated Israeli strongpoints still held out against attacks by Egyptian armor and infantry supported by well-directed artillery fire.

The Israeli situation on the Golan sector of the front was equally precarious. The Israeli mobilization, as we have seen, had provided heavy reinforcements. But despite their arrival, the Syrians did not give way as the Israelis, who had a low opinion of both of their principal antagonists, expected. The Syrians "read" the pattern of Israeli attacks: heavy assaults from the air, accurate artillery fire, and finally headlong assaults by the tanks.

These tactics had worked in the past. They worked now, but slowly and at considerable cost. The Israeli air force sought to knock out the Syrian SAM-6 batteries to win air superiority over the battlefield. This was done, but the air force suffered heavy losses. By Monday evening, the Israeli armor had managed barely to recover its own brigade headquarters at Naffal. Even so, the Syrian armor still held Khusniye in the southern Golan, which was the center of a tank concentration.

Despite their losses, the Syrians were still on the offensive. Early on Tuesday morning their tanks moved in the dim predawn light to begin a series of attacks which constituted a major offensive. The fighting that followed was as violent and protracted as any in the war.

The Israeli lines around Kuneitra were penetrated by one Syrian division. Another pushed past Khusniye in the south. The situation on the Kuneitra front was stabilized after several hours of heavy fighting and the Syrians' retreat. By this time the tank crews on both sides were battleweary; their reactions were not as quick as they had been at the start.

The Syrian armor persisted. Around 7 A.M., T-64's, Syria's most modern tank, crashed into the Israeli front and established a position north of Kuneitra. Again, the Israeli air and armored formations counterattacked. Syrian losses were high; the Israelis estimated that eighty tanks had been knocked out. Now the Israelis turned their attention to the southern thrust around Khusniye.

Here the qualities of initiative and small-formation enterprise which had been inculcated into the Israeli armored forces proved decisive. A formation cut off the nose of the Syrian column, and as dawn broke, the Israeli air force began to hammer the mass of tanks, armored personnel carriers, and artillery from the air. By dusk the Syrian attack had been broken.

The fighting continued into the night of Tuesday, Oct. 9. The Syrian offensive, although stalled, still had potent reserves. The Israelis estimated that 400 enemy tanks had remained out of the battle, providing the force necessary for a renewal of the offensive. And there were other weapons available to the Syrian high command.

Just before sunup on Tuesday, Oct. 9, a Frog-7 was launched from Syria. The Frog is a Soviet-made surface-to-surface missile with a range of forty or more miles. The missile hit Kibbutz Gevat, near Nazareth in the center of northern Israel. The damage was extensive, but there were no casualties since adults and children were sleeping in underground shelters. But the Frog attack reminded the Israelis that Syria's resources for an air and missile war remained largely intact. Although the Frog that hit the Kibbutz Gevat attracted the greatest attention, sixteen more were lobbed into northern Israel in the next three days. The greater part of the damage was done to civilian targets.

Israel reacted rapidly. Six F-4 Phantoms, flying in flight groups of two aircraft, swept across the desert south of Damascus to attack with rockets and cannonfire the Syrian Air Force Headquarters and the Ministry of Defense just after noon on Tuesday. The attackers did some damage to their military targets. They also hit a residential area, the main radio station, and the Soviet cultural center.

The attack signaled the rapid acceleration and expansion of the Israeli air offensive, operations that would take Israeli fighter-bombers away from the massed batteries of SAM-6's protecting the advanced army formations. Banias, the Mediterranean terminal for Syrian crude-oil shipments, was wrecked; two oil refineries at Homs were damaged; and fuel tanks at Adria, Latakia, and Tartous were either destroyed or badly damaged. The power stations at Damascus and Homs were severely damaged; the former supplied a fifth of Syria's electricity. The attacks went on, and in the process Syria's industrial capacity was severely reduced.

Meanwhile the tactical air attacks against Syrian missiles were strengthened. By Tuesday evening the Israelis estimated that their bombers had destroyed half of the batteries around Golan while the Phantoms and Mirages, flying high for cover, had knocked down twenty-seven Migs in a day's fighting over the Golan. Israel lost one plane.

The Syrians had ample reserves of SAM-6's, although the apparatus supplied by the Soviet Union was weak in high-altitude identification of targets. But the combination of attacks over the battlefield and on Syrian industrial targets forced the Syrians, as the Israelis had hoped, to disperse their SAM batteries around the country.

The war on the Golan lapsed into an active stalemate. The Syrian armor had been so badly mauled by Israeli tanks and aircraft that it was incapable of launching a new offensive, even if the planners in Damascus had been able to propose something more innovative than the headlong drive against the Israeli tanks that had smashed previous attacks. The Israelis were in little better shape. The tank crews had fought themselves into a stupor. The armor and the artillery needed ammunition and fuel. The forces on the Golan were adequate to meet a further Syrian attack. They were not yet in a logistical or personnel situation that would permit an Israeli offensive.

There was no stalemate on the southern front in the Sinai.

Sharon tried an attack on Tuesday (Oct. 9) and was checked with heavy losses. The object was to relieve some of the outposts still holding out on the Bar Lev Line, particularly two fronts near Ismailia. An armored battalion, the 190th, encountered heavy Egyptian fire from the Egyptian Second Army. Gonen, the Israeli commander on the front, did not reinvest in defeat with additional armor, probably because his resources were low. But he did call in air strikes.

Sharon, as always, demanded more tanks and men to expand what was clearly an unsuccessful attack. Gonen held back. Sharon appealed to General David Elazar and finally to Moshe Dayan. Neither gave way. Israeli reinforcements in the area amounted to a paratroop brigade below the Mitla Pass. Inevitably the 190th Armored Battalion was lost and its commander captured.

It was now apparent to the Israeli high command that this was far different from earlier wars against the Arabs. The combat quality of the Arab soldiers and airmen was far higher than in previous wars. The enemy had displayed skill in employing sophisticated equipment provided by the Russians. Their tactics, while somewhat rigid, had not offered the Israelis opportunities for dazzling coups on the battlefield. It was a different war. The Israelis had to think now about how to win it.

Dayan, the Minister of Defense, restless, imaginative, seeing four options when ordinary men saw one, was sure that the first priority was to eliminate Syria, as he said, to "silence the front." He was confident that on the Golan at least "we've got the Syrian thing behind us." He was less optimistic about the situation in the Sinai. Israel did not have at that time, he told a group of newspaper editors, the resources to drive the Egyptians back over the Suez Canal. The Egyptians had more tanks across the canal than Israel could bring to bear against them, and the tanks were supported by artillery, missiles, and infantry equipped with antitank missiles. Israel retained air superiority, but the planes were encountering "difficulties" because of the lavish deployment of Egyptian SAM batteries.

With or without Dayan's reflections, it was clear that the Israelis in the Sinai were in an adverse tactical situation. They could not afford a battle of attrition. They lacked the assets for a massive counterattack. Their only obvious option was to pull back to a line closer to the mountains and there prepare for a counteroffensive. Meanwhile, there was always the air force. If the Syrians could be first held and then rolled back from the Golan, then much of the air force and some of the armor could be transferred to the Sinai sector of the front. At the time it seemed a long shot.

Dayan alone among the Israeli leaders seems to have grasped the psychological implications of the first four days of fighting. This, he told the Israeli newspaper editors, had "revealed to the entire world that that we are not stronger than the Egyptians. The halo of superiority, the political and military principle that Israel is stronger than the Arabs, and that if they dared to start a war, they would be defeated, has not been sustained here."

Dayan wanted, he told this writer years later, to lay the facts before the Israeli people, trusting as Churchill had in 1940 that the national reaction would be a popular effort to sustain the battle. This did not happen for reasons locked in the political plans of Mrs. Golda Meir, the Prime Minister.

The primary question, of course, was what should Egypt do with its tank and missile forces concentrating east of the Suez Canal. No one on either side minimized the extent of the Egyptian victory in the opening days of the war. The Egyptian bridgehead extended from Port Said to Port Suez. The Israeli defense had been broken. As we have seen, Israeli forces east of the canal were small in number and had been badly mauled in some engagements. Ahmed Ismail, Egyptian War Minister and Commander in Chief, had one of the greatest opportunities in war since the Germans broke through the French defensive lines and crossed the Meuse in 1940.

What did he do with it? Nothing more enterprising immediately than the consolidation of Egypt's positions across the canal. This, in the end, gave the initiative to the Israelis. This strategy, if it deserves the name, was not unopposed. Lieutenant General Saad el-Shazli, the Egyptian chief of staff, argued heatedly for a resumption of the offensive toward the Sinai passes. He wanted to abandoñ a set-piece strategy and exploit Egypt's successes before the Israelis had time to concentrate armor and infantry in the Sinai and divert air squadrons from the attacks on the Golan. Ismail turned him down. It was his duty, he said, "not to run risks," as though war itself is not one gigantic risk. He went further. He told Mohammed Heikal, editor of *Al Ahram,* the best-informed and most influential Cairo newspaper, that he was not prepared to move at all.

From Ismail's standpoint, the results of the canal crossing had not been as significant tactically as he had planned. The tanks had not reached the sand ridges twenty miles to the east of the canal but had penetrated a maximum of sixteen miles and generally only to slightly over twelve miles. The Israeli counterattacks, although generally unsuccessful, had forced the Egyptians to retire in some areas. There was a sense of resignation in Ismail's nonstrategy. He had done what he could. Let Allah take care of the immediate future.

The Israelis were not waiting on the future. The first step was to reshuffle the command—a natural move in a deteriorating situation. Elazar, deeply concerned over the friction among his generals, designated Haim Bar Lev, a lieutenant general who had been chief of staff, to assume "special duties." These duties, it developed, included backing Gonen in the Sinai. There were other changes, some cosmetic, some sensible; but these did not balance Israel's worsening overall situation. On Wednesday, Oct. 10, Iraq entered the war and King Hussein of Jordan ordered mobilization but did not take the final, irretrievable step of declaring war. At the same time Israeli intelligence, doubtless with an assist from the United States, concluded that the Soviet Union was prepared to make up the Syrian losses in SAM's. The Israelis that day launched heavy air attacks on both fronts. But the war machine was short of supplies and, probably more important at that juncture, of reserves. For supplies it could look to the United States.

Although the Egyptian position was theoretically the more menacing, the elimination of the Syrian threat had priority. The Egyptians, after all, were many miles from Israel. The Syrians were frowning down on northern Israel. Therefore the Syrian armor must be driven off the Golan.

The battle went on throughout Wednesday. By nightfall the Israelis had won. It was not a cheap victory. The Israeli armor advanced into heavy fire from Syrian tanks and from infantry armed with RPG-7 antitank weapons in the battle for the Khusniye positions. Tank after tank was knocked out. In the end the Israelis won by launching their armor in a costly frontal attack. The Syrians withdrew still firing, with the tanks repeatedly reforming to fight stubborn rear-guard actions.

The clash at Kuneitra was easier. The Israeli armor simply smashed up to the road from Narrak and into the town where the garrisons that had held out from the first day of the war were relieved.

The heaviest Syrian losses may have been suffered in the retreat. The Israeli air force caught the retreating Syrian columns and inflicted heavy punishment. By nightfall the Israelis were everywhere masters of the battlefield. Their problem was, would they be strong enough to penetrate the Syrian defenses on Thursday? They reckoned without the combative resilience of the Syrian forces.

At dawn on Thursday four helicopters bearing Syrian commandos were caught as they tried to land behind the Israeli lines. This small but significant victory owed much to Israeli monitoring of the Syrian radio. But complete though it was, the success did not prevent the Syrians from launching an armored counterattack in the north along the Damascus–Kuneitra road. It was a serious attack, but it lacked the weight of earlier Syrian drives. The Israelis stopped it and then sent tanks in a flanking movement to attack the Syrian rear. So fast did they go that they found themselves between the Syrian forward line and the rear areas. The Syrian offensive in the Golan was over.

It had been costly. The United States Defense Department estimated that Syria had lost 8,000 men, the great majority of them dead. There were 600 Syrian tanks destroyed on the battlefield and another 500 abandoned.

The effect on Israel's strategy of this victory was to enable the high command to begin the transfer of armor from the Golan to the Sinai. This region, henceforth, was to be the principal theater of operations.

Operations there did not begin without a heated row among the commanders on the spot. Sharon, as usual, was in the center of it. He was confident that given the resources, he could cross the canal into Egypt and turn the war around. He attacked Bar Lev as a political soldier and railed against the military authorities in Tel Aviv for their blindness.

Sharon stated his views after the war. "Our aim," he said, "was to check them in Sinai while we attended to the Syrians. I personally thought this was a mistake and expressed my views several times. I saw that we did not have unlimited time. I saw that the Egyptians were not pressing forward, but were digging in; and that a cease-fire would find them strongly entrenched."

Sharon was overruled, by Gonen, Bar Lev, and Dayan in ascending order of authority. But Egyptian operations were giving authority to his views. By Thursday Ismail had begun the transfer of most of the tanks remaining on the west side of the canal to the east side. These tanks had been intended to guard Egyptian rear areas against any sudden Israeli incursion. Now they were east of the canal, leaving the security of the lines of communications to scattered infantry formations. The movement made possible the subsequent Israeli crossing of the canal. It also appears to be a surprising reversal of Ismail's "play it safe" strategy.

Sharon, who had held the southern command for four years, had thought long and seriously about a canal crossing from east to west. It struck him as the best means, at this time and in this situation, for enabling Israeli armored and infantry forces to return to their usual tactics of sudden attacks. "By carrying the war to the west bank, we would be in our element," he said.

But he had to wait.

The Israeli high command wanted time to transfer armor and infantry from the Golan. It also expected that Ismail would continue the movement of forces onto the east bank of the canal. Every company of infantry, every squadron of tanks that crossed would give an Israeli invasion a better chance. At the same time, Tel Aviv was worried by events outside its control. The Soviet airlifts to Syria and Egypt had begun on Thursday, Oct. 11, with the promise of resupply of the weapons lost in the opening five days of the battle. As yet, Israel had not received a similar air supply from the United States.

The resupply of the Arab forces was significant. The Soviet high command, assisted by the KGB operatives in Syria, had discerned that the country was close to defeat. Recognition of this resulted in tank shipments by sea through Latakia and the arrival of Mig-21's at Syrian airfields. By Friday, Oct. 12, it was estimated in Washington that one hundred airlift flights into Syria and Egypt were preparing those states for a resumption of the war on a major scale. Washington's estimates may have been out of line. If the records of the air control supervisors in Belgrade and Cyprus are accurate, they were. But Soviet aircraft in an emergency have been known to ignore flight control zones and fly direct to their destination.

The United States, on the other hand, was slow in resupply. After a personal appeal by Mrs. Meir, President Nixon agreed to send both ammunition and other supplies to Israel. The first transport flight landed at Lod Airport near Tel Aviv early on Friday morning. The second act of the war ended with both combatants apparently insured against any decisive reduction in their stocks of armaments. Israel was in position to begin the operations that would bring the war to a decisive and triumphant end.

Israeli losses already had been heavy. By Sunday, Oct. 14, the Ministry of Defense announced that 656 soldiers had been killed thus far. This was a serious underestimate. Probably at least 100 or more were also dead. The war had been in progress for only eight days. One factor in the losses that emerged after the war was the high incidence of officer deaths. These were far higher than American officer losses in Vietnam and approached those of the British and Germans on the battlefields of World War I, "the hell where youth and laughter go."

Finally, on that Sunday, the war was moving into the final act. At dawn on Sunday the Egyptian armor, preceded by a ninety-minute artillery barrage, started an offensive to the east. It precipitated a major armored battle.

The Israelis were prepared. The movement of 500 tanks from the west to the east bank of the canal could not be hidden. Ismail now had well over 1,000 tanks on the east bank. The Israelis had fewer deployed on the battlefield, but the reinforcements were on their way from the Golan.

The Egyptian attack was a sight none who saw it will forget. A huge cloud of dust arose as the tanks moved out of their positions. The Israelis went out to meet them. The tank battle that followed was won and lost primarily on the abilities of the Israeli armored commanders, the rigidity of Egyptian tactics, and the technological

margin of the Israeli tanks—a narrow margin but still a margin—
over those of their enemies.

One aspect of this technological superiority little noted at the time
was that the Centurions (British) and M-60's (American) with
which the Israeli forces were equipped could depress their guns ten
degrees below the horizontal. The Egyptians' Soviet-made T-55's and
T-62's had guns that could be depressed only four degrees. In
fighting that took tanks over ridges onto the field of fire, this gave
the Israelis a considerable advantage. Moreover it developed that in
a tank battle of maneuver, much as in a war at sea, the Israeli tanks
were better adapted to operations across the rolling terrain of the
Sinai. Finally, the Israeli tanks were equipped with automatic range-
finding systems, primitive compared with today's systems, but far superior to the Egyptian and Syrian method of estimating range by vision. The Israeli tanks could open fire in seconds. In tank warfare it
is the first shot that counts.

Despite these advantages in personnel and equipment, the battle
was not easily won by the Israelis. The Egyptians attacked from
out of the darkness and had the Israeli tanks silhouetted against the
dawn. The major attack north of the Gidi Pass was preceded by air
strikes and an artillery barrage. Neither was particularly effective.

"They threw a great many shells and launched a great many
rockets and bombs," an Israeli colonel said as we walked over the
battlefield. "But although they are good artillerymen, they were not
getting many hits with shells, and our fighters prevented their
bombers from mounting a really punishing attack."

The tanks fared better at the outset. Both sides described it later
as a "charge," but it bore little resemblance to the traditional charge
with cavalry squadrons in line. Some tanks made good going, up to
eighteen miles an hour. Others were slowed either by Israeli fire or
treacherous terrain. But the Egyptian commanders persisted, thrusting onto a plateau between Little Bitter Lake and Gidi Pass. There
for an hour the tanks fought it out, with the Israelis bringing down
what artillery they had and the Egyptians deploying mobile guns.
The battle lasted for well over an hour. The Israelis claimed that
205 enemy tanks had been destroyed, and that same day Cairo radio
admitted that one hundred Egyptian tanks had been hit.

The exact figures are unknown, but it seems probable that Egypt
lost between 170 and 180 tanks that day, which means it also lost
the crews, most of them veterans. Adding mechanical breakdowns to

tanks destroyed in action, it is probable that the Egyptians lost about thirty percent of the tanks sent into the action. This was a serious loss. At the outset the Egyptians had an advantage of approximately two to one in tanks. By nightfall that edge had been sharply reduced.

In retrospect Ismail's decision to launch his armor against the most redoubtable tank force in the Middle East was a mistake. But as we have seen, the Egyptians *had* to deepen their bridgehead across the canal or be condemned to incessant bombing and shelling while the Israelis built up their armored forces. Ismail and his commanders must have realized that once their tanks left the protection of the SAM batteries in the bridgehead, they would suffer from Israeli fighter-bombers. Moreover it proved impossible in the battle for the Egyptians to support the armor with infantry armed with antitank missiles. So all the cards were stacked against the Egyptians. They lost the battle and with it, the war.

Cairo could not hope for a renaissance of Syrian efforts. Wrecked Egyptian tanks were still smoldering on the Sinai battlefield when on Monday, Oct. 15, the Israeli forces slipped off the Golan Heights and pushed through to Sasa, a scant twenty miles from the outskirts of Damascus. The Syrians, orally, were still full of fight. But President Hafez el-Assad's regime had to be propped up by oratory. The Russians were sending equipment and ammunition, but out there on the Golan were hundreds of dead veterans who would have known how to use both. The entrance of Iraqi and Jordanian forces into the battle on Tuesday could not balance those losses.

In any event, the attack launched by the two latecomers on the flank of the Israeli forces pounding into Syria had little effect. The offensive was hardly the sledgehammer blow that Cairo and Damascus expected. Jordan sent the Fortieth Armored Brigade. Iraq's contribution, stripped of propaganda rhetoric, was not much greater —one armored and one infantry brigade. It was the Jordanians, with their well-trained tanks crews, that the Israelis feared.

The Jordanian armor attacked at first light on Oct. 16. The target was the Israeli force pushing up the Kuneitra–Sasa road. To the east of the Jordanians were the two Iraqi brigades. Two Syrian brigades were deployed along the old cease-fire line to meet any Israeli attack out of Naffal. The dispositions and the battle plan were satisfactory. When the battle opened, everything went wrong.

Syrian bombers hammered the Israelis in the hills just north of El

Harra. The bombardment lasted ten minutes and had little effect on the Israelis, who took shelter in the massive concrete strongpoints that the Syrians had built. The bombing was followed by an artillery barrage fired by sixteen Syrian and three Jordanian batteries. Under its cover the armor was to go forward, but at this juncture the Jordanians discovered that the Iraqis had no plans for an attack.

The Jordanians, under increasingly heavy Israeli artillery fire, decided to start the attack on their own. Two battalions of Centurion tanks, about sixty vehicles, pushed forward at 7:30 A.M. The Iraqis finally sent one battalion into the fight at about 10 A.M. A second battalion, deployed on the front line, never moved.

Relieved of Iraqi pressure ("We could hardly believe it," an Israeli major said later), the Israelis hit one of the two advancing Jordanian battalions with antitank missiles, destroying ten tanks. The second battalion had better going and by midday was about to assail its first objective when the commander realized that he was about to be cut off by advancing Israelis. The Jordanians retreated. The danger of a new offensive launched by Syrian, Jordanian, and Iraqi troops on the Syrian front was over.

The Israeli crossing of the Suez Canal, the last offensive of the war, was not, as some thought at the time, an inspired last-minute dash by Sharon. On the contrary, as General Adan points out, the Israelis since the middle 1960s had been studying the problems of water crossings and had purchased bridging equipment and what Adan calls "uni-float rafts" in Europe.

The concept of a canal crossing was rooted in the Israeli strategy that developed in the days after the tank battle near the Gidi Pass. Adan writes that "virtually no one on the Israeli side doubted that the war would be decided only after we had crossed to the west bank and destroyed the main enemy force." As in all such situations in war, timing was essential. Timing was influenced not only by events on the battlefields, north and south, but by diplomatic maneuvers in Moscow, Washington, London, and at the United Nations.

Adan notes that on Oct. 13 the Israeli high command received reports that Britain was about to submit a cease-fire proposal to the United Nations and that "we were apprehensive that this was liable to be adopted while the military balance in the field was not in our favor."

Sharon, we know, already had selected the site for a canal crossing. This was a spot between Lake Timsah and the Great Bitter Lake. But another commander, Adan, equally experienced, called for a strategy that would launch two assaults across the canal, not one. Sharon's plan prevailed. Late on Oct. 14 he was ordered to launch his attack across the Suez Canal.

Surprise was not complete; as noted previously, it seldom is in war. The Egyptians knew that the most fertile field for attack was the gap between their Second and Third Armies, a gap which extended almost twenty-five miles between Deversoir and Abu Sultan. But the gap could be closed. Meanwhile Sharon's men had to fight their way through the Twenty-first Armored Division and the Sixteenth Infantry Division. The first of these had been savaged by Israeli tanks and aircraft in the fight in the Sinai. The infantry, however, were astride the roads leading to the canal from Sharon's positions around Tasa. This was eighteen miles northeast of Sharon's preselected crossing point. The problem was clear. The Egyptians had to be flushed out of their positions by the Israelis to give Sharon's force a clear run to the crossings.

His forces, although strong, were just enough for the crossing. Sharon had three armored brigades, each of about eighty to eighty-five tanks (the table of organization called for more, but there had been serious losses in a week of fighting); a brigade of infantry and engineers laden with bridging equipment; and barges for crossing the canal.

The Israeli planners had given Sharon very little time to accomplish the twin objectives of reaching the canal and building a bridgehead. To do this, he planned to employ one armored brigade in a demonstration that would divert the Egyptians and to push his second brigade down the road running southwest from Tasa to the Great Bitter Lake.

The road was important because it ran into the main highway along the canal a few thousand yards from the two secondary roads that led to the crossing point selected. The general area where the roads met was known to the Israelis as the Chinese Farm. It had been the site of Japanese irrigation experiments; and the Israeli troops, mistaking the documents they found, dubbed it the Chinese Farm. It was to be the focus of the greatest armored battles of the war.

If the Israelis were able to win control of the road network, they were in good shape. Sharon could send his infantry across the canal to establish a bridgehead on the west bank and then feed his engineers into the battle to establish a viable crossing. One brigade, only one, was assigned to meet and defeat Egyptian tank counterattacks in the area of the Chinese Farm.

Sharon, it is suspected, paid less attention to the task of keeping open his lines to the potential bridgehead than to the crossing itself. The force selected to make the crossing was under Adan: three brigades of tanks and infantry and paratroopers in the rather dilapidated half-tracks that served the Israelis as carriers for their combat infantry.

Things began to go wrong. The paratroop brigade, which was supposed to cross the canal in rubber dinghies, reached its staging area eighteen miles east of Tasa. The dinghies were not there. The brigade, according to plan, was supposed to cross the canal at 11 A.M. It was not until 2 P.M. that a reconnaissance party located the dinghies.

Things began to go right. One of Sharon's tank brigades north of the Tasa–Great Bitter Lake road struck westward toward Ismailia. This was the intended diversion, and it resulted in heavy fighting with the Egyptian Twenty-first Armored Division. The Egyptians fought tenaciously. The Israelis advanced but at considerable cost.

The attack had been launched at 5 P.M. An hour later Sharon's Second Armored Brigade pushed in a curve to the southwest, probing for the gap between the Egyptian Second and Third Armies. When the tanks reached the lakeshore road, they turned north with the canal on their left flank. For a time they were unopposed; then they encountered heavy Egyptian fire from artillery, missiles, and tank guns and were forced to deploy off the road. It was the beginning of the great armored battle that was to last for two days.

The task of Colonel Amnon Reschef, the brigade commander, was to check the Egyptians and prevent their penetration to the two side roads that led to the canal. Sharon's mission was to force the main road leading from Tasa to the crossing point. Neither commander was successful. Reschef's men could not establish a perimeter defense. Sharon was slow in getting his attack started. Only at midnight, hours behind schedule, did the force designated to cross the canal move out. The Israelis hit the Egyptians from the rear on the Tasa road, joined the paratroopers in their personnel carriers, and with the engineers and their equipment following moved up the road beside the canal and reached the water's edge. About 200 men, led by Sharon, paddled across the canal, at this point about 100 yards wide, and entered Africa. A single-word signal, "Acapulco," announced the establishment of a meager bridgehead on the west bank.

The invaders encountered no opposition. But the gun flash to the east indicated that a significant battle was developing in the Sinai.

Reschef's advance battalion had been held by the Egyptians and had suffered losses in tanks and men. A tank brigade ordered to secure the area north of Nahalal junction was heavily engaged by Egyptian armor and artillery. The vital road from Tasa was subject to sudden attacks by Egyptian infantry. In the circumstances, the crossing of the canal in force, the principal objective, again fell behind time. The paratroopers were ferried across the canal at dawn, but there was no sign of the vital bridging equipment. If the Egyptians had had the wit and the resources, they could have destroyed Sharon and the first crossing force then and there.

The major crossing of the canal was an epic of engineering skill. Barges ferried thirty tanks and about 2,000 infantry across to support Sharon's tiny party. To the Israelis' surprise, no Egyptian counterstroke developed. Four Egyptian tanks, apparently on a reconnaissance mission, had been knocked out by the paratroopers' missiles in an early morning encounter. Elsewhere the front remained quiet as the Israeli force was slowly built up. Too slowly. The fighting on the east bank had grown in intensity and was preventing the movement of Adan's main armored force across the canal.

There, in the Sinai, the Israelis were barely holding their own against Egyptian tanks and missile-firing infantry. It takes some hardihood for Sharon to state that all was going according to plan. The Egyptian reaction had been quicker and more powerful than anticipated. All now hung on the Israelis' ability to hold open the main road from Tasa, down which reinforcements for the west bank must pass.

Adan noted that by the morning of Oct. 16 the forces fighting on the north of the road were "exhausted" and many of the tanks were out of fuel. The paratroopers on the west bank had it easy in comparison. The Egyptians still were in ignorance of the Israelis' plans. The few troops encountered by Sharon's force were easily mopped up. But the Israeli position was nonetheless dangerous. No bridge had yet been thrown across the canal, and some of the bridging equipment had been damaged by Egyptian artillery fire on the way to the canal. Over the whole front on both sides of the canal, the Israeli casualties had been heavy.

Napoleon sought lucky generals. Sharon was lucky. His tiny bridgehead force survived because in the early hours of the crossing no considerable Egyptian units arrived to attack it. The Egyptians' failure appears to have been the result of poor communications. In November 1973 an Egyptian officer said that a peasant near the crossing had perceived what was happening and had run through the night to the nearest telephone to call the Egyptian command. The telephone was out of order! President Sadat, alerted by premature Israeli radio claims of victory, had called Ismail. The latter said that he had heard that "three infiltrating Israeli tanks" had managed to cross the canal.

Sharon's tactics once he had a force across the canal called for a rampaging offensive into Egypt. He should have known that he did not have the forces available for such an adventure. But he persisted and defied Gonen's order to dig into defensive positions until Adan's armor arrived. On the contrary, Sharon sent raiding parties out to attack Egyptian SAM sites, munitions dumps, and outposts. The bridgehead on the west bank was left to a small covering force, too small to defeat any sizeable Egyptian counterattack. These adventures had one positive result: Sharon's freebooters knocked out four SAM sites, assuring the Israeli aircraft of security from missile attacks during the canal crossing.

The question is why didn't the Egyptians move? Early failures in communication do not explain their lassitude. Probably they were hypnotized by the scope of the operations east of the canal. There the Israelis, despite heavy losses, had gained ten miles and won control of the Tasa–Great Bitter Lake road. General Abdel-Moneim Mwassil, commander of the Third Army in the south, apparently was unaware that an enemy force was operating between his army and the Second Army.

The answer is that the Israelis by crossing the canal, admittedly in insufficient strength, had imposed on the Egyptians exactly the sort of battle they were incapable of fighting. This was no set-piece engagement like the Egyptian crossing of the canal on the first day of the war. This was a contest in which bold initiatives, even by small forces, could turn the tide. Neither the Egyptian officers nor their Soviet mentors were conditioned militarily for this kind of war.

The London Sunday *Times* insight team, the authors of *The Yom Kippur War,* focus on another Egyptian failing. Lateral communications between battalion, brigade, and division commanders were infrequent. Units fought the Israelis when they appeared and fought well. But there was no coherence in the Egyptian tactics. Above all hung the dead hand of Soviet doctrine. The command center was Ismail's war room. So rigid was the chain of command that an Egyptian brigadier general reported that his tank brigade had been half an hour from the Gidi Pass in the previous week's fighting with the way open for a determined push. He had asked to be given the initiative. The order, he said, went to division, then to army, and finally to Ismail's war room. When permission finally was obtained, it was too late. An Israeli brigade, strongly supported by artillery, had closed the gap which the brigadier had perceived.

Rigidity of command may have saved Sharon's bridgehead once its importance registered on the Egyptian high command. An operation calling on the resources of the Second and Third Armies had to be approved by a general order signed by four staff officers. The signatures were secured, ultimately, but it was not until Tuesday, Oct. 16, that the Egyptians mounted their major counterattack on the eastern approaches to the canal crossing.

Concentration on those approached signaled a return to sound military judgment. If they could be knocked out and Sharon's supplies cut, then the forces on the west bank would be isolated and reduced almost at leisure. The fighting, called by the Israelis the Battle of the Chinese Farm, was the bloodiest of the war.

The Second Army threw its full weight into the counteroffensive from the north. The Third Army, belatedly bestirring itself, struck from the south. Adan's division, earmarked for the canal crossing, and what was left of Reschef's brigade fought the battle through Tuesday night.

Darkness hurt both sides. The Israelis' superior gunnery was negated by the darkness. Similarly the Egyptian infantry with their missiles were unable to hit. It was a battle of groping and grappling, not of tactical deception. Shazli, the Egyptian chief of staff, pulled together elements from three battered units and pushed them into the Israeli forward positions. There they were shot to bits by Adan's tank gunners.

Sharon's contribution was important, although relatively unnoticed at the time. By eliminating the Egyptian SAM sites on the west bank of the canal, he had enabled the Israeli air force to operate with impunity over the battlefield. Under this air cover and because of the extraordinary efforts of the Israeli armor, the bridgehead on the east bank held, then slowly expanded. By midday Wednesday, Oct. 17, the Israelis finally threw a bridge across the canal and three brigades of Adan's armor supported by two brigades of infantry rolled across.

The heavy fighting around the Chinese Farm had secured the route to the bridgehead. Now the Israelis were "in Africa" in force. What would they do with their victory?

They could go north and cut off the Second Army from its bases. That would mean an advance of about forty miles over terrain that offered the Ismailia Canal and irrigation works. Or Adan's force could swing south and isolate the Third Army from its bases. In that direction the going was better and the Israeli left flank would be on the Bitter Lakes with no chance of attack. Once in position, the Israelis would trap the Third Army.

Israel chose the southern option. But by the time Adan's tanks began their move, time was running out for the Israelis, diplomatic time. The Americans and the Russians had agreed that the war must come to an end. The political factors in that decision are outside this chronicle. But it is obvious that the subsequent cease-fire saved Egypt—Syria with Damascus in peril was out of the war—from even greater disaster.

The Israeli forces west of the canal were pushing slowly north and had the main Cairo–Ismailia road under artillery fire. Adan's forces were streaming south, dismantling missile sites as they went and driving the Egyptian rear guards before them. Israeli F-4's and Mirages ruled the skies: seventeen Egyptian fighters were destroyed in a single day's operations.

By Sunday, Oct. 21, the war was now more than two weeks old, the Israeli bridgehead over the canal was eighteen miles deep and twenty-five miles long. The Israeli vanguard was pushing slowly toward the Cairo–Port Suez road, the main supply line of the Third Army, which was now in an increasingly vulnerable position.

The Egyptian position was desperate. There was no way in which their forces east of the canal could be turned around to launch a counteroffensive on the Israeli forces now astride the waterway. For that maneuver the Egyptians needed time. Time was running out.

The Israeli government had now agreed after much heart-searching, to accept the United Nations Security Council resolution calling "upon the parties to the present fighting to cease all firing and to terminate all military activity immediately . . ."

Aggressive to the last, the Israelis fought one more action before the UN resolution halted the war. On the morning of Monday, Oct. 22, helicopter-borne infantry attacked the Syrians in position holding the ridge below the summit of Mt. Hermon. They paid for it with casualties that were heavy for that war or any other. But they took the position.

Sudden, unexpected victories on the Suez Canal and the Golan Heights, stubborn defense, a costly and unsuccessful renewal of the offensive on both fronts, a flawed but in the end successful resumption of the offensive by the Israelis—that is the story of war. It was won by the Israelis and, equally, lost by the Arab commanders. If the war had any purpose, it was that this generation of Egyptians and Israelis learned from it the futility of further conflict. Future generations may or may not accept the lesson.

BIBLIOGRAPHY

CHAPTER ONE

Falk, Edwin. *Togo and the Rise of Japanese Sea Power.* New York: Longmans, Green, and Company, 1936.

Hough, Richard. *The Fleet That Had to Die.* New York: The Viking Press, 1958.

Wilson, H. W. *Battleships in Action.* Boston: Little, Brown, 1969.

CHAPTER TWO

Churchill, Winston. *The World Crisis.* New York: Scribner's, 1951–59.

Edmonds, H. H. *Military Operations, France and Belgium.* London: Macmillan, 1922–28.

Falkenhayn, Erich von. *General Headquarters 1914–1916.* London: Hutchinson, 1919.

Falls, Cyril. *The Great War.* New York: G. P. Putnam's, 1959.

Foch, Ferdinand. *Mémoires I.* Garden City, N.Y.: Doubleday, Doran, 1931.

Kluck, Alexander von. *The March on Paris.* Buenos Aires: L. Bernard, 1921.

Liddell Hart, Sir Basil Henry. *The Real War 1914–1918.* Boston: Little, Brown, 1930.

Poincare, Raymond. *Au Service de la France.* Paris: Plon-Nouritt 1926–33.

Schwarte, M. *Der Grosse Krieg 1914–1918.* Leipzig: J. A. Barth, 1921–23.

Terraine, John. *The Great War 1914–1918.* New York: Macmillan, 1965.

CHAPTER THREE

Churchill, Winston. *The World Crisis*, Vol. 3. New York: Scribner's, 1953.

German Ministry of the Marine. *Der Krieg sur Zee, 1914–1918*. Berlin: 1922–66.

Harper, Rear Admiral J. *The Truth About Jutland*. London: Murray, 1927.

Jellicoe, Admiral of the Fleet Earl. *The Grand Fleet 1914–16*. London, New York: Cassell, 1919.

Liddell Hart, Sir Basil. *The Real War 1914–1918*. Boston: Little, Brown, 1930.

MacIntyre, Captain Donald. *Jutland*. London: Evans Bros., 1957; New York: Norton, 1958.

CHAPTER FOUR

Blake, Robert. *The Private Papers of Douglas Haig*. London: Eyre and Spottswoode, 1950.

Churchill, Winston. *The World Crisis*, Vols. 3–4. New York: Scribner's, 1953–54.

Ellis-Williams, Major Clough. *The Tank Corps*. New York: George H. Doran, 1919.

Fuller, John Frederick Charles. *Tanks in the Great War*. London: J. Murray, 1920.

Hierl, Constantin. *Der Weltkrieg in Umrissen*. Charlottenburg: Verlag Offene Worte, 1924–26.

Liddell Hart, Sir Basil. *The Real War 1914–1918*. Boston: Little, Brown, 1930.

CHAPTER FIVE

Beaufre, Andre. *1940: The Fall of France*. New York: Knopf, 1968.

Benoist-Mechin, J. *Sixty Days That Shook the West*. New York: Putnam's, 1963.

Chapman, Guy. *Why France Collapsed*. New York: Holt, Rinehart, and Winston, 1969.

Churchill, Winston. *The Second World War*, Vol. 2. Boston: Houghton Mifflin, 1948.

Ellis, L. F. *The War in France and Flanders 1939–1940*. London: H. M. Stationery Office, 1953.

Guderian, H. *Panzer Leader*. London: M. Joseph, 1952.

Horne, Alistair. *To Lose a Battle*. Boston: Little, Brown, 1969.

Liddell Hart, Sir B. H. *History of the Second World War*. New York: Putnam's, 1971.

Manstein, Erich von. *Lost Victories*. London: Methuen, 1958.

Middleton, Drew. *Our Share of Night*. New York: The Viking Press, 1946.

Shirer, W. L. *The Collapse of the Third Republic*. New York: Simon and Schuster, 1969.

Spears, Sir Edward. *Assignment to Catastrophe*. New York: A. A. Wyn, 1954–55.

Weygand, M. *Recalled to Service*. Garden City, N.Y.: Doubleday, 1952.

CHAPTER SIX

Churchill, Winston. *The Second World War*, Vol. 2. Boston: Houghton Mifflin, 1949.

Clarke, Ronald. *The Battle of Britain*. London: G. G. Harrap, 1965.

Collier, Basil. *The Battle of Britain*. London: B. T. Batsford, 1962.

Collier, Richard. *Eagle Day: the Battle of Britain*. New York: Dutton, 1966.

Deighton, Len. *Fighter*. New York: Knopf, 1978.

Galland, Adolf. *The First and the Last*. New York: Holt, 1954.

Middleton, Drew. *The Sky Suspended*. New York: Longmans, Green, 1960; London: Secker & Warburg, 1960.

Richards, Denis. *Royal Air Force 1939–1945*, Vol. 1. London: H. M. Stationery Office, 1953.

Wheatley, Ronald. *Operation Sea Lion*. Oxford: Clarendon Press, 1958.

Wright, Robert. *Dowding and the Battle of Britain*. New York: Scribner's, 1970.

CHAPTER SEVEN

Brown, David. *Carrier Operations in World War II*, Vol. 2. Annapolis: U. S. Naval Institute Press, 1975.

Fuchida, Mitsuo and Masatake Okumiya. *Midway: The Battle That Doomed Japan*. Annapolis: U. S. Naval Institute, 1955.

Lord, Walter. *Incredible Victory*. New York: Harper & Row, 1967.

Morison, Samuel Eliot. *History of United States Naval Operations in World War II*, Vol. 4. Boston: Little, Brown, 1947–62.

Nimitz, Chester W. and E. B. Potter. *The Great Sea War*. Englewood Cliffs, N.J.: Prentice-Hall, 1960.

Tuleja, Thaddeus V. *Climax at Midway*. New York: Norton, 1960.

Winton, John. *Air Power at Sea*. New York: Crowell, 1976.

CHAPTER EIGHT

Chuikov, V. I. *The Beginning of the Road.* London: MacGibbon & Kee, 1963.

Erickson, John. *The Road to Stalingrad.* New York: Harper & Row, 1975.

Mackintosh, Malcolm. *Juggernaut: A History of the Soviet Armed Forces.* New York: Macmillan, 1967.

Samsonov, General Alexsandr M. *The Battle of Stalingrad.* Moscow: "NAUKA," 1968.

Zhukov, Marshal G. K. *Reminiscences and Recollections.* New York: Harper & Row, 1969.

CHAPTER NINE

Alexander, Field Marshal Earl. *The Memoirs of Field Marshal Earl Alexander of Tunis 1940–1945.* London: Cassell, 1963.

Barnett, Corelli. *The Battle of El Alamein.* New York: Macmillan, 1964.

Bryant, Arthur. *The Turn of the Tide.* Garden City, N.Y.: Doubleday, 1957.

Carver, Field Marshal Lord. *El Alamein.* London: B. T. Batsford, 1962.

Churchill, Winston. *The Hinge of Fate.* Boston: Houghton Mifflin, 1948–53.

De Guignand, Sir Francis. *Operation Victory.* New York: Scribner's, 1947; London: Hodder & Stoughton, 1947.

Irving, David. *The Trail of the Fox.* New York: Dutton, 1977.

Mellenthin, Friedrich Wilhelm von. *Panzer Battles 1939–1945.* London: Cassell, 1955.

Montgomery, Viscount Bernard L. *El Alamein to the River Sangro.* New York: Dutton, 1949.

————. *Memoirs.* Cleveland: World Publishing, 1958.

Rommel, Erwin. *The Rommel Papers,* edited by B. Liddell Hart. New York: Morrow, 1969.

War Office. *The History of the Second World War, the Mediterranean and the Middle East,* Vols. 3 and 4. London: War Office, 1960, 1966.

CHAPTER TEN

Collier, Basil. *The War in the Far East 1941–1945.* New York: Morrow, 1969.

Evans, Sir Geoffrey Charles. *Slim as Military Commander*. New York: Van Nostrand-Reinhold, 1969.

Evans, Geoffrey and Anthony Brett-James. *Imphal*. New York: Macmillan, 1962.

Kirby, Stanley Woodburn. *The War Against Japan*. London: H. M. Stationery Office, 1957–69.

Mountbatten of Burma. *Allied Forces*. London: H. M. Stationery Office, 1951.

Reeves, James and Desmond Flower. *The War 1939–1945*. New York: Harper & Row, 1960.

Slim, Field Marshal Viscount. *Defeat into Victory*. London: Cassell, 1956.

CHAPTER ELEVEN

Bradley, Omar N. *A Soldier's Story*. New York: Holt, 1951.

Butcher, Harry C. *My Three Years with Eisenhower*. New York: Simon and Schuster, 1946.

Eisenhower, Dwight D. *Crusade in Europe*. Garden City, N.Y.: Doubleday, 1948.

Irving, David. *The Trail of the Fox*. New York: Dutton, 1977.

Lewin, Ronald. *Ultra Goes to War*. New York: McGraw-Hill, 1978.

Montgomery, B. L. *Normandy to the Baltic*. London: Hutchinson, 1949.

Morgan, Frederick. *Overture to Overlord*. Garden City, N.Y.: Doubleday, 1950.

Ruge, Friedrich. *Rommel in Normandy*. Stuttgart: K. F. Koehler, 1959.

Ryan, Cornelius. *The Longest Day*. New York: Simon and Schuster, 1959.

Speidel, Hans. *Invasion, 1944*. Tübingen: R. Wunderlich, 1949.

Wilmot, Chester. *The Struggle for Europe*. New York: Harper & Row, 1952.

CHAPTER TWELVE

Acheson, Dean. *Present at the Creation*. New York: Norton, 1971.

Appleman, Roy E. *South to the Naktong, North to the Yalu*. Washington: Military History Office, 1961.

Marshall, Samuel Lyman Atwood. *The River and the Gauntlet*. Westport, Conn.: Greenwood Press, 1970.

Rees, David. *Korea: The Limited War*. New York: St. Martin's Press, 1964; London: Macmillan, 1964.

Truman, Harry S. *Years of Trial and Hope*. Garden City, N.Y.: Doubleday, 1956.

CHAPTER THIRTEEN

Fall, Bernard. *Hell in a Very Small Place.* Philadelphia: Lippincott, 1967.

Roy, Colonel Jules. *La Bataille de Dien Bien Phu.* Paris: R. Julliard, 1963.

CHAPTER FOURTEEN

Giap, General Vo Nguyen. *The Military Art of Peoples' War.* New York: Monthly Review Press, 1970.

Halberstam, David. *The Making of a Quagmire.* New York: Random House, 1968.

Hoopes, Townsend. *The Limits of Intervention.* New York: D. McKay, 1969.

Taylor, Maxwell. *Swords and Ploughshares.* New York: Norton, 1972.

Westmoreland, General William C. *A Soldier Reports: Report on Operations in South Vietnam, January 1964–June 1968.* Garden City, N.Y.: Doubleday, 1976.

CHAPTER FIFTEEN

Momyer, General William W. *Airpower in Three Wars.* New York: Arno Press, 1979.

U. S. Air Force. *Air War—Vietnam.* New York: Arno Press, 1978.

CHAPTER SIXTEEN

Adan, Avraham. *On the Banks of the Suez.* San Rafael, Calif.: Presidio Press, 1980.

Glick, E. B. *Between Israel and Death.* Harrisburg, Pa.: Stackpole Books, 1974.

Haykal, Muhammad. *The Road to Ramadan.* New York: Quadrangle/ New York Times Books, 1975.

Rothenberg, Gunther E. *The Anatomy of the Israeli Army.* New York: Hippocrene Books, 1979.

Sunday Times Insight Team. *The Yom Kippur War.* London: Deutsch, 1975.

INDEX

About the Author

Drew Middleton describes the "best break" of his early newspaper career as ". . . being sent to France with the British Expeditionary Force in October 1939. Thereafter I had five and one half years instruction in war at the hands of the German army, air force, and navy." Middleton escaped from France in 1940 with one of the last British units and was in London during the Luftwaffe's attempts to destroy the RAF prior to invading the British Isles. He was in the thick of things when the Germans, their invasion plans frustrated, turned their massive *Blitzkrieg* raids from military targets to the civilian population.

"My interest in the military started with World War II and has continued ever since. At one time or another I knew Eisenhower, Bedell-Smith, his Chief of Staff, Montgomery, Bradley, Alexander, Spaatz, 'Bomber' Harris, Curtis Le May, and dozens of others. You listen and you learn."

As a foreign correspondent, he traveled extensively in Europe, Africa, the Middle East, and Asia. He was successively New York *Times* bureau chief in Moscow, West Germany, Britain, France, the United Nations, and finally European Affairs Correspondent in Brussels.

Mr. Middleton is now the distinguished "Military Analyst" of The New York *Times*.